The Knights Templar in the Golden Age of Spain

The Knights Templar in the Golden Age of Spain

Their Hidden History on the Iberian Peninsula

Juan García Atienza

Translated by Federico E. Rodriguez Guerra

Destiny Books

Rochester, Vermont

Destiny Books
One Park Street
Rochester, Vermont 05767
www.DestinyBooks.com

Destiny Books is a division of Inner Traditions International

Originally published in Spanish under the title *El Legado Templario: Una historia occulta* by Ediciones Robinbook, s.l., Apdo. 94085-08080 Barcelona
First U.S. edition published in 2006 by Destiny Book

Library of Congress Cataloging-in-Publication Data

Atienza, Juan G. (Juan García)
[Legado templario. English]
The Knights Templar in the golden age of Spain : their hidden history in the Iberian peninsula / Juan Garcia Atienza ; translated by Federico E. Rodriguez Guerra.
p. cm.
"Originally published in Spanish under the title El legado templario: una historia occulta"—T.p. verso.
Includes bibliographical references and index.
ISBN 978-1-59477-098-2 (pbk.)
1. Templars—Spain—History. 2. Spain—History—711-1516. I. Title.
CR4755.S6A75 2006
946'.02—dc22

2006004924

Printed and bound in the United States

10 9 8 7

Text design and layout by Jonathan Desautels
This book was typeset in Sabon with Copperplate and Al Juliana as the display typefaces

Contents

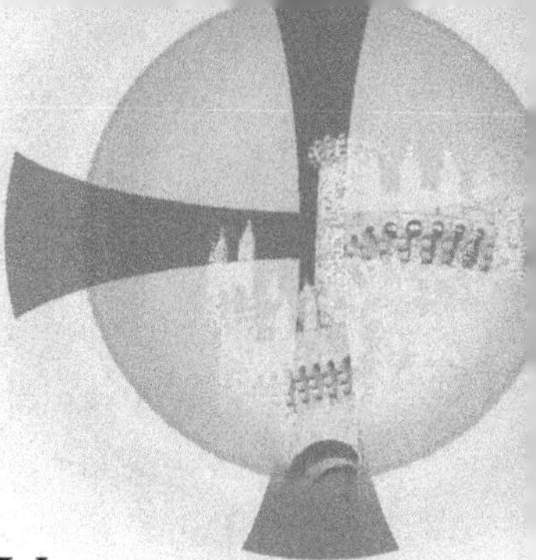

INTRODUCTION

Some years ago, when I became interested in studying the Order of the Templars, I was convinced that its history was but a footnote to the great history of the European Middle Ages and that, for this reason, it moved in tandem with the developments that took place during the less than two hundred years of Templar public life. Yet, little by little, I realized that in the history of medieval Europe, there were many questions that would find only hypothetical answers unless the Templars were given the importance that academic historiography persists in denying them. In fact, the Templars not only made up a part of the Middle Ages, but in great measure shaped the period and gave it meaning as well. For instance, when we consider the possible influence or the eventual intervention of the Templars in many historical events—which has been systematically ignored or rebuffed—these events acquire a raison d'être that would constitute but a few of history's quirks without the presence of the White Friars.

Before such evidence, I have laid out the reason for the persistent silence that official investigation maintains in reference to the authentic importance of the Order in Europe's transformation in the twelfth and thirteenth centuries. My conclusions, though probably incomplete in many cases, have allowed me to trace a whole series of motives that explain this constant veiling and silence surrounding the role of the Order.

A Shortage or Absence of Documents

Despite the abundance of archival Templar documentation, there still exist unrecoverable gaps that, on the one hand, provoke reasonable doubt about key circumstances of Templar history and ideology. On the other hand, it seems that some fundamental aspects of the Templars' identity—including the specific locations of their settlements—have been deliberately obscured for motives that have also been obfuscated.

These deficiencies have frequently incited controversies that have ended in stalemate, at least officially, without anyone being able to pronounce a definitive conclusion that could be acknowledged in history texts. This has occurred, for example, when some have tried to determine that monuments such as the funerary chapel at Eunate, in Navarre, or the Church of Vera Cruz, in Segovia, are works of the Templars. When we resort to an in-depth study of these examples of sacred architecture and, above all, when they and their transcendent purpose are compared to those of other structures that offer no documented doubts regarding construction, we conclude that there has been a deliberate shrouding of both the origins of these chapels and churches and the motives for their erection. We might guess that the reason for all this secrecy and uncertainty is due to the fact that those who later possessed these structures did not want anyone to know how or why they had become owners of works that were created by others.

Well-founded suspicions such as these lead us to a second motive that might explain the silence that looms over Templar ideology and works and their decisive influence on the history of the medieval world.

Those Who Create History Desire a Leading Role

This can be seen even today: Those whose circumstances or personalities in part transform the world or their own countries stubbornly refuse to confess any of their shortcomings. And when the time comes for them to expose their actions to the public and proclaim their ideology, they take credit for decisions, plans, deeds, victories, and enterprises that, more often than we suspect, come from other sources or have been suggested by those who have realized the success of their intentions precisely by remaining anonymous while letting others promote what appear to be their own ideas and hopes regarding their future or the future of the world.

One example that comes to mind and which we will fully discuss in this book is already recognized by more lucid historians: James I, the Conqueror, was absolutely touched and influenced by the Templars, whose ideology contributed to his own ideas that took shape at his castle in Monzón. Yet either by his own choice or from exterior pressure, he barely mentioned the Order when the time came for him to record the history of his reign in the *Libre dels Feyts* (Book of Deeds), though it seems evident that all his policymaking was suggested directly or indirectly by the Templars, who saw the possibility of fulfilling through this king the fundamental designs of the Order, including the establishment of a universal theocratic empire capable of transforming the historical structures underpinning their time.

The Hidden Silence of Intentions

Of course, James I, like so many other medieval characters touched by the Templar spirit, could not by documentation or oral chronicle make public any of these designs. Such universalistic ideologies are never explicitly exposed when they are actually conceived, due to the fact that their publicizing would entail traumatizing the powers that be, who would then rush without haste to destroy these ideologies while they are still in the long-range implementation phase. In a way, this is what must have happened to the Order of the Temple; this is what provoked its condemnation and abolition on the part of the Church, monarchs, and kingdoms that had previously embraced the Templars as long as they believed them to be simple servants to the institutions that held power.

Could we imagine, here and now, the true intentions of organizations such as the CIA, certain fundamentalist sects, or some multinational conglomerates without awakening a generalized feeling of objection and disapproval in the face of what we suppose to be the definitive and irreversible end of the structures we believe govern us? Without a doubt, we could not, and we are living this truth in our own time: The world survives immersed in all types of corporate self-interest through which those from diverse social strata imagine themselves as protagonists of their own transformations. But if these social strata, apparently autochthonous, are threatened with annihilation for the sake of a new universal order that would necessarily uproot and eradicate the small national, labor, institutional, and political powers on which we base our existential designs, we can be sure that all of them, or a great number of them, would unite so that such an elimination would never become possible.

Among these structures, nationalism has always formed a primary unifying nucleus. There has been secular fostering of the endogenous, and what supposedly came from the outside was always rejected in a more or less violent manner. This nationalistic mode of operation, which does not form part of any determined moment in history but is instead essentially timeless, constitutes another of the motives by which France always considered the Templars as her own. There has been a tendency to minimize or ignore the function of the Order in medieval Europe as a whole and, specifically, the development of the Order on the Iberian Peninsula.

Nationalist Obsessions

It seems to have always bothered the majority of studious Spanish historians—and hardly any of them have been able to conceal it—that in crucial moments of Spain's past, the country and its people may have been influenced by a power or a determined ideology (other than that of Rome and the Church) that was alien to their own structures. In some way, Spanish citizens have tended to consider as malignant what comes to them from beyond their own seas or borders. But in this regard, Spaniards' attitudes are no different from the dominant feeling in any other country. This perspective has led to such paradoxes as the secular and absurd idea of the Reconquista* paired with the notion of Spanish Muslims as foreign invaders, despite the fact that after centuries of presence on the Iberian Peninsula, these Muslims were as Spanish as the Christians that dominated the northern territories. Likewise, Spaniards have been convinced of the antipatriotism of the Frenchified countrymen of nineteenth-century Spain, most of whom were viscerally convinced of the necessity to "Europeanize" the country in order to pull it out of the cultural darkness in which it had sunk as a result of the isolation fostered by the Church's Council of Trent and its most archaic offices.

Due in great part to the persistent chauvinism of Spain's neighbors on the other side of the Pyrenees, the Templars have always been seen as a more or less—let us say less—French institution rooted for a century and a half in peninsular Christian kingdoms. As such, their presence in the context of Spanish history has been minimized, as has that of the European Crusaders, who sporadically intervened in the fight against Islam as part of what was merely a mercenary collaboration toward celestial glories. (When their mission ended, they returned to their lands and allowed Spanish monarchs to rule, without outside pressure, on the political matters that affected their kingdoms.)

I understand that when setting out to impart from a classroom or proclaim from a text the glorious deeds of local history that must be taken as a retroactive defense of present institutions, the indiscriminate exaltation of national pride must have absolute priority. I am also willing to admit that it is convenient at times to balance shortcomings with the silences to which Spanish history has secularly submitted itself in the European context. It is also understandable that the black legends†

*This refers to Catholic Spain's struggle (from 718 to 1492) to reconquer lands that had existed under Muslim rule.

†[The term *black legends* usually refers to Spanish atrocities committed against Indians, Protestants, and so forth, though many times a black legend is not based on truth. For instance, some of these false stories include those of Spaniards starving Dutchmen to death in rooms above restaurants so that the smell of roasts would add to their misery. —*Trans.*]

provoke passionate cajolery and firm barriers by those who uphold them, because more objective conclusions can be reached.

Yet I also believe that we confuse just claims with blind defense and, what could be worse, the supposed reality with the indiscriminate exaltation of nationalist attitudes and their known champions. This is as dangerous as—or more dangerous than—wrapping ourselves in a romantic fantasy that takes history as a simple structure on which to hang a universe of idealized sentiments. In the name of supposed historical rigor, this confusion allows us to give unlimited credit to some documents, which are then taken at their word, and permits us to forget that no written record, not even a simple bill, is itself objective, but is instead a response to someone's desire or an attempt to record a personal or collective will.

In the face of this path of study, which I deem a dead-end street, perhaps we should deal with historical fact from a new perspective. This would entail not abandoning but rather adding to old paths we have trodden thus far, creating new avenues such as collective memory, popular legend, myth, and even the introduction of evident false "truths" into the events of the past—methods that have been systematically renounced by rational investigation but which can help us resolve the mysteries of undocumented history and ask questions that historians all too frequently reject when discovering answers has proved difficult.

Some call this collection of investigative methods *inner history.* It is a valid name, much as is the term *parapsychology* for the study of so-called paranormal phenomena, for both inner history and parapsychology employ mediums and tackle questions that reject historiography and the psychology of conventional, official, or academic sciences.

Alas, there is but one discipline we can call history, just as the one way to study the soul is called psychology. We must recognize that in either discipline a human being may not always move in the strictest confines of rationality, but instead acts, exists, and move irrationally, in the realm of the intuitive, within an anathematized, chauvinistic universe in which the only thing that is admitted by decree and without reluctance is what has been erroneously dictated by strict reason that sets accepted conclusions as valid. It is precisely this universe that has supplied the final motive for our historiography to avoid an in-depth study of the Order of the Temple.

Fear of Intuition

History cannot be denied in the face of evidence. Inner history—let us keep using this term as long as its methodology and discipline are denied incorporation into the scientific mainstream—snakes its way among clues* that frequently lead to surprising conclusions, which, being so, are not believed or accepted by the historical authority in vogue. But what is incredible is often considered uncertain until the moment it is confirmed by evidence. The conclusions of inner history should be considered hypotheses for continued investigation as long as the available clues can coherently reconstruct reality—no matter how different these conclusions might be from those established by the researcher's usual tool: documentation.

This lack of belief in unexpected conclusions can be called *fear.* But it may have more to do with adopting a comfortable posture merely because it is the official one and, therefore, the only one that allows for achieving academic prestige in our cultural context. In any case, the attitude seems like fear; at least historians seem to be transmitting fear: an uncontrollable reticence in the face of what is considered untried and what cannot be admitted, for if it were, it would require so many changes in books that the majority of these texts would lose their appeal as accepted knowledge.

I understand this fear and why the scholars who conduct the academic research on which our current cultural system is based cling to its accepted principles, despite their suspicion that something fundamental is changing in the collective consciousness that will sooner or later force this research to fit our perspectives about general knowledge and

*[In Spanish the word *clave* also means "key" or "code." I have used *clue* throughout to better reflect the author's multiple readings of *clave.* —*Trans.*]

the different disciplines that compose it and break it down to its basic elements. If inner history is distinguished from conventional historiography, it is due to the unavoidable obligation of the researcher to delve deeper and compare materials outside the mainstream of history. Naturally, this requires a profound change within scholars, obliging them to know—or at least not to ignore—materials that at times are radically different from those that constitute their specialty, and then to abandon once and for all the specializations that have so greatly limited the horizon of our knowledge.

It is, for example, a fact—every day more evident and worrisome—that medievalists ignore ancient and modern history. Without blinking, they then mention that many of the events that form their specialty are a consequence of attitudes and ways of thinking that were forged centuries before the age to which they have limited their study. But it would be impossible for them to take on rigorously the subjects that form their research unless they take hold of related disciplines. Without an understanding of these, they cannot comprehend the greater part of the motives that have contributed to a specific episode of the history within their specialty.

Illustrating the necessity of this broader understanding, the great Robert Graves, who spent many years on the island of Mallorca, in his prologue to a book by the Sufi master Idries Shah writes: Reading the medieval chronicles of James the Conqueror, he was surprised to learn that the surrender of the plaza of Ciotat (Palma) came to pass when the Catalan-Aragonese monarch promised those under siege that a common bat would form part of the emblem of the city when the Christians occupied it. Graves consulted Shah on this, and the master told him that the flying creature is a fundamental symbol in the transcendent ideology of the Sufis, who see it as being capable of envisioning light in the midst of darkness. This detail, probably unknown to many medievalists, and perhaps considered not worth knowing, has a fundamental if not rationalist importance: In his promise, the conquering king demonstrated to the Moors of Mallorca that he knew their traditions and that he would enter the plaza ready to respect them.

To understand instances like these, which repeat themselves throughout history, the researcher must be willing to throw a stone in the pond of knowledge and follow to their limits the rings that spread from its point of contact with the water, for these waves consist of so many other forms of knowledge that may have been forgotten. Every day, the knowledge we acquire of our world grows in inverse proportion to our capacity to embrace it: The vast amount that there is to know prevents us from remaining abreast of all that is discovered, published, and revised. It is easy to become lost in the labyrinth of information that we have created. But we have also deliberately complicated our world, with the result that we have abandoned holistic and humanistic attitudes. Like a butterfly in a chrysalis, we have concentrated our awareness on a small, narrow cell of knowing, and from this narrow place we never emerge to see what may happen in another cell nearby.

I would like to ask for patience from those who read this book, for in it, using all my strengths (which are not many) and what little I have been able to learn, I attempt an intra-historical dive, throwing overboard ahead of me the reticence of academic historiography regarding this type of investigation. I am grateful to all researchers for the work they have accomplished without setting out to accomplish it. While they worried about rents and donations and battles in courts and councils, they exposed the clues that have been there all along, though they may have resisted interpreting them, fearing reproach from the ivory tower. The majority of the facts that I have used in my study, which I will lay out for the reader, are within everyone's reach. Some have been published; others gather dust in national and local archives. I did not resist reading between the lines, searching beneath those apparently banal events that hide decisive meanings for the interpretation of the intentions of a collective such as the Templars. Readers will be able to come to their own conclusions, but of this they may be assured: The Order of the Temple played a decisive role in the development of the historical course of the Iberian Peninsula in the twelfth and thirteenth centuries. Whatever the academic texts and studies suggest, the historical, political, religious, and cultural adventure of the Iberian Peninsula would have been very different if the Templars had not lived among its people.

PART 1

THE OPPORTUNE MOMENT

Ce fut au temps du mois de May,
Qu'on doibt fouïr deuil et esmay,
Que i'entray dedans vn vergier
Dont Zephirus fut iardinier.
Quand devant le jardin passoye,
Ie n'estois pas vestu de soye,
Mais de pauures draps maintenu,
Pour n'apparoir en public nu.
Et m'esbattant auec desir
De chasser loing mon desplaisir,
Ouy vng chant harmonieux
De plusiers oyseaux gratieux. *

JEHAN DE LA FONTAINE,
LA FONTAINE DES AMOUREUX DE SCIENCE
(*THE FOUNTAIN OF THE LOVERS OF SCIENCE*), 1413

---

*It was in times of the month of May,
When one must shoo away sorrow and fainting spells,
I entered inside a garden that had Zephyr as a gardener.
When I passed that luxuriant garden,
I was not dressed in silks,
But in poor rags, so as not to appear naked in front of others.
Debating myself, desiring to break loose of my sorrows,
I heard the harmonious song of various small birds.

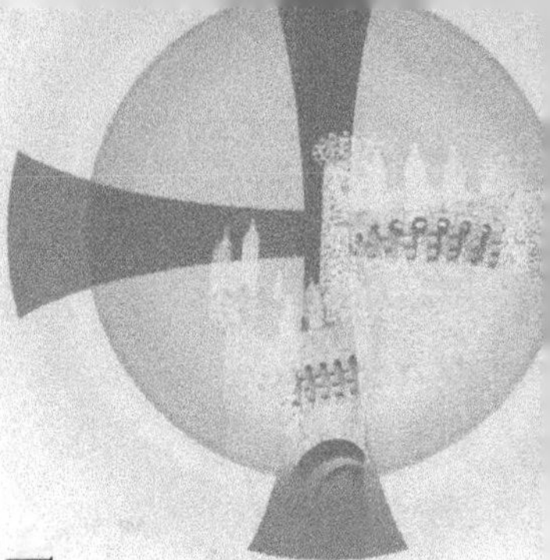

1
Clues to the Millennium

History is created by the human species that lives it and marks stages of splendor or crisis according to its dimensional sense of time. Using subjective measures, no less real as parameters, humanity gives itself limits, summits, and canyons to conquer as events occur. As it navigates these temporary obstacles or easy courses, it projects its fears and hopes toward a future that is supposedly marked by destiny or Providence.

Waiting for the Year 1000

Contrary to what was dramatically contended by the researchers of the Romantic Age, for medieval man the arrival of the first millennium of Christianity was not a threatening terror but an expectation of change. Although not without an element of fear, this expectation was widespread among believers. As for the triumphant Church itself, according to all testimonies and what we can infer, it set the date of the millennium as the start of its effective power over the Christian community.[1] At this time, the Church's spiritual hierarchy subscribed to the concepts of *parousia* (Christ's Second Coming) and the messiah. Parousia was first used to warn those who had not yet submitted to and embraced

Christianity. The idea of the messiah was used by the Church itself to assume a Christlike sacredness in order to prepare its theocracy and definitively rule the destinies of humanity.

At the time of his Second Coming, Christ, it seemed, could count on an authentic monastic militia, Cluniac Benedictism, which had been ready since the time of St. Odo (927)* to consolidate the power of Rome, feudalism, and an empire that considered the Church its own. At this time the Church was corrupted by its own leaders, who submitted to tacit obedience in exchange for the protection kings could provide the institution. Another trump in the Church's possession was its intellectual dominance over the surrounding world. The majority of those who could read and write were found within its ecclesiastical state. For this reason it constituted by itself an elite with the ability to rule, using its great powers to impose its dialectical criteria and influence on the will of its parishioners.

Although millennial sentiment directly affected the whole of European society immediately prior to the tenth century, it was largely a product of the Church. To develop it, the Church availed itself of some gospels whose interpretation fell outside any critical capacity of the populace. The words of these scriptures were taken as a divine omen not of what would occur when the thousand years of the Incarnation came about, but of what should be done so that the threat of the end of the world would not come to fruition. To avoid this demise, it was necessary that the Church of Rome achieve complete triumph in its bid to definitively rule the destiny of believers—a goal that certainly was not without a profound magical and thaumaturgic aspect. It was not by chance that special powers and secret knowledge were attributed to the pontiff of the millennium, Sylvester II (Gerberto de Aurillac, 999–1003), which he supposedly obtained during the early years of his esoteric development in Toledo, a city traditionally considered to be the cradle of ancestral magical knowledge.

Much more than a time of potential and definitive horrors, the year

*St. Odo was the second abbot of Cluny, succeeding St. Bernon and organizing and enlarging the monastery.

1000 was the Church's projected date for the start of a New Order whose goal was widely announced during the two hundred years preceding the millennium. Thus, no one could excuse himself from awareness, and to ensure this, the Church actively disseminated commentaries on the Apocalypse: those of Beatus of Liébana, who came from within the community of Christians threatened by the Evil One (which the Church personified as Islam), and those written around the time of the Carolingian court (whose power had grown to such an extent that it threatened even the authority of the Church). Various key testimonies of the millennial sentiment were established in the tenth century as the precise date drew nearer.[2] The Last Days were formally announced in the Council of Trosly (909) and in the writings of the Cluniac abbot St. Odo (927–42). For his part, in his *Libellus de Antechristo* (954) the monk Adson, perhaps by design, uncovered the Church's goal, which proclaimed that the Antichrist, announcer of the definitive Judgment, would make his appearance at the decline of the Carolingian Empire (at that time but a shadow of that envisioned by Charlemagne).[3] Some scholars who have examined St. Odo's text affirm that the monk was convinced he had exposed the decadence of imperial authority. Yet his work pales next to that of Bernard of Thuringia, a hermit who providentially arrived in Würtzburg in 960, announcing the definitive date of the Second Coming.

Among the Years of Christ

The year 1000 came and went, along with its associated worries, suspicions, fears, and auguries that never came to pass. For Christian Spain it marked the end of the terrible military expeditions mounted during the summers by the Saracen leader Almanzor. These decimated the kingdoms and territories of the north during the last twenty years of the millennium. Almanzor himself lay dying in Medinaceli in 1002, the same year in which the German emperor Otto III died, inaugurating a profound change in the relations between pontifical Rome and the Empire. The Church silenced the few remaining allusions to the end of the world, but the idea was still alive in Christendom, and in all of the disasters that occurred during the first thirty-three years of the new millennium, many began to see proof of the evangelical prophecy coming to fruition.

We will never know for sure if the fears and suspicions that grew in those years were a depth charge fired surreptitiously by the Church to create a state of confusion from which it could emerge with reinforced power. It is certain that with the plagues, sea monsters, eclipses, and celestial omens that were punctiliously noted by the Cluniac Raúl Glaber in his *Historia,* the Benedictine friars of the abbey of Burgundy widened unopposed their field of influence. In doing so they attracted the indiscriminate admiration of the peninsular rulers (whose monasteries had not yet embraced the Benedictine Rule): The Benedictines discreetly promoted the fight against the multitude of Moors who destroyed the Holy Sepulchre in 1009, threatened Sicilian Christendom from Al Andalus (Muslim Spain), and infiltrated slowly but surely the pontifical domains until the opposition of this rising threat became the only engine in papal politics. Curiously, at the turn of the millennium, when the Church saw the need to remove society's foundations and terrorize it materially with the threat of extinction, it was not precisely Rome, the visible head of Christendom, that manned the trenches in the battle allowing it to emerge as a political force imposing its theocratic principles. In fact, at that moment, Rome lived in its flesh and through its pontiffs the same decadence and decay that served as bait to the millennial idea of impending doom. Popes of that time came from the patrician families of the imperial city and were elected for the local influence they could exercise. They practiced nepotism and simony, forgetting their function as leaders of a theoretically universal parish, and sought protection of their position in which spiritual responsibility had been widely replaced by relaxation and good living.

In the meantime, monks, from their accepted authority and asceticism, began a kind of ecclesiastical reform, closing ranks around the pontiff because the papal office, however corrupt a symbol, was the visible representative of the whole of Christendom. These monastics agreed to ignore the poor example presented by the pontiffs' depravity, dependence on protection provided by external powers, and abuse of an authority they had no right to exercise. What mattered above all else and at all costs was the maintenance of the institution of the Church, which included cleansing it of all impurities and returning to it its lost prestige.

In a way, in its circumstances at the time, the Holy See joined itself to the millennial idea without intending to do so. Its return to an authoritative position would depend on the kind of pontiffs who emerged after the millennial anguishes of the end of the world had passed. Only then, as some prophecies suggested, would there be installed a strong, wise, just, and all-powerful Church under the protection of the Holy Spirit. Only then could there be tacit condemnation of all who would not profess in body and soul the faith of which they would be effectual representatives.

The Unstoppable Ascent

The key years of the millennial threat coincided with the emergence of unique monastic figures on the European landscape. Between 995 and 1048, St. Odilo, the fifth abbot of Cluny, directly influenced the rise of several monks who left their mark on the history of the Church at a time when the majority of believers did not even know the name of the pontiffs who governed Christendom. St. Romualdo, seemingly running from Roman influence, created the ascetic order of Camandula. In the Hispanic provinces, Oliba gathered the mitres of the bishops of Ripoll and Cuixá and the bishopric of Vic to create the foundations of the Catalan state, and regarding Navarre and Aragon, don Sancho y Paterno went to the monastery in Cluny to drink from the original wellsprings of Benedictine reform and bring them back to his lands to establish the European monastic spirit there. In Castile, Domingo de Silos (d. 1072) established Benedictine discipline through miracles in the Mozarabic monastery, which fate had placed in his hands. Far from the Reconquista, Raúl Gabler, the wandering monk, visited all the central European monasteries, taking note of how to impress the laity for which he wrote. Juan of Vadières (c. 933) returned to obeying Hungarian Christian rule. Guillermo de Volpiano raised armies of militant monks in the regions of Normandy and Lombardy.

By the time the millennium and the date of the ten centuries of the Passion of Christ had passed, the whole of Europe was in fact a spiritual fief of Cluny, and the kingdoms and feudal lordships were unconditional donors to Cluniac monasteries and priories in exchange for the prayers and Masses of Cluniac monks, which were all, without exception, considered the greatest examples of virtue and the most effectual intermediaries between the parish and the promised Glory. For many, the millennium coincided with the empire of Cluny.

But this spiritual empire was forged not only from a Christian fundamentalism created by the monks in their eagerness to restore ecclesiastical glory. The Cluniac monks were aware that throughout the first thousand years of a growing Christianity, the believing common folk were the bearers of both the faith that had been inculcated in them from the pulpit and a host of ancestral beliefs born in the deepest part of the collective unconscious. Parishes traded equally in holy orthodoxy and ancient traditional values—those same values that the Church attacked indiscriminately. It was for this reason, and under Cluny's influence, that parishes began promoting the importance of relics (almost to the point of declaring them magical) and pilgrimages to the Axis Mundi (Santiago, Rome, and Jerusalem), the centers of the world touched by the transcendent ideal. Relics, which were invested with thaumaturgic powers rather than merely testimonial ones, were palpable proof of the holiness in which faith originated or were latent examples of those who sacrificed themselves for the theocratic ideology to which all parishioners must reach. The Axis Mundi embodied the goal of those Christians who aspired to a certain level of holiness. In their mere desire to reach this level or to have a place among the just in Glory, they understood they must suffer sacrifices in the form of an initiation that, theoretically, would transform their spirit, making it worthy of heavenly favors and an instant vision of the Final Judgment at that precise place on the axis that joins earth with the heavens.

Within this strictly orthodox rationale for pilgrimage and relic worship there was also a kind of fulfillment of sacred impulses in the collective consciousness of the believers. The sacred object that must be venerated and the sacred place that must be visited have formed a primal part of religion since the origins of civilization. After the first millennium, Christianity, which began its journey purporting remake humanity's religious past, awoke to incorporate to a great extent these primal elements produced by an unrestrained collective impulse and never officially supported by recognized Church authority.

Cluny found itself squarely behind this resurgence of the ancestral religious impulse. While its monasteries became the principal accumulators of relics, which attracted parishioners with their offers of transcendence, the Order installed itself on the roads frequented by pilgrims making their way to sacred destinations. In this way they established official routes that obliged these travelers to stop at or pass by monasteries that the Cluniacs had won to their reform.

But this implementation was only part of a wider and more ambitious political maneuver. Cluny sought to claim for the Church absolute power over Christendom and, once it was obtained, to engage in the conquest of the world on a grand scale, creating a kind of universal government dominated by the Church and ruled by the monastic class. After it gained control over the populace, it aggressively promoted its following in order to influence the governments of Europe and foment their weakening, which, logically, would reinforce monastic political influence over the rulers of the divided countries. The history of Spain during this time—with events such as the fractures among the Catalan counts; the division of their kingdoms by Sancho III, the Elder; Portugal's independence; and the breakup of Castile and León, all of which curiously coincided with the arrival of Cluniac Benedictism on the Peninsula—could be substituted, in lieu of documented proof, as evidence for the enormous power that Cluny assumed in all of Europe's ministates shortly after its arrival in each.

All these maneuvers, which the Cluniac order undertook simultaneously in the rest of Europe, though on a smaller scale than on the

Iberian Peninsula, seemed to work toward a very concrete goal: With the maximum moral authority of the Church behind it, Cluny probed the possibility of finding the formula that, in a determined moment, would allow unification of the Church and the world under the maximum authority of the Roman pontiff. The pope, in turn, would be protected by the sweeping force of a king carefully chosen from among many rulers and capable of acting as a universal defender of Christendom once the theoretical power of the Roman-Germanic Empire (which pretended to rule over the indisputable authority of the papacy) was neutralized.

The Cluniac Popes

To the disgrace of Cluniac monks, during the years that closed the millennium, theocratic ideology and the pontifical crown were in the worst hands. Benedict VIII, a member of the high Roman patriciate, was succeeded by John XIX (1024–32), a member of the same family. In a climate of unprecedented nepotism, John XIX was succeeded by his brother Benedict IX, who came to the throne at twelve years of age and in a short time came to be known as the "small Heliogabalus" because of his evident congenital degeneration, which may have contributed to his amoral excesses.

The Germanic emperors, however, seemed to approve of this degradation; they protected the popes of this period and excused any depravity as long as they received from the pontiffs a solemn coronation, which gave their rank a seal of sacredness. This promoted an empire with the authority to boast but not convince. As the heads of Christendom, the popes surely could have put a stop to this exchange of favors, but doing so would have ended the not very ethical means by which they assumed power. Sylvester III bribed his way to the Holy See, and while both he and the boy pontiff, Benedict IX, were alive, Pope Gregory VI, a rich Roman arch-prelate, ascended the throne of the Church. It became clear to Gregory VI that the Church had to experience a deep change of heart in order to be able to recuperate its battered prestige. At this same time, on the sidelines and in the shadows there stood a young Cluniac monk named Hildebrand.

The need for reform, which preoccupied Pope Gregory VI, was not backed by imperial interests. Holy Roman Emperor Henry III still had in the Eternal City two popes to whom he could turn: Benedict IX, who occupied Santa María Major, and Sylvester III, who lived at St. Peter's, while the domain of the new pontiff, Gregory, was reduced to San Juan de Letrán. It wasn't very difficult for the emperor eventually to remove Gregory to Germany, where he died in Cologne in 1047. The Cluniac Hildebrand later succeeded Gregory, becoming Pope Gregory VII in 1073, but in the meantime, in Rome the patrician infighting for the seat of Peter continued.

Clement II directly followed Gregory VI; he was given the office of pope entirely on the whim of Emperor Henry III and died within a few months with neither loss nor glory. His immediate successor, Dámaso II, could not defend himself against Benedict IX, who desperately fought to recover his full power. In the meantime, change seemed to be at work beyond the German frontiers: In February 1049, a relative of the emperor, an Alsatian, arrived in Rome prepared to take over the reins of the Church. He was crowned Pope Leon IX, and the chaplain who accompanied him on his voyage to the pontifical see was none other than Hildebrand of Cluny.

The installation of this new pope coincided with the death of Abbot Odilo of Cluny and with the naming as abbot of Cluny the greatest promoter of Cluniac power, St. Hugh (1049–1109), whose fifty years in the position coincided with the most profound transformation experienced by the Church during its history to that time.[4]

Hildebrand (who, as we have learned, became pope himself in 1073) kept himself on the immediate sidelines of the pontiffs who had been appointed by the emperors—Victor II, Stephen IX, Benedict X, and Nicholas II. He exchanged his imperial influence for protection from the Normans, who dominated the old Muslim territories of Sicily and Calabria. This course of action, interrupted by the maneuvers of rival armies who fought among themselves in a battle for influence over Christendom and the Vatican's blessing, was nothing more than a means to clear the way for the Church—and, therefore, Cluny—to assume the theocracy that was the goal of the abbots of the monastery of Burgundy.

When Alexander III was named pope, Hildebrand was his chancellor. During Alexander's twelve-year pontificate (1061–73), the Roman liturgy, which still had not been recognized by some of the kingdoms of peninsular Spain, was established universally in Western Christendom. In addition, the Vatican promoted the development of the most ascetic monastic orders, including the reformed Benedictines and the Calabrese hermits. Alexander bowed to Roman aristocracy, closely connected to former popes, and was disgusted with those entrenched in their positions; he happily accepted the weakening of emperors and Normans alike by wars that would benefit only the unstoppable ascent of papal prestige. When Hildebrand was finally elected Pope Gregory VII, the Church was ready to fight for its theocratic ideal, with the goal of placing itself as the foundation of that universal empire which Cluny had silently promoted. The struggle of Gregory VII against internal meddling by Henry IV, which, according to some, made Gregory the most important pontiff in all of Christendom, suffices as proof of this willingness to fight. And although Gregory's efforts failed and he ended his days in Salerno after placing himself in the custody of Abbot Desiderio of Montecassino, his call was a true Cluniac declaration of war: Ultimately, it was the monks of the Benedictine Order who dug the foundations and built the structures of the glorious edifice of power that soon stood ready to take the reins of the Occident's destiny.

An Introduction to Holy War

There has been more than enough insistence that the Crusades be defined as a visceral reaction to Islam's domination of the Holy Land and the subsequent impossibility of access to Jerusalem for those Christian pilgrims who were full of desire to reach that Axis Mundi of the gospel narration. Naturally, many historians echoed this rationale, until investigative trends persisted in uncovering the economic reasons behind that medieval epic, which served to remove the sacred aspect of the motives put forward by the chroniclers who wrote under the influence of the Church's interests.

The metahistorical reality, if it could be so called, is different still, and its analysis could open new investigative roads. To get a fuller picture of the authentic (and secret) motives of the Crusades, let us look, at least superficially, at the circumstances on the Iberian Peninsula in the years surrounding the millennium.

At this time, Iberian territory was geographically and politically divided into two presumably opposed belief systems: Christianity and Islam. The Muslims occupied more than two thirds of Spanish territory, whereas the northern third was Christian, divided among fledgling states that were powerless and capable of surviving only by forming themselves as a barrier between the Peninsula and the rest of Europe, which essentially relegated Iberia to oblivion. This is verified by non-peninsular chroniclers and historians who did not consider Hispania part of Europe; instead it was merely the wall that allowed the rest of the West to exist without an immediate Muslim threat.

This state of isolation in Iberia produced an unusual situation relative to the rest of Europe: Al Andalus—that is, Muslim Spain—sheltered within it almost as many Christians, or *mozarabes,* as Muslims. Likewise, almost as many Muslims—*mudéjars*—as Christians inhabited the small kingdoms of the north. In addition, on one side of the border—however imprecise—there could be found numerous Sephardic colonies, for many Jews had arrived in Hispania at least since the conquest of Jerusalem by Titus, and these communities served Christians and Muslims and provided an effective emulsion of beliefs and effects that made the peninsular Christians feel closer to their Andalusian neighbors than to their fellow Christians on the other side of the Pyrenees. Wars, when they erupted, were of a political nature or were due to mere territorial or economic needs. In the meantime, Hispanic Islam absorbed Christian esoteric spirituality through its Sufi masters, and the monks on both sides of the dividing line drank in with enthusiasm the manuscripts of the old tradition, which Islam had rescued in the East.

For the Cluniac fundamentalist ideology, this way of living on the Iberian Peninsula was a threat, or at least an obstacle, to the desire to bring the known world to the universal submission of the powerful Church. This was a situation in many ways similar to that in the Orient, where Christian beliefs bloomed under the political dominance of Islam. Armenians, Coptics, Monophysitists, Maronites, Jacobites, Nestorians, and some minor sects could speak openly in these environments, safe from the strict Roman orthodoxy that wanted to bring them back to the bosom of Christendom's dominance as it liberated Islamic territories.

Today, we have many details regarding how Cluny started to infiltrate the Iberian Peninsula in the last years of the millennial period (c. 1027), steadily earning the goodwill of the region's Christian monarchs and transforming its religious image into one of traditional monasticism while it prepared to launch the Christian states into the great Reconquista.[5] The Cluniac leaders were trying to foment on all levels the idea of a holy war that, in theory, would forcibly Christianize the known world and, at the same time with the cooperation of officials, create an army whose mission would be to defend the Church and win territories for its glory. In place of wages, the Church would give the members of this army, as "Crusaders," the promise of salvation, thereby making them warriors of the Cross and fighters for the universal theocratic ideal.

The only differences formally distinguishing the Western Crusades from those of the East were that in the Holy Land there could be found the remains—or the memory—of the very roots of Christianity and that an expedition to the East would demand a more laborious preparation, at least theoretically; it seemed the enemies of the faith on the Iberian Peninsula were merely "around the corner." To reach their goals in Palestine, the Crusaders would be required to make a very long trip during which they would have to cross the Byzantine Empire, which was governed mostly by a Christianity that no longer recognized Roman authority. Thus, regarding the presumptuous soul-saving adventure of the East versus that of Iberia, the deployment of means was considerably greater and the risks were more evident in the former. In addition, an Eastern

Crusade came with a difficulty regarding its conclusion: While the conquered territories of the Iberian Peninsula would always belong to the monarchs who had organized the campaigns, those of the Orient would have to be divvied up and political leaders to run them would have to come from among the Crusaders.

A Well-Outlined Plan

The papal regimes supported by Cluny, beginning with Alexander II and his chancellor, Hildebrand, started to worry seriously about the creation of a strong army exclusively dedicated to serving the theocratic interests of the Church. An ameliorating situation, interestingly, was furnished by the Normans, one of the groups that had only lately been incorporated into the Faith and had been famous in past centuries for its indiscriminate raids on Christian and Islamic territories on the European Atlantic shore, where they had established bridgeheads that were soon to become new kingdoms: Great Britain, Normandy, and Calabria.

The Normans were the first force launched in Italy by Hildebrand and Pope Nicholas II against imperial aspirations for continued dominance over the destinies of the Roman pontificate. The Normans took from the Muslims their last strongholds on the Italian peninsula and attacked them on neighboring islands—Malta, Sicily, and Sardinia—eventually arriving on the African coasts, assisted by ships from Pisa and Genoa, which launched attacks very similar to those executed by Islamic corsairs against the coasts of their Christian adversaries. The popes, even Gregory VII, supported without hesitation these enterprises and those that followed. Indeed, Cluny's pontiffs—Victor III, Abbot Desiderio of Montecassino, and Urban II—were even directed by Cluny to incite war against Islam, as they had done on the Iberian Peninsula.

But the Church required from all Christendom a total affirmation of the rebirth of Christianity and the Church as well as an acceptance by all sectors of society that would leave no doubt as to whose side anyone was on, no matter how humble or remote the individual who heeded the call. Many historians are still amazed at the massive response of all Europeans to the call to arms of Urban II at the Council of Clermont-Ferrand in 1095. In looking at this time, some point to the rebirth of Christian consciousness, a return to the ideology of martyrdom, including the sudden identification of the faithful with a Church finally rising from his own ashes. Even considering these factors, it is difficult to imagine how the pontifical message could expand so quickly and be embraced with such fervor and to such an extent three quarters of a century after the destruction of the Holy Sepulchre by Caliph Al-Hakim's Fatimites. There is no doubt that the Crusades were one of the goals that Cluny had proposed, if not from the instant of its emergence, then from the moment it established itself as a disciplined order reconfiguring universal precepts belonging solely to the Rule of St. Benedict. Because Cluny controlled the visible representative of the Church (the pope), for the Cluniacs, as for the pontiffs, holy war was the ideal medium and only possible way to achieve universal theocracy. To this end, they gathered all those who held positions of power over the society of their time and who were thereby capable of dragging the populace into an enterprise that would immediately benefit the Roman Church spiritually, politically, and materially. The Iberian experience, which was for Cluny a type of dress rehearsal for the performance in the East, demonstrated that it was possible to call on Christians to a common enterprise, as long as it promised salvation for the populace, who would follow leaders selected with care from among those who had ambition and exhibited other specific requirements and who were imbued with an almost supernatural, messianic charisma.

The Crusades, then, did not involve the Empire or monarchs, who would have claimed for themselves the glory and the benefits of the enterprise to the detriment of the aspirations of the Church. Rather, they involved the second-born of the great families and the heirs of mythical traditions, whom the populace had converted or would come to convert into knights touched by the aura of the superhuman—men capable of leading the masses anxious to reach messianic goals that would change the roots of the existential perspectives of the world. Above all, personally and collectively these masses were cleansed of the mark of sin, the terrible ghost of condemnation created by the Church, which could impede for all eternity the way to the promised Glory.

A chronicle of the Crusades that appeared in Castile probably around the beginning of the fourteenth century and the assured adaptation of other, older and contemporary Latin and French chronicles could play a significant part in the weighing and revising of the history of the beginning of that fundamental event relative to the history of the Middle Ages as a whole. The Castilian tale *La Gran Conquista de Ultramar* (The Great Overseas Conquest),[6] which has been published in various manuscript versions, first in Salamanca in 1503, certainly constitutes the most complete compendium of that transcendental adventure, with an immense added value contributed by certain traditional accounts from those who accompanied the principal leaders of the first expedition. In chapter 29 of *La Gran Conquista de Ultramar,* we are told of many noble knights who "crossed" themselves, eager to depart to the Orient after Urban II's ardent proclamation during the Council of Clermont in 1095. Among them, we see a brother of the king of France, the count of Flanders, Robert of Normandy; William the Long Sword, a brother of the Norman king of England; the counts of Bearn, Aubergy, Chartres, Flowers, and Orange; the lords of Montpellier, Caumont, and Bonneville; and many others, including the man who would become the undisputable hero of that first divine adventure to the East: Godfrey of Bouillon.

The Predestined Leader

Historians cannot agree on why Godfrey of Bouillon was elected king of Jerusalem when the immediate goal of the Crusades had been fulfilled. Some gloss over the subject altogether as something too difficult to determine, while others avoid declaring their thoughts on the matter by suggesting cryptically that the reasons are impossible to publish. The more sincere scholars claim not to understand how the thirty-six-year-old man from Lorraine reached such a position (though he in fact refused to be crowned and accepted only the title Defender of the Holy Sepulchre). It seems he did not have many special merits—certainly others had worked harder than he—nor did he come from stock that might earn him a vote of blind confidence (though he was a very distant descendant of Charlemagne). The only fact we officially know of him is that when he was still very young, he was allied with Emperor Henry IV against Pope Gregory VII in the struggles over the latter's investiture. Before leaving for the Holy Land, he and his brothers Eustace and Baldwin resigned all their goods and properties, as if declaring that they had no intention of returning to their country of origin. If the chroniclers' words are true, Godfrey's very election, conducted by an assembly of unnamed Crusaders' representatives, seems due to the exaggerated devotion he displayed in public and in private. The text of *The Great Overseas Conquest* tells us that those closest to him were continuously engaged in endless prayer and that when they entered a church, everything went by the wayside, even scheduled appointments. Thus "the knights passed much time, taking so long that their eating was ruined."[6]

The election of Godfrey of Bouillon as visible head of this overseas adventure that transformed medieval history is the first clue that Cluny's theocratic plans were not completely realized. First, Godfrey was a noble who, from the early years of his youth, had shown his partiality to imperial ideas and had actively collaborated with Henry IV in the emperor's fight against the investiture of Hildebrand as Pope Gregory VII, whom Henry managed to imprison during the attack on Rome. In addition, according to what the contemporary chroniclers say, Godfrey's origins accumulated legendary elements connecting him to traditional myths that had no place in the structures laid out by Cluny for the future political roles of the Church and the papacy. According to these myths, which *The Great Overseas Conquest* recounts minutely through ninety-one chapters in Book 1, Godfrey of Bouillon was the grandson of the Knight of the Swan, who, in Western tradition, was connected to magic—some heterodox, some pagan—to form part of a myth whose elements can be found in narrations including the epic novel *Los Siete Infantes de Lara* (The Seven Princes of Lara) in Castile and the Germanic tale of Lohengrin, the son of Parsifal, which encompass a significant component of medieval sentiment.[7] To declare Godfrey of Bouillon a descendant of the Knight of the Swan was to attach him to an ancestral sacredness that could be tapped only by those who were predestined, who carried the sign* identifying them as chosen by the gods to effect great transcendental deeds. It was surely Cluny's intention, however, to create a king of the world from the orthodoxy imposed by Rome, not from a tradition that the Church could not control. And there was no doubt that Godfrey's predestination, only now coming to light, was an association carefully prepared and executed.

Interestingly, shortly after the turn of the millennium, at the end of the tenth century and into the eleventh, there appeared in Calabria an eremetical movement.[8] It was born at the same time as the Cluniac reform movement, but contrary to the leaders of Cluny, its founder, St. Nile (born c. 905), followed the Rule of St. Basil, which was explicitly forbidden by the Roman Church when the Rule of St. Benedict was established under Pope Gregory Magnus in the sixth century. In Apulia we can still find the remains of St. Nile's *lavra,* monasteries constructed to resemble those in which gathered the hermits in the deserts of Thebes and eastern Jordan under primitive anchoritic Christianity.[9] The Calabrese cenobites lived near Islamic and Norman influences until the monks of Montecassino granted them a place in which to congregate and live apart from the vicissitudes of the history and geography of their time: Velleluce, the Valley of Light. In one of the hills near this locale there can be found the remains of Mercurion, a pagan sanctuary dedicated to Hermes, the syncretic divinity originating in Egypt whose cult, with its esoteric knowledge that made Hermes famous as messenger of the gods, extended throughout the Mediterranean basin. Curiously, the hermits of St. Nile (we must take notice of the derivation of this saint's name) acquired the reputation of great astrologers among the people of southern Italy; they were considered capable of foretelling the destiny of the faithful.

Although the Calabrese hermits always maintained themselves apart from the world and its avatars, they eventually counted among their group close to three hundred cenobites, and they obtained from Pope Paschal II, in 1105, a privilege of exception that officially authorized them to continue to follow the Eastern Rule they had chosen a

*Note the French phonetic differentiation between *cygne* and *signe.*

century before. They did not expand much throughout Europe, and there is hardly any information on their German branch established in Burtscheid by the Calabrian monk Gregory.[10] Toward the year 1060, however, the approximate birth year of Godfrey of Bouillon, a group of the Calabrese hermits repossessed the French lands to the north of France and installed themselves in what is now Belgium, in the forest of Orval, which formed part of the domains of the duchess Matilde of Tuscany and Count Godfrey the Gibbous, the adoptive parents of the man who would be recognized as the leader of the First Crusade. Tradition points toward evidence that one of these cenobites of St. Nile was Peter the Hermit, who forecast the Crusades at the same time that Urban II issued his call and whose journey to the Holy Land—which preceded the campaign known as the Gentlemen's Crusade—was accompanied by an impressive army of forty thousand indigents. Unhappily, most in this army died along the way, as if preparing the road to salvation that the organized warriors would follow soon after.

It seems that the Calabrese hermits abandoned their refuge in Orval sometime around 1108, as silently and mysteriously as they had arrived, and that immediately the newborn Order of Cister, founded in part by Stephen Harding, third abbot of Cîteaux, and having as its spiritual and ideological leader St. Bernard of Clairvaux, took over the site and built on it one of its most important abbeys. But it seems that not all the hermits of St. Nile returned to their places of origin. The chronicles of the Crusades, among them *The Great Overseas Conquest,* allow us to glimpse the Calabrese hermits among those who victoriously entered Jerusalem. One of these Calabrian victors was the bishop of Mantran, who, according to the chronicle, found the miraculous clue suggesting that, despite the aspirations of other important leaders in the Crusades, the king of Jerusalem should be Godfrey of Bouillon.

The *Castilian Chronicle*[11] tells us that among the members of the assembly who were in doubt about who would be deserving of the title of king, the voice of the Calabrese bishop imposed itself, proposing that all clerics and leaders go in penitence to the Holy Sepulchre and that any military leaders who wanted to elucidate who would be leader bring with them unlit candles: "[L]et us all pray to God that he who pleases him be the king of Jerusalem, and that he demonstrate later his virtue with a miracle over his candle, in a manner that it remains lit; and he whom he lights, we will raise to honor Jesus Christ." The *Chronicle* continues that the knights did penance and fasted with barley bread and water, each one eating "three bites and no more," and that when night fell, they gathered in the Holy Sepulchre, illuminated only by the lamp at the altar, and prayed that the Lord grant them the light while they sang *Veni Creator Spiritus*. Suddenly, a horrendous clap of thunder was heard, "and later came a bolt that entered through the church as if it were fire and in passing lit the candle of Duke Godfrey of Bouillon."

The Scene Is Set

Urban II lay dying while the Crusaders took Jerusalem. He could not contemplate from this world the results of the great operation that he launched from the field of Hermes of Clermont, an enterprise that, theoretically, was to make the Church the absolute owner of Christendom and an aspirant to governing the world. But there were profound changes to come—changes that Cluniac ideology had not yet noticed. The principal clue at that time was strictly political: Cluny had spent its ascent to power influencing and standing at the side of European monarchs so that these men, upon rebelling against the Empire, would opt for total obeisance to the papacy, which, in turn, would designate from among them, because of their fidelity and devoted defense, those worthy of heading the destinies of the Church's universal government so carefully structured in the millennial age.

Now, however, with the results of the First Crusade in sight and the return of many of those who had departed for the Holy Land under the cry of "*Dieu le voit!*," the scenario played out very differently. Politically, Cluny, with its monks still placed strategically in Rome, was being contested by both the populace and the nobility, who saw themselves left behind by the ostensible demonstrations of power exhibited by an order that seemed to care only for the accumulation of riches and the offering of favors to the highest bidders. In all of Europe—and especially on the Iberian Peninsula—the lower nobility as well as the populace were retiring their unconditional support for the black monks. Faced with the obligation of turning in their tithe and earning their place in heaven through sacred charity, they preferred to donate their means to humble monks who had passed through the monastery and returned to lifestyles resembling traditional eremitism. For example, the lists of donations noted in the archives of the Galician monasteries[12] clearly demonstrate a slow decrease compared to those of royal provenance.

The Cluniacs, who converted the holy war into an essential expression of their ideology, lost control in Palestine and started to do the same on the Iberian Peninsula. Europe's monarchs worried about a monasticism that took hold of every available cenobite and the greater part of the episcopal sees and, through its influence, tried to bend the behavior of the states and its rulers to the insatiable will of a faraway abbey independent of any jurisdiction.

The emergence of the Cistercians in the years surrounding the First Crusade was an affront to Cluniac predominance. Like the Cluniacs, the Cistercians set for themselves the goal of theocratic control of the world. In principle, its greatest promoters—Robert of Molesme, Stephen Harding, and Bernard of Clairvaux—planned to achieve this end by means of tenets that Cluny had forgotten: austerity, work, and economic independence from those in positions of power. They felt that monks, and with them the Church as a whole, could achieve universal domination and victory over the forces opposed to their ideology only if they worked for these goals on their own, if the power they achieved emerged from their own convictions, and if they could do without the accumulated dependencies that Cluny had not managed—or did not want—to eliminate. According to the Cistercians, asceticism and work were the source of energy and power.

Of course, there was no need to reject what Cluny had already achieved. In reality, the ideological scaffold erected by Cluny was perfectly sound when the time came for the Cistericans to act. Both the plot and the ideological message of the sacred drama of the time were perfectly functional; only the stage, the actors, and the method of performing required altering. The Cistercians set about integrating and contemporizing strict Christian faith and tradition—that is, without disowning the principles that sustained the essence of Christianity, they showcased how these aspects could seamlessly and undogmatically mingle with humanity's ancestral tendencies. Mystical living, equal in many aspects to the initiation process that the Church ostensibly disowned, returned with the Cistercians—or at least, it became an intention—to constitute one of the fundamental bases of the transcendental experience. Regarding the power to influence and win over, which no ideology could entirely abjure, Bernard and his Cistercians discovered that after a thousand years of Christian faith, the return to the arcane Mother was fundamental to creating an ecumenical and universal religious sentiment. The Cistercians, who foresaw the return to the earth through work, lived and propitiated as never before the cult to Mother Earth through the resurrection of the cult to the Mother of God. Since the Second Council of Nicaea, this worship had been confined to theological writings that were never divulged and were known and discussed only in the bosom of the highest ecclesiastical authority.

The Cistercians, who would very soon start to place popes in the Vatican, did not lose the theocratic password; instead, they reinforced it with the addition of some modes of behavior that, at least in principle, made way for other methods of confronting faith and transcendence.

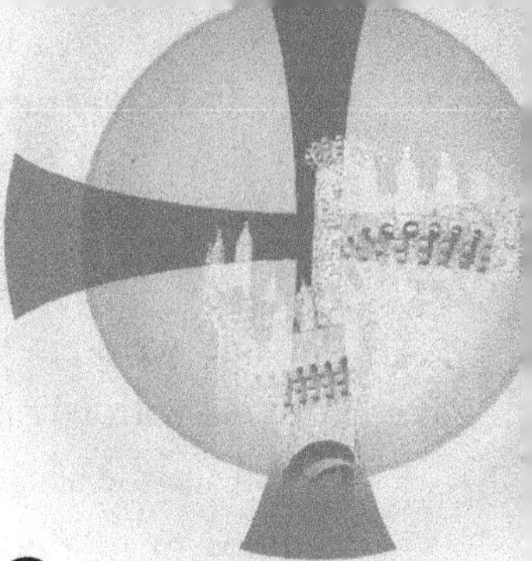

2
The Clues to God's Militia

From its undisputed summit of authority, the Roman Church had spent half its history preaching the principles of love for God and neighbor and peace and harmony among human beings. It spent the other half coming up with both excuses and reasons not to fulfill these precepts and a justification for violence, torture, discrimination, and the struggle to the death for power as they worked toward achieving the world's submission to its theocratic will.

From Peace to Holy War

The words attributed to Jesus in the gospels are always words of harmony and love. Even when he proclaims that he has not come to this world to bring peace, or when he suggests the necessity of breaking with romantic and family ties, he preaches not war or hate, but rather the necessity that human affections be channeled to the Divinity through primordial love. The years of persecution were years of victimization, of allowing people to be killed for an ideal but not to kill for the same. Only when the Church looked at the possibility of using its authority for the salvation of the world, thanks to Constantine the Great's progressiveness and his solar exaltation, did the cross emerge as the theoretical protagonist of a victorious war: the Battle of Milvian Bridge, with *In hoc signo vinces.**

The writings of the great Christian theologians of antiquity are plagued with complicated mental processes that attempt to give justification for the senseless phenomena of violence and war. These thinkers claimed to follow evangelical teachings with the intention of creating a different world based on the idea of salvation—a concept that had never before emerged with such force in any religious structure. The excuse they cited (a very human one) was this: self-defense. The ideology included removing the mark of sin from those who kill or create violence either in defense of what they consider just or in punishment of those who operate on the margins of justice. Naturally, no one in the constellation of holy fathers of the time doubted what was just. As in our day—for we are the direct inheritors of two thousand years of ecclesiastical power—what is just is established by those in power. Just are those who follow the rules that come from that power. A just war, like those proclaimed by Augustine of Hippo, is one that avenges injustice. Yet not Augustine nor Isidoro of Seville nor the popes who applauded them nor the councils that backed them and elevated their words to those of the rank of precept ever mention either what is meant by justice or what kind of justice determines who is just. Nevertheless, the idea of justice is understood and all must accept it, with its inevitable consequences of prizes for some and punishments for others.

As we have seen, the convenient concept of a just war remained current in the Christian world until the fulfillment of the millennium. During this time, popes and the Church approved or dismissed the struggles among the laity as they benefited or threatened Church interests. But up to the millennium the ecclesiastical state had not intervened in any war, even though it suffered some passively, especially at the time of the barbarian invasions. This fact did not stop Church representatives from advocating campaigns such as Charlemagne's expeditions, or from justifying aggressions that allowed its expansion. In the midst of

---

*["By this sign you shall conquer," which refers to Constantine's pre-battle vision of a heavenly cross. —*Ed.*]

all these acts of violence, however, it was the laity who had intervened at their own risk; the clergy, pontiffs, and monks limited themselves to pronouncements of justification or condemnation.

In 1027, Abbot Oliba, bishop of Vic, declared in the document *Peace and Truce* that it was forbidden by religious authority for anyone to "assault his enemy from the noon hour of Saturday until the prime hour of Monday, with the goal that all should be able to fulfill Sunday's duties; that no one assault for any reason clerics or nuns that go unarmed, or those men who with their families come and go from church; no one should dare assault or violate the churches or the houses within a radius of thirty steps."[1]

This document, reflecting the firm will of a segment of ecclesiastical authority to control the warring actions of the laity and to determine the legality of such actions, was subscribed to and implemented in the whole Christian world through the insistence of Abbot Odilo of Cluny in 1041, which thereby exerted a certain amount of control over the duration of those wars that the Church had no interest in ending but instead confirmed and adjusted to its own interests. In effect, it allowed war when and how it suited Christendom and its representatives.*

A just war, however, would not satisfy the Church, Cluny, or Rome when it came to the involvement of its representatives in the theocracy these institutions projected. Authorizing or forbidding an engagement is not the same as promoting or preaching it. A new situation must be created, and it was found in Spain: the full-scale dress rehearsal for holy war, *jihad,* all-out conflict with the enemies of the religion, a struggle that would ensure the moral impunity of those who killed and eternal Glory for those who died in the battle against the enemy.

Holy war found its catechism in the vibrant call of Urban II at Clermont, which Hildebrand, together with St. Hugo of Cluny, had put to good use in the struggle aginst Henry IV and his predecessor Alexander II, when the peninsular Christian armies were incited to recuperate for

*This decree for peace and a truce was for a long time thought to have been the work of St. Odilo, until the discovery made by Father Albareda, which demonstrated Oliba's authorship.[2]

Christendom the lands taken by Islam three and half centuries before. Thus it is the declaration of Clermont that defines divine battle and to whom it is charged:

> To whom go there and lose life in the enterprise, during the trip by land or sea, or in the fight against infidels, may at that hour their sins be forgiven, by the power that by God our Lord himself has been conceded to me [. . .] Who until now lived in criminal enmity against his fellow believers, turn your weapons against the infidels and take to its victorious conclusion that war that should have been initiated a long time ago; who until today were bandits, make yourselves soldiers, deserve now the eternal prize; who dissipated their strengths with grave harm to body and soul, employ them now and win a double reward.[3]

From Crusader to Warrior-Monk

By the power and grace of pontifical power and Cluniac ideology accepted without question by the militant Church, the laity, which came from all parts of society, had, as in the times of martyrdom, an opportunity to reach heaven on the fast track. The past did not matter for those who answered the call to arms, for it was clear that sins would be forgiven through the devoted exercise of violence, war, and extortion, and the stains of humanity could be made sacred and be integrated into the most pure Christian sentiment. It sufficed to change the ordinary meaning of some terms—in time, this practice would become habitual, as it is now—so that killing became a bit of *opus Dei as*, pilgrims fullfilling God's supernatural goals, which are reinterpreted as needed by his most renowned representatives.

We should keep in mind, however, a very special circumstance: Members of the ecclesiastical estate—abbots, priests, bishops, and monks—were expressly forbidden to take arms, though no one seemed scandalized when a cleric beheaded Saracens. Officially, war was the function of the laity, no matter how holy the ends, how sacred the warriors, or how holy their patrons, as was Santiago Matamoros (Moor Killer) or St. Millán in Spain, who from the heavens decided victory in compromised battles. As for members of the laity, when facing certain stimuli—the possibility of bounty, for instance—they could forget their sacrosanct function and give in to the desire to pillage (to their benefit and to the detriment of the rights acquired from the Church, which, feeling fleeced of what it considered its patrimony, still had to keep its promise to ensure the salvation of those who plundered in its interests). The religious consciousness of the warrior stopped at the designation of an enemy whose annihilation would guarantee salvation.

Things changed when, thanks to Cluniac strategy, the Holy Sites were conquered, the penalties suffered in the campaign were compensated by bounty, and the Crusaders opted either to return to their homes or to establish themselves in the new territories, creating duchies, counties, lordships, and even kingdoms structured in the image of the feudal world they had left behind in Europe. The Church and the few Crusaders conscious of the authentic intentions provoked by the call to holy war awoke to an unfavorable situation for the intended theocracy. The recognized ideal at the time, like a battering ram capable of knocking down the walls of the Axis Mundis called Jerusalem, apparently was coming apart and had widened once again the breach that existed between the laity and a religious authority that attempted to control its behavior. The crusading knights' particular interests once again differed from and even opposed the essentially ecumenical interest of a Church that was anxious to impose itself as the one decisive power in Christendom's universe.

The problem and its eventual, convenient solution resided in making war compatible with monastic vocation. Monasticism's vow of poverty was the only means by which a troublesome knight could be made to place above all else reordered precepts of indiscriminate obedience to avoid the temptations that might arise during bellicose activity and its consequences.

Without a doubt, the scheme that was decided on was one that mirrored Islam's structure. In Islam, holy war—jihad—was directly related to the teaching of the Koran, while the teaching of the gospels decidedly called for peace and harmony among human beings.

In the Islamic world of the Orient, the Maghreb, and Al Andulus, the *ribats* were fortified convents, collectives of warrior-monks who were prepared to join the elite corps of Muslim armies. In them the teachings of the Koran were tirelessly imparted at the same time that individulas were conscientiously preparing for a holy war, which the Prophet had proclaimed a fundamental goal of Islam. As it was conceived by the adepts of the ribats, jihad was seen in principle as a purification translated into a struggle within ourselves against the passions usual to the human condition, which was then channeled into an all-out war for the universal triumph of the Islamic ideal. The warrior devotees did not go to a ribat to spend their lives cloistered, however, as the Christian monks did, but rather to receive the sacred warrior initiation that would later allow them to face the enemies of their faith in a battle which, as much as killing and dying could, had much to do with the mystical. They transformed the notion of war into a transcendental act emanating directly from divine will.

Although contemporary chronicles do not usually speak of it, it is more than likely that in their struggle against the peninsular Moors, the Christian warriors heard of Islam's warrior-monks. Toponomy has left us many names that speak of the places where these ribats were built: San Carlos de la Rápita (at the mouth of the Ebro River), Calatrava (a transformed Qalat al-Ribat), and Rábida of the Huelva region, as well as the names from Soria, Rabanera and Rábanos. All these are associated with areas on the Peninsula where Islamic warrior-monks faced Christian troops in the Middle Ages.

Templars before the Temple

The Crusaders must have had more than just secondhand information about the ribats and the warrior-monk's efficiency and religious courage, for their fame and even some basic attempt at imitating them started to spread, especially among those who, after their mission had ended, had returned to their home countries touched by the sacredness of the adventure through which they had just lived.

Despite the fact that Pope Urban II vetoed the Spaniards' intervention in the Crusades, alleging that a similar holy war was already taking place on the Iberian Peninsula under the auspices of Cluny, numerous knights and nobles from Castile, Catalonia, Navarre, and Aragon answered the call. Most of these were integrated into the host armies of Raymond IV of Toulouse, who was accompanied in this enterprise by the Castilian princess Elvira, daughter of Alfonso VI.[4] Some historians affirm that Count Enrique of Borgoña, married to Teresa, another daughter of Alfonso VI and founder of what was to be the kingdom of Portugal, was also in the Holy Land during the First Crusade. This seems doubtful, however, given the numerous problems the count met in his attempt to gain as much independence as possible for the territories granted him by his father-in-law.

The Crusaders from the Peninsula returned to their original kingdoms steeped in miraculous legends and laden with relics, some of which in time started to acquire fame (including the images of Our Lady supposedly carved by St. Luke and, above all, numerous fragments of the True Cross). Tradition says that these relics are what inspired the count of Portugal to join the Crusades—for it is told that Godfrey of Bouillon himself gifted the count with several relics and the emperor of Byzantium gave him the very arm of St. Luke, the Evangelist, who today is venerated in the cathedral of Braga.[5] Similar tales about the inspiration of relics are told of Prince Ramiro, father of García Ramirez, the Restorer, king of Navarre and son-in-law to El Cid Campeador's daughter, Elvira. Prince Ramiro apparently fought valiantly in the Crusades and was present at the taking of Jerusalem, which he entered by passing through the Gates of the Lions. Legend tells us that he reached the Pool of Bethesda and found on its dry floor an image of Our Lady carved, of course, by St. Luke, and a fragment of the Living Cross. In 1110 he made provisions in his will for the housing of such relics and charged the abbot of the monastery of San Pedro of Cardeña, Pedro Virila, with building a church that was to be called Our Lady of the Pool. He also asked that there be created in his name a brotherhood of knights to watch over the temple and venerate the relics. His descendants and relatives would form part of this brotherhood, as would people of good birth who committed themselves to a life of charity and to the defense of the Faith against its enemies. This brotherhood would constitute something like a knightly order dedicated to fighting for the Christian religion. It was specified in the will that this order would never grant membership to plebes or descendants of Muslims or Jews or those lacking the aristocratic and devout spirit demanded by the fraternity.

This military or knightly order proposed by Ramiro had no rules and asked for no proof of commitment other than some kind of declaration of intent. Its parallel might be the Order of the Jar, founded in Nájera by the grandfather of Prince Ramiro, the king don García, on the basis of a miracle that supposedly revealed to him the image of Holy María the Royal some seventy years earlier. Ramiro's so-called order, certainly the first founded by a layperson in the Middle Ages, was also based on the commitment of its members to defend the name of Our Lady from attacks and ambushes from enemies of the Faith.

It was an event in Aragon during the reign of Alfonso I, the Battler (who will appear again later in our story, in relation to the Templars), that for a long time convinced some historians that the Templars had established themselves in this peninsular kingdom before receiving official approval for the Order at the Council of Troyes in 1128. Professor Lacarra has published documents in which there is mentioned a "Militia Templi Iherosimilitanis" or "Salomonis," an order that existed before the Templars were introduced on the Peninsula, which made him suspect the presence of a contingent of Templars in Iberia before the Order was formally recognized.[6] In reality, as later studies have discovered, this "order" was a brotherhood of knights from Aragon and France who, infused with the spirit of the Crusades, were charged by King Alfonso with defending the frontiers of the kingdom of Valencia from the attacks of the Moors.[7] This brotherhood (Confraternitas Caesaraugustane Militae), was installed in Monreal del Campo and was also headquartered at Belchite[8] and Zaragoza. It was effectively conceived as an order in the style of the ones that had started to appear in the Holy Land. The sixteenth-century Spanish historian Zurita y Castro confirmed this when he specified that the king "proposed to establish another in imitation of the order and militia of the Holy Sepulchre."[9]

What these creations fundamentally prove is that the Christian world, and in a unique way the Hispanic environment, had, with Cluny's tacit blessing, accepted the necessity to channel the meaning of holy war through committed collectives controlled by the Church via vows or rules. These rules obligated their followers to take up the fight against the infidels as part of a vital mission rather than as a solution to the problems of conscience experienced by those who went to war as a means of acquiring lands, riches, and honors at the expense of an enemy of the Faith against whom all sorts of excesses could be committed. This effort at association, which emerged from a desire to institutionalize the path to theocracy promulgated by the Cluniac pontiffs, would find in the Templars a model of the formal structure of what should constitute God's authentic militia. Orders like the Templars convinced the Church it could reach by its own means those summits of power it long held as a goal without having to depend on a secular force that could turn its back at any moment on the interests of Rome in favor of its own ends, however distantly related to the Church's goals they might be.

The Birth of the Templars

As much as we would like to be able to read between the lines of history, we will never be able to know with certainty if the Order of the Poor Knights of Christ and the Temple of Solomon emerged due to the Church, the concrete monastic system that provided the structure of its ideology, or from a particular initiative that the highest ecclesiastical hierarchy adopted once it realized the role it could play in the attainment of papal goals. History gives sufficient clues for us to suspect, with a high degree of certainty, that the Templars did not appear by chance, the whim of its founders, or some predesigned intention of the Church. Everything seems to point to a deliberate proposal by Hughes de Payns and his initial companions of the possibility of forming a fraternity in which the search for knowledge would join forces with military and economic power to achieve, through its prestige, a synarchy* in which the Church could take part as a source of spiritual authority—a fraternity of brothers who could act as unconditional guardians and firm watchmen should the time come to close ranks and defend it.

The Templars' synarchic plan undoubtedly had many similarities to Cluny's theocracy in terms of an ideal and goal to be achieved by the Church. But its philosophy soon diverged from that of Cluny thanks to the founding Templars' nine-year initiation in the Holy Land. The Templars were never averse to claiming certainties that might divert from the strict dogma on which the Church had propped its authority. Instead, many of its structures point toward an attempt at unifying Christian beliefs with those held by Islam and Judaism, of fusing beliefs seen as anathema by Christian fundamentalism toward the idea of making a more ecumenical, transcendent belief system with Jerusalem as its great center. Jerusalem, after all, was a city held sacred not only by the three great religions born of the one Book, but also by the marginal movements that emerged from primitive Christianity, those belief systems that had been shunned in the West but which clearly blossomed in the lands of the Fertile Crescent.

The nine years that passed between the time when Hughes de Payns and his companions went before Baldwin II, Latin king of Jerusalem, asking to be installed in the ancient stables of Solomon's palace (then occupied by King Baldwin) near the Temple Mount, and the Order's approval by the Council of Troyes (1118–28) suggests an accumulation of apparently unanswerable questions that point to a perfectly structured plan. The spiritual and familial vincula of its main founders to Bernard of Clairvaux, who in those years may have intervened in the Holy Land's public affairs and military matters, their insistance on occupying the space that formed part of the Temple of Solomon, and their propagation of Bernard's fame throughout Europe, seemingly without taking any action to further it, were all shrewd promotional maneuvers. (Such

*A government made up of various princes, each one administrating a section of the state.

actions are identical to the kind of promotional efforts that precede the launch of certain consumer products in the advertising world today.)

A good deal of intrigue accumulated in the years preceding the approval of the Order. Apparently the Templars did not give any signs of bellicosity during the nine long years prior to their acceptance by the Church. As the chroniclers of the Crusades indicate, they went before Baldwin II with the intention of becoming involved in the protection of pilgrims and the paths they traveled—of becoming a sort of rural police. Intriguingly, the king of Jerusalem wrote Bernard a letter in which he asked the Church for protection and assistence in recruiting men for the defense of Christ's sepulchre and to fight in the Holy Land. He then gave this letter to the Templars to take to Troyes.

Here are some other details that reinforce the obscurity of Templar origins and intentions:

- The insistence that there be exactly nine knights, between the time of their introduction to the king of Jerusalem and the approval of the Order, prompting some—Hugo de Champagne, for example—to join the Templars in 1125
- The evidence that none of the founding Templars was involved in the conquest of Jerusalem and that all of them arrived in Palestine when the Crusade had actually ceased operations
- The surprising fact that the Order had barely been approved when Templar membership exploded, including the alleged en masse joining of neophytes. The period of novitiate, which for the founders had been nine long years, was now waived, allowing new members to immediately acquire posts and responsibilities that they used to gain access to lords and monarchs while soliciting donations and expounding their ideology.
- The unexpected praising of certain Templar virtues by Bernard of Clairvaux in *De Laude Novae Militiae* (In Praise of the New Knighthood)—virtues that they were still theoretically about to unveil and which confirmed their role as the undisputed protectors of the Church's interests and defenders of official Christendom

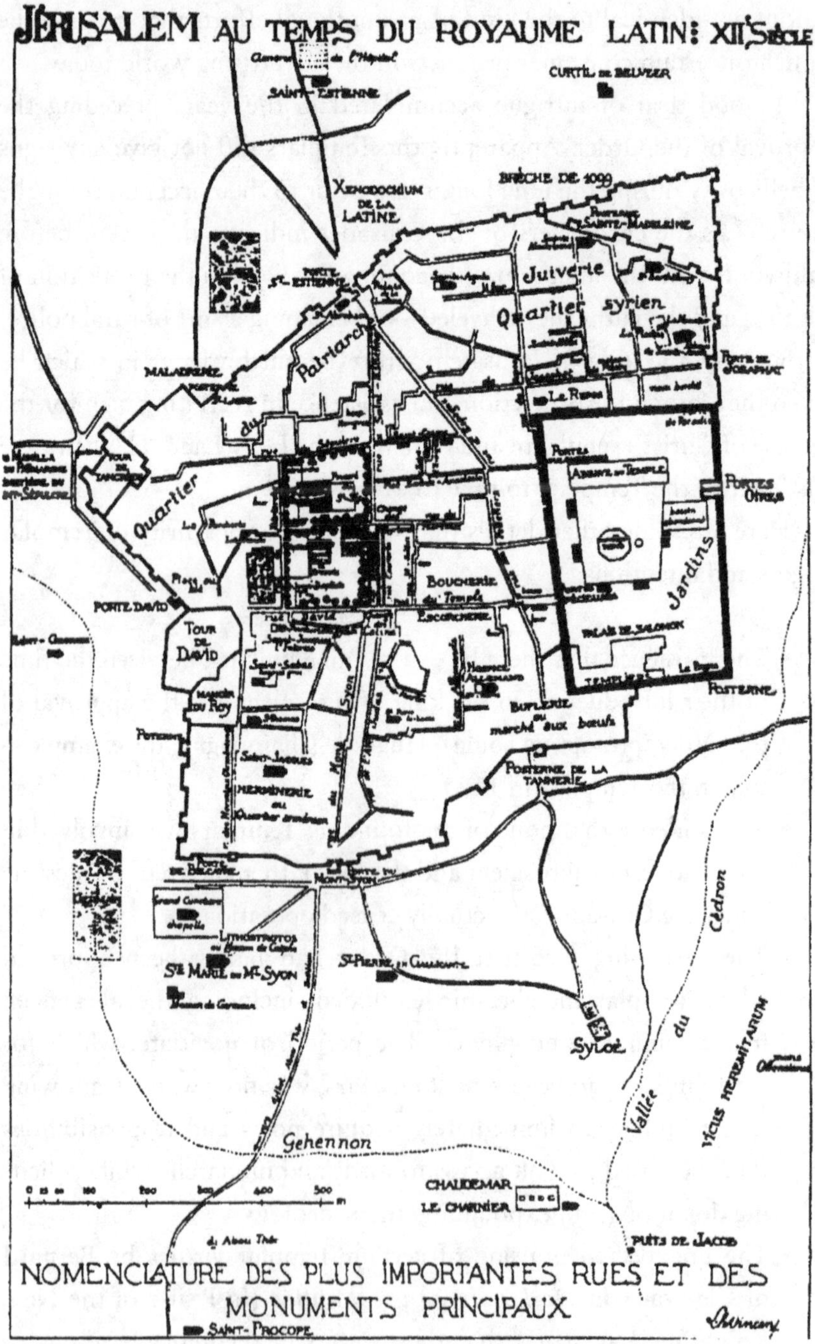

Fig. 2.1. Map of Jerusalem at the time of the Crusades. The compounds marked on the right in bold were Templar properties. Drawing by S. Lambert.

From the Temple to the Rule

When Hughes de Payns and his companions went before King Baldwin to ask for permission to establish quarters in Jerusalem, they chose as their base of operations the site previously occupied by the Temple of Solomon. The monarch immediately responded affirmatively to their petition. Some say that the location of the Temple was a direct offer from the king. Even at that time, it was seen as an important historical locale, and the Templars' location there was viewed as an important historical event.

In time, the royal palace relocated next to the Tower of David and the king ceded the entire Temple complex to the Templars, thereby lending them two transcendent associations: First, even after its destruction by Titus, the complex of the Temple had always been the preeminent sacred place of Judaism. In fact, the Wailing Wall continues to be Israel's principal place of prayer, and a Hebrew tradition holds that the arrival of the Messiah will take place when the Temple is rebuilt. Second, the mosque of Al-Aqsa, built at the beginning of the eighth century (705–15), stood on the Temple's esplanade and served as a provisional residence for Baldwin II. The Dome of the Rock, also part of the Temple complex, was raised between 687 and 691 on the rock on which Jacob had the vision of the ladder and from whence Muhammad catapulted himself to the heavens on the back of his mare, Buraq.

Simply enumerating the conflicts inspired by the Temple complex in our time suffices to show that this place, sacred to both Jews and Muslims, embodies a holiness outside of time. During the Middle Ages it was one fifth the size of the entire city. It is surprising that nine knights could occupy it for nine years without recruiting servants or others who could defend it from attacks or plundering.

Called Moriah by Muslims, the site of the Temple Mount looks today much the same as it did during the time when the Templars used it as their home until the Holy City was lost. As in antiquity, at the time of the Templar occupation there remained only part of the exterior wall of the destroyed Temple of Solomon, the Wailing Wall, along with a portion of the basement, which can be entered from the left side of the Wailing Wall and still serves as a place of study and gathering for Jews involved in religious practice. The rest of the Mount formed the upper esplanade, consisting of both Muslim and Jewish religious structures. The Templars turned the Al-Aqsa Mosque into their residence as soon as King Baldwin gave them his blessing. They used the Dome of the Rock as an oratory, consecrating it in 1142 as the Temple of the Lord and adding to it a large patriarchal golden cross placed at the highest point of the dome.[10] This base became a kind of "mother temple" of the Order and, as such, its image was reproduced on numerous Templar seals. Thus, because of the Templar associations with the Dome of the Rock and despite the naysaying of many scholars, it is not farfetched to acknowledge the Templar order as the father of those octagonal and polygonal temples that appeared throughout Europe during the twelfth and thirteenth centuries. The impetus for the construction of these buildings is found not in a desire to raise a structure with occult or esoteric implications—however much some researchers might insist on it—but instead can be put very simply: In these European buildings—places like Santa María de Eunate and the Ermita de San Saturio and the Church of the Vera Cruz of Segovia—the Templars were paying homage to their central see and calling to mind those places in which they prayed.

We must consider that all groups formed with the intent of standing apart from the society to which they actually belong and over which they aspire to rule will necessarily work with elements that distinguish them and are their exclusive property. These elements range from the use of a group of unique symbols to the adoption of codes of conduct that benefit these groups but are not applicable to the collective over which the group hopes to hold sway. This phenomenon has been repeated time and again throughout history, by the priestly class in Egypt to Freemasons today. The courses of action these collectives followed to attain their goals rather than being what we might call magical were instead simply different from the paths followed by those who do not form part of a fraternal nucleus that exists with the secret goal of dominating a larger group.

There are many examples of this action: Today we know—and there exists sufficient corroboration of this—that Hitlerian Nazism crafted a particular cosmography that had nothing to do with that generally accepted by science. Benito Mussolini and his "black shirts" devoted themselves to performing magical rituals that theoretically would elevate them to the summit of power.* If we know that so many groups, personalities, sects, and regimes followed such seemingly irrational paths with the hope of attaining their goals through magical, "secret" behavior, we cannot deny that the Templars may have operated similarly. There is no doubt that throughout its history the Order exhibited signs of following behavioral structures that were different, to say the least, from those considered legal in a society that proclaimed itself devoutly and firmly Christian in its beliefs.

It is my conviction that the Order of the Temple was created for a very concrete end that manifested itself discreetly from the time of its beginnings. One solid proof of this is that at all levels among the powerful from the moment of its inception, the Order inspired controversy, passions, and even hatred until its demise brought about by evidence (whether truthful or only partially so) concerning a kind of heretical behavior that its era's society and rulers could not tolerate. The apparent justification for the Order's persecution was the Templars' avoidance of accepted rules, but in reality, it may simply have been motivated by the perception of the Order as an obvious threat to established and recognized authority.

The document that speaks for the first time of the Templars' master plan for a new world order is the very Rule of the Temple. There has been much insistence—to which I myself have subscribed—proposing Bernard of Clairvaux as the author of this Rule. Its seventy-two points take their cue from the Rule of St. Benedict as filtered through Cistercian precepts. Close examination, however, reveals a number of clues indicating that in all probability Bernard limited himself to making corrections

*Let us remember that Benito Mussolini's personal magician was the occultist Julius Evola, just as Hitler's was the pseudoscientist Horbiger, inventor of the hollow earth theory, and as Juan Perón's was the magician López Rega, creator of the Triple A.

or additions to what the Templars drafted in Jerusalem. They based it on chapters of the Cistercian code but adapted it to the military foundations of the Order, unifying these with its conventual nature as well as (somewhat discreetly) with the long-term goals laid out by the Order's founders. We can find evidence of this unification in the fact that the text of the Rule transformed itself gradually from that approved initially to the point that substantial differences can be detected between the Latin Rule adopted by the Council of Troyes in 1128 and the first French version preserved in manuscripts drafted a short time after the Order became official. Subtle but important differences can be discerned among the later translations of the Rule for use by English, Italian, Castilian-Portuguese, and Catalan-Aragonese Templars. These differences, however coded, indicate that the Order's program varied considerably based on its host country. Similarly, today's large multinational companies exhibit small but important variations in each of the different countries in which they are based.

One of the Order's variations concerns the treatment to be conferred on excommunicated knights. According to the Latin Rule, these men could be received in the Temple as a means of atoning for their sins, but only with prior approval from the bishops of the cities in which they were recruited. But in later versions of the Rule, such as the French and Castilian versions, permission to join the Order had to be granted solely on the master of the chapter; bishops had no say or vote. This difference, seemingly merely formal, indicates on the one hand that this alteration in practice occurred in 1139, when the Templars began answering only to the pope, discarding all other ecclesiastical oversight. But it also reveals that the very fact of having been excommunicated was no obstacle to joining the Order, whose ends were above the clerical framework then in use and depended on a project much more vast than the mere fulfillment of liturgical or formal demands of canonical law.

Another point of the Rule that lends itself to erroneous and misguided interpretation can be found in numbers 46, 47, and 48 of the Latin and Castilian Rules (55 and 56 of the French Rule), which forbid the Templar knight to hunt with the help of birds, bow, crossbow, or dog and forbid hunting of any type except that of lions (number 48), the hunting of this beast being authorized due only to its symbolic meaning in the scriptures,* where it is identified with the lurking devil. Considering that by the time the Templars arrived in Palestine, lions had already disappeared from the area and, of course, from Europe, this specificity in the Rule seems absurd and unnecessary—that is, unless we interpret this struggle between knight and beast as a spiritual conflict leading to the combatant defeating his own impulses and desires. In this way, the knight was accepted on his own as a member of the Order; his work was crowned with success.

*I Peter 5.8: "Your adversary, the devil, roams as a roaring lion, looking for someone to devour."

PART 2

How to Plan a Project

And from thence forward, they grew much in country estates, as you can now see. And [they called] themselves the Order of the Temple, because they were the first close to the temple, and could not not fail beyond the seas and in that land of Christians, where there was not this order, or houses, and friars and great income. And in the beginning, they remained wise and humble, like those men who left the century of God; much later as the riches grew, they left what they began, and fell into great madness, so that later they left the orders of the patriarch of Jerusalem; and later they cheated the pope so much that they ceased to obey the patriarch and all the prelates, those who were entrusted with the assets of the Church.

La Gran Conquista de Ultramar
(The Great Overseas Conquest),
Book 3, chapter 169

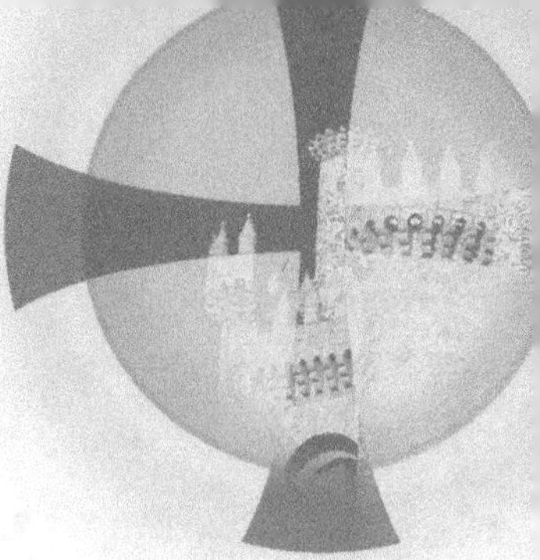

3
Like an Oil Stain

Scholars are always pleased to find documentation to supply all the facts necessary for the study of a subject, leaving no gaps or doubts, freeing them from dependence on undocumented hypotheses or on the equivocations of the chroniclers, who speak of events from their own chronological perspectives, however subject these were to diverse pressures that compelled them to adopt views we consider obsolete today. Unfortunately, there are still historical episodes about which we do not have proper documentation, perhaps because in their time they occurred with little notice, or perhaps because vested interests conspired to ignore them or to judge them according to their own criteria. This is what happened in Spain with the Templar order, whose first incursion there remains buried in silence and contradiction. This has allowed the emergence of a number of harebrained hypotheses that eventually became regarded in some quarters as fact. These, in turn, influenced attitudes, opinions, and tendencies that have produced confusion difficult to overcome in attempting to establish any certainties that can be backed by facts.

Penibetic Nationalism*

I must recount here a historical lie that I believe no one believes. I cite it to demonstrate how we ourselves can be affected by attitudes that lead us to reproach historians of other lands. This lie may also give us a measure of the importance the Order of the Temple has to Iberia. There are those who have no qualms about distorting the historical record to create the scenario by which Spain—especially Catalonia—was the historical and perhaps ideological cradle of the Templars.

I read this story by chance in a small and almost forgotten little work on the Templars put out by a publishing house in Burgos that is no longer in business and written by an author whom I tried to contact with no result.[1] While nosing around the manuscripts in the National Library, the author of this work found a seventeenth-century tale in which a don Esteban Cobera describes to the count of Guimerá the history and the details surrounding the Lignum Crucis† that is preserved in the Church of San Esteban de Bagá, in the foothills of the Catalan Pyrenees.[2] I wrote about this manuscript, enumerating the many references it made to an account of the origins of the Order of the Temple, quoting all the facts and sources I had used. I let others know of it and only later found out that a number of these people brought it to light (once again) as if they had just discovered it, without giving credit even to the author who originally discovered it. I will repeat this story, once again emphasizing how it came into my hands.

In spite of being quoted in neither the *Anales* of Zurita y Castro nor the work of Fernández de Navarrete,[3] the manuscript in question, echoing some ancient tradition of the territory of Bagá, recounts the story of brothers Hugo and Galcerán de Pinós, the sons of the admiral of Catalonia and lord of Bagá and his wife, Berenguela de Montcada, and participants in the First Crusade in answer to the call of Urban II.

*[The Penibetic Mountain Range extends from the Sierra Nevada to Cape Tarifa in the Sapnish region of Andalusia. —*Trans.*]

†Wood of the cross.

In Jerusalem they put themselves under the command of Raymond IV of Toulouse and became part of the Catalonian army led by the counts of Rousillon and Cerdaña. The brothers fought in the capture of Jerusalem (1099) and entered the city by St. Stephen's Gate. Later, during their stay in Jerusalem, the older brother, Hugo, joined other crusading knights to establish a fellowship dedicated body and soul to the protection of pilgrims. King Baldwin II gave to this fellowship as a headquarters some buildings situated in the dependencies of the old Temple of Solomon, which led these men to be called Templars. Their founder, once head of the new Order, changed his surname to reflect his place of origin and thus became Hugo de Bagá or, in Latin, Hugo de Baganis or Paganis. The French then came to call him Hughes de Payons or de Payns. Hughes eventually sent his own brother back to their birthplace in Spain, bearing the Lignum Crucis, with the specific charge of founding the Church of San Esteban, which would house the relic, and to start recruiting knights for the Order that he had established in the Holy Land.

The story is complemented by a miracle that is traditional in peninsular hagiography: Don Galcerán de Pinós fell into the hands of the Saracens when he took part in the first conquest of Almería, a small Hispanic crusade promoted by Count Ramón Berenger IV of Barcelona that took place in 1145. Legend says that as ransom for the Catalan knight the Moor asked for one hundred cows, each with flanks of a different color from the rest of its body; one hundred white horses; one hundred pieces of gold cloth; and one hundred damsels—a difficult price to pay and an impossible amount to gather. While his vassals tried to assemble this ransom at all costs, even sacrificing his properties and women, don Galcerán placed himself in the hands of the martyr St. Stephen, through whose gate he had entered Jerusalem years before. It is said that God deigned to accede to his prayers, dropping him safe and sound at the port of Salou, just as his father was about to ship the costly ransom solicited by the infidel.

We must recognize—all nationalistic feelings aside—that the framework of the story concurs with traces remaining in a whole series of traditions that can still be found on the Peninsula, under the guise of

Fig. 3.1. The monument to don Galcerán de Pinós in Bagá

rites and festivals, significantly in those very places once ruled by the Templars. We should recall that the cult to the Lignum Crucis, kept in a reliquary in the shape of the patriarchal cross, goes back to St. Helena, mother of Emperor Constantine. Worship devoted to alleged pieces of the True Cross appears not only in Bagá but also in places such as Ponferrada, Segovia, and Caravaca—all of them with important connections to the Templars who once owned them. As for the rescue episode, it has a counterpart in the myth of the tribute of one hundred damsels, a Christianized version of fertility rites that were practiced on the Peninsula long before Christianity took hold and which continued to be recounted specifically in places such as Tomar and San Pedro Manrique—also important Templar possessions at one time.

There seems to be no document besides this late-seventeenth-century manuscript to confirm the strange story of the Catalan identity of the founder of the Templar order. Instead, many testify to the existence of

Fig. 3.2. The Lignum Crucis of Bagá, brought from the Holy Land by don Galcerán de Pinós by order of don Hugo de Pinós, who is said to be the founder of the Knights Templar.

Hughes de Payns of Borgoña, which has been properly noted by medievalists,[4] and leave no doubt that the Pinós family was involved in the Order from its genesis through constant donations* and final symbolic gestures such as the surrendering of armor and horses to the Templars in 1179—which implies that at least some of the members of the family were either lay members of the Temple or active members of the Order. The length of this relationship (1154–1279) is further evidence of the curious connection between the Templars and the Pinós family. Thus it does not seem unrealistic to assume this relationship began at the very birth of the Order in Palestine.

I believe Hugo de Pinós of Bagá's story was a local concoction drawn from the fact that the Templars had been created largely by Frenchmen, though it is believed there were Spanish Templar knights from the very dawn of the Order. That the names of these Spaniards remain unknown could be due to the Gallic researchers looking out for France's interests. It also speaks volumes given that Spain was the first country in which the Templars began to be mentioned. This can seen in the Militia Christi of Monreal (see chapter 2). Likewise, Barcelona was the first Spanish county in which a ruler died as a member of the Order (Ramón Berenger III), and the Spanish surname Gondemar is the first non-French name found among those in the first fellowship of soldiers of the Temple of Solomon.[5]

The Establishment of the Templar Order in Aragon and Navarre

The rest of the countries in the West still needed to be convinced to support the Templar order. Since shortly before the moment of their official knighting in Troyes, Europe was aware of and awaiting the Templars, for they were seen as representatives of a new ideology capable of pulling Christendom triumphantly from a crisis that the Crusades

*The family gave the Templars a house in Lérida while the castle of Gardeny was being refurbished.

had not been able to overcome and the Cluniac pontificate had not even foreseen. Alfonso I, the Battler (1073–1134), king of Aragon and Navarre and later of León and Castile, was even more attentive to the messianic principles on which the the Temple of Solomon was established. Here was a monarch who knew how to structure his politics according to imperialist perspectives that were very close to the idea of a world government that would strive for a goal of universal unity, religious as well as political—a goal that was a heartbeat in the very origin of the Order. He not only established Templar-style fellowships to comfortably roam his lands, but when the time came to think of the future of his kingdom without him—he ruled over Aragon and Navarre after renouncing his plan for a Spain unified through his marriage to Urraca de Castilla—he also conceived the absurd idea of turning his territory over to those military orders from the Holy Land that promoted the great synarchic project that he himself, surely, had already constructed.

Given what we historians know about the character of Alfonso I, we cannot accept his testament without trying to understand the motives that would bring him to write a document so absurd in the political context of his time. After listing the donations that would be made to different monasteries in his kingdom, this testament, first published by Moret in his *Anales de Navarra* (Annals of Navarre) says:

> Therefore, after my death I leave as heir and successor to me the Sepulchre of the Lord which is Jerusalem and those who observe and guard and serve God there, and to the Hospital of the poor which is of Jerusalem, and to the Temple of Solomon with the knights who keep vigil there to defend the name of Christendom. To these three I concede my whole kingdom. Also the lordships which I have in the whole of the lands in my kingdom, both over clerics as well as over laity, bishops, abbots, canons, monks, magistrates, knights, burgesses, peasants and merchants, men and women, the small and the great, rich and poor, also Jews and Saracens, with such laws as my father and I have had hitherto and ought to have . . . I also add

> to the Templar Cavalry the horse belonging to my person, with all my weapons. And if God gave me Tortosa, all of it shall completely be for the Hospital of Jerusalem . . .[6]

This testament, dictated in front of the walls of Bayonne in 1131, was ratified shortly before the Battle of Fraga, in 1134, which would be the only defeat in the long years of the peninsular crusade of Alfonso I as well as the immediate cause of this death, which occurred a short time after the crusade due, it seems, to the wounds he received in combat. In addition to being a kind of premonition, the ratification of the will became a type of public confirmation of intentions, barring the possibility that the nobles of his kingdom, as the tacit executors of the royal will, would choose to ignore his actual intentions.

Upon his death, however, something happened that exceeded traditional medieval custom: The obsequies due a man of his rank were not rendered. His body was spirited away from any possible homage of his subjects and was taken for burial, in quasi-secrecy, to the monastery of the regular canons of Montearagón. His will was ignored. The populace did not hear of his death until his brother, Ramiro, a Cluny monk who at that time was bishop of Roda and Barbastro, was made sovereign. Everything surrounding this transfer of power was rushed: the papal dispensation that freed Ramiro—from that moment on, Ramiro II—from his vows and his immediate wedding to Inés de Poitiers. A daughter, Petronilla, was born the following year and was offered in matrimony in 1137, when she was not yet two years old, to the count of Barcelona, Ramón Berenger IV, who immediately became prince of Aragon and virtual regent of the kingdom. The secularized monk Ramiro returned to monastic obedience without hesitation, after officially reestablishing the dynastic continuity of Aragon and the definitive union of his kingdom and the county of Barcelona. The Catalan-Aragonese crown had been crafted thus and the two realms would remain as one throughout the Middle Ages. The Catalan prince Ramiro, to whom contemporary chroniclers gave the title Saint, was charged with dealing with the military orders, presumably the legacy of Alfonso the Battler, which he officially installed throughout the kingdom, giving numerous fortified plazas in exchange for their renunciation of the rights that the controversial will and testament had given them barely three years earlier.

We should now turn our attention to some very special circumstances of this precise instant in history that seem to lack any reason for their connection: The father of the new prince of Aragon, Count Ramón Berenger III, was married to one of the daughters of El Cid Campeador. Ramón Berenger IV was, therefore, a grandson of the famous Castilian hero. The other daughter of Rodrigo Díaz de Vivar (El Cid), Elvira, contracted nuptials with Prince Ramiro of Navarre, whose adventures as a Crusader have been frequently recounted, and these two became the parents of García Ramírez, who was in charge of the castle of Monzón under the reign of Alfonso I. After the sovereign's death, he assumed the crowns of Aragon and Navarre and was made king by the people of Navarre, who refused to accept the decisions of the nobles of Aragon when the time came to annul the succession of the dead monarch. Ramírez came to be known as García Ramírez the Restorer. His castle of Monzón was certainly one of the first donations made by Aragon to the Order of the Temple, and, curiously, it seems he kept watch over La Tizona, El Cid's sword, which was later given to the Templars by James I, the Conqueror.[7] While he was a marginal figure from a strictly historical perspective, thanks to the mythologizing of history for medieval Spaniards—and even today—Rodrigo Díaz de Vivar was and has been seen as a kind of paradigmatic holy war figure.

The Messianic Power of the Symbol

Despite academic historiography's persistent attempts to demonstrate the opposite, it is clear that history, more frequently than not, is set in motion by symbols and intentions, as if its protagonists obeyed preestablished codes or latched on to old, ancestral laws that are more easily understood through intuition than through reason. I am of the opinion that if the tale of the medieval Templar adventure has been partially ignored and even omitted by more academic studies, the main cause comes from an absurd desire to present events solely from a rationalist perspective, resorting to the essentially superficial aims and facts that are usually published in documents. Deeper motives have to be extracted from contexts that are never divulged, and when they do appear (in apparently literary or legendary parables), they relate—between the lines—facts that would never be openly stated.

This period of the Middle Ages—the twelfth and thirteenth centuries, which correspond to the the birth, heyday, and decline of the Templars—can hardly be understood without measuring the power and influence of the symbol in human relations, gauging its social and bellicose consequences and influence on political decisions.

We might wonder what brought about the union of Aragon and Catalonia, even at the cost of Navarre seceding, under the short reign of Ramiro the Monk. We will see that this alliance, propitiated beyond potential and immediate conveniences, occurred for some internal, hidden reason about which no official parchment offers testimony.

In principle, Alfonso the Battler's will had to be disobeyed by the living forces of Aragon. The state would not allow itself to be ruled by a group of military orders from Palestine under the direct domination of the recently acknowledged Templars. It is clear, however, that the Templar order, despite its newness as an institution, arrived full of a messianism that had already inspired two rulers, Alfonso of Aragon and Count Ramón Berenger III of Barcelona, to perform, upon their deaths, the symbolic act of turning over to the Order their horses and armor—both essentially emblematic of their power, social rank, and position as heads of their respective territories.[8]

As Zurita y Castro confirms, it seems the very first move made by the Aragonese when pressured by Alfonso VII of Castile to take ownership of the Battler's inheritance was to give the crown to a noble, don Pedro de Atarés, for whom they invented a quick and distant kinship with the deceased monarch.[9] To his real importance as a leading member of the Militia of Monreal—referred to as Templar in the papers of Alfonso I—a very evocative name was added: that of the renowned, remote, and almost legendary Juan de Atarés, a hermit and holy man on whose tomb and memory the monastery of San Juan de la Peña was built. This monastery was also said to be the resting place of the Holy Grail, considered the fundamental symbol of esoteric Christianity and container of the profound knowledge of the transcendental essence of truth, as the Arthurian romances would soon proclaim. Here we find symbolism and its representations creeping beneath immediate reality while conforming to political events.

Members of the nobility of Aragon, in their desire to ingratiate themselves with those of Navarre, who had already displayed their intention to secede and name their own king, abandoned the idea of putting don Pedro de Atarés on the throne, yet they did not consent to the sovereignty of García Ramírez, who was backed by the strong forces of Pamplona. They must have foreseen the loss of their starring role, and perhaps they even believed that by removing Ramiro from his monastic vocation, they had the possibility of increasing their power and managing the kingdom as they pleased. Many of them formed part of the Militia of Monreal, established by Alfonso I in the image of the Palestinian Templars, and they could well have believed that by deed, if not by law, the possibility of the fulfillment of Alfonso's testament existed with the election of a monastic king, and that this fulfillment would be in their favor and not in that of their actual fellow knights from Jerusalem.

These intentions and the way in which Ramiro was forced to smother them turned into a parable subtly bathed in symbolism. From this secret and undocumented struggle emerged the legend of the Campana de Huesca (Bell of Huesca).* Even though Zurita y Castro mentioned it, he clearly presented it for the record, not because he believed it had any credibility: "From the death of these knights there is no memory, not even of its cause. Perhaps in certain ancient Catalan Annals . . . mention is given that the Potentates of Huesca were killed, in the era of one thou-

*[The Bell of Huesca refers to the legend in which Ramiro summoned to the court in Huesca all the region's wealthy noblemen on the pretense of dedicating a bell that, when rung, would be heard throughout the land. Upon their arrival, the noblemen were beheaded and their heads were hung as "clappers" in an underground vault. No facts have borne out the veracity of this legend. —*Ed.*]

sand one hundred and seventy four; that was the year of the Nativity of Our Lord of one thousand one and hundred and thirty six."[10] Some lines earlier the same Aragonese chronicler has revealed to us that "the graves, which one author affirms are in the Church of San Juan in the city of Huesca . . . by them is shown, they were of Templar knights, of whose Order and convent was that house the first; and they have no emblem or sign of those lineages, that were the most principal of the kingdom."

Operation Templar

Out of this accumulation of internal tensions, initially inspired by the polemical last will and testament of the Battler, a solution emerged three years later. Aragon rejected the Templars as the inheritors of the kingdom, but Ramiro II, as provisional monarch who was conscious of his transitory role, put the kingdom in the hands of a regent prince who was a native of Barcelona: the son of a Templar knight in whose house Ramón Berenger III had died. This knight was of the same Order that had settled in Barcelona, in the castles of Granyena and Barbara, which had been donated by Count Armengol de Urgel and the count of Barcelona himself, respectively.

Ramón Berenger IV never possessed the title king of Aragon. Ramiro II, who had acted as monarch (although technically only as consort),* reserved the title for himself even after abandoning the throne and rejoining the Cluny order at the monastery of San Pedro el Viejo of Huesca. During the same year that Ramiro donned his habit again, his son-in-law, as if obliged by compromise, or maybe as a promise, wrote to Grand Master Craon to ask for ten knights to organize a Templar militia in his Catalan-Aragonese domains. Along with other knights of the kingdom, he committed himself to a year of service to the Order as a lay member, without mentioning the prickly matter of the inheritance of Alfonso I, which the Holy See, in its permanent anxiousness to expand its own political power, was insisting be implemented in the strongest

*This refers to the engagement between Ramón Berenger IV and Petronila when the count was nineteen and the princess two years old. The wedding was celebrated in 1150.

terms. Yet a trip by Cardinal Guido of San Cosme in 1136, on orders of Innocent II, did not resolve the matter.

In 1140, the patriarch of Jerusalem, William I, and the grand master of the Order of the Hospital of St. John of Jerusalem (the Hospitallers), Raymond de Podio, renounced the rights presumably derived from the Battler's will. In exchange, they received from Ramón Berenger IV houses and goods in both Catalonia and Aragon.[11] Finally, in 1143, in Gerona, there took place a meeting with Templar representatives in which the Order, through its direct representative, Pedro de Rovira, formally renounced its rights of inheritance in exchange for the confirmation of the properties and goods the Order had acquired in Catalonia; the possession of the castles of Monzón, Chalamera, Montgay, and Remolins; the promise of another castle in Corbins once it was conquered; the annual rent of a thousand *sueldos* [more commonly known as the Spanish doubloon —*trans.*] in Zaragoza; 10 percent of all the rents that its possessions produced; one fifth of the bounty from all the campaigns in which the Templars participated; a fifth of any lands that would be conquered with Templar support; and the incorporation in the Templar name of the confraternities of Monreal and Belchite. In addition, the testament of the Battler would be pronounced settled if the marriage of the count and Princess Petronila produced no descendants.

But the Templars continued making use of their *voluntary* renunciation of their rights to the crown of Aragon. The prince consort promised not to interrupt their struggle against Islam and not to sign peace treaties or truces without the explicit consent of the Templar order, which had already established which areas in the Islam world it would conquer and govern.

The Holy See, with Honorius II as pope and Cardinal Guido present as pontifical legate at meetings, demonstrated an obvious lack of any realistic theocratic vision (of which the Templars conversely had more than their share) and refused to sanction these Templar agreements until fifteen years later. The Templars, however, conscious of the enormous advantages the agreements gave to the Order, approved them without reservation. Among those present at the approval were Éverard de Barres, the future third grand master; one of the Order's founders, Geoffroy de Saint Omer; and the future first grand master of the new Catalan-Aragonese province, the aforementioned Pedro de Rovira.[12]

Soon after the new kingdom of Navarre seceded, García Ramírez, the Restorer, ascended the throne. Thus, for obvious reasons, it is not surprising that none of the documents concerning the first years of the restructuring of the state makes any mention of Templar establishments in the territory: In the first place, Navarre likely had to reject adhering to the mandate imposed by the testament of its last sovereign, which kept it conjoined with Aragon—meaning that any Templar presence was probably considered an immediate threat to the stability of a kingdom struggling for its independence. In addition, as a sovereign territory, Navarre no longer had any border with Islam; its Reconquista was, in fact, over, and it was precisely the idea of a Reconquista, no matter how circumstantial, that immediately facilitated Templar penetration into the rest of the peninsular kingdom. Navarre was thus of secondary importance; it lacked any circumstance that would justify the urgent presence of the Templar order spurring on a holy war that could no longer serve Navarre as an excuse for territorial expansion.

Yet the Templar order had within its organizational principles another, more compelling reason to settle in Navarre: its condition as an Order dedicated to the protection of pilgrims. Since the inception of the pilgrimage to Compostela, many of the travelers arriving from France and northern Europe had passed through Navarre. Even as early as the mid-eleventh century, with the strength of Cluniac influence at that time, the French Road they created crossed the whole of Navarre's territory, although one of its branches (the one entering the Peninsula through Somport) extended from Aragon's territory. The excuse of protecting pilgrims was more than enough motivation for the Templars to settle in Navarre's lands, which is precisely what happened. The first possessions that we know of were remote from the pilgrimage road. There were donations made by Sancho the Wise, son of García Ramírez, of which Father Moret speaks in his *Annals:* "We discovered only one before he [King Sancho] left for the day in the month of March in Tudelo, and it is in favor of the Templar knights, and he must have made use of some of them in this endeavor. Give it to them, shall they dig irrigation ditches and dam up the Fontellas in the Realengo del Rey, on the Ebro, and they can cut wood in Fontellas grove."[13] The text shows us that this territory, which contained an enormous extension of land between Fontellas and Ribaforada, was donated to the Templars in the seventh year of the reign of King Sancho the Wise, which corresponds to 1157, when Hughes Rigalt was Templar grand master for the kingdoms of Spain.

Silent Discretion and the Risky Game of Valor

When it comes to establishing the beginnings of the penetration of the Order of the Temple in the eastern part of the Iberian Peninsula, there is no documentation illustrating a policy that proceeded on an even keel until the Templar militia was dissolved. The course of establishment in the western part of the Peninsula—in Castile, León, and Portugal—seems composed of loose ends and fragments in which the Templars themselves appear and disappear like a historical Guadiana,* emerging at specific moments as if to give notice of their presence and disappearing at others, which, for motives we can only surmise, served to keep them in the shadows, overlooked in the great events taking place around them.

It was during this century that Castile experienced its last years as an entity separate from the kingdom of León. Among medieval chroniclers there remains a persistent lack of information concerning Templar activity in Castile at this time. But this absence is punctuated by one specific event that is seen as a smear on the history of the Order and a glorious blossom hanging on the reputation of the native military orders that were born in the Templar shadow and, in many cases, in its image and likeness.

---

*[The Guadiana is one of the longest rivers in Spain. —*Trans.*]

This event began with the early entrance of the Templars in Castile through the donation of the plaza of Calatrava made to them by King Alfonso VII, son-in-law of Ramón Berenger III, in 1129, as the Templars battled the Almoravids, a Bedouin tribe from Yemen that subscribed to the most orthodox Sunni doctrine. It continued with the later abandonment of this fortress by the Templars in 1157, before the Almohads'* invasion. The Templars were immediately replaced by the military order that took the name of the plaza (the Calatravan order) and which was established by the abbot of Fitero, Raymond, with the collaboration of the cleric Diego Velázquez.

The chronicle of Archbishop Jimenez de Rada recounts how, knowing of the news that the Almohads had advanced on Toledo,

> . . . the friars of the order of the Temple, which occupied the fortress of Calatrava, facing the possibility that they would not be capable of resisting the charge of the Arabs, appealed to King Sancho† to take charge of the fortress and the village of Calatrava, for they did not have the necessary forces to face the Arabs and they had not found any potentate willing to assume the risk of the defense. There was at that time in Toledo a cleric, Raymond, abbot of Fitero, accompanied by a monk called Diego Velázquez, of noble origin and a former expert in all things military, and King Sancho. On realizing the king's concern about the danger facing Calatrava, he counseled the abbot to ask the king to give them control of this territory; and although in the beginning the abbot showed himself reticent, he acceded to the monk's pleas . . .[14]

The king fearfully agreed, and Archbishop Juan contributed help from his own patrimony. The archbishop continues: "He arranged that it be made public that indulgences would be earned for all the sins of

*[The Almohads had their origin in the puritanical Muslim sect founded by Ibn Tumart. Though fanatical, they were less so than the Almoravids, whom they replaced. —*Ed.*]

†Sancho III, the Chosen, king of Castile (1157–58), at the deaths of his father, Alfonso VII, and brother Fernando II de León.

those who would go to the defense of Calatrava." But the Moors did not show up: "And then many that were animated by their devotion, their dress lightened as demanded by military mobility, entered that order, and immediately started to accost and attack the Arabs, and with the help of God, they were given strength by the impetus of the monks."

Pedro Rodríguez Campomanes, the eighteenth-century Spanish historian, accepting everything recorded by the earlier chroniclers,[15] repeats the charge that the Templars of Calatrava "had deliberately forsaken it, on not finding itself with sufficient forces to defend it." He then ends by telling how many knights, having enlisted on the orders of the abbot of Fitero, to whom King Sancho donated the fortress, the village, and its lands, "had from here on a glorious beginning as the one from Calatrava, that such glorious deeds he performed to help banish from Spain the abominable name of Mahomet." Moret[16] branded the Templars "terrified by the risk that threatened."

Another scholar of Spanish military orders repeats the story to the letter, arguing for the inopportune nature of that abandonment because the king "had to await the war prepared for him by his brother, don Fernando, king of León, co-aligned with the one of Navarre."[17] In other words, in accepted and immutable history, this was sufficient motive to promote a native order, to the detriment of Templar prestige, but it also justifies the idea that the Templars merit mention merely as a footnote to that make-believe holy war that allegedly liberated Spain from the Saracen scourge. Digging for other, more realistic motives to understand and judge this event should not be a futile task, for the abandonment of Calatrava does not square with Templar principles, especially during a time—barely thirty years after the canonical approval of the Order—in which its knights must have felt imbued with the spirit of the Rule and its constitutions. In particular, number 232 of the Rule specifies that those brothers who abandoned the pennant, the war standard, and ran away in fear of the Muslims would lose the right to remain in the Order.[18]

To gain insight into the reasons for their alleged abandonment of

Calatrava, we need only investigate the circumstances that produced the donation of Calatrava to the Templars and why they abandoned it thirty years later. As the Templars arrived in Spain, the peninsular crusade was entangled with the Almoravids. They had already taken North Africa and had imposed in Andalusia the religious behavior of a radicalized Islam that made no concessions to the cultural refinements predominating in the courts of the emirs of the Taifa. In a way, the Almoravids could be considered barbaric tribes recently Islamized and, because of this, intolerant of the permissiveness and much more spiritualized faith of their Andalusian coreligionists, who were developing a mixture of Islam, Mesopotamian Sufi mysticism, and a healthy dose of syncretism in harmony with Christian and Jewish spirituality.

For the Templars, as for other Christians, Jews, and Muslims who did not share this theology, this fierce, intolerant, and blind fundamentalism was precisely the doctrine they were called upon to combat. What is more, this kind of doctrine imposed a basic impediment to the Templars' undeclared goal of religious unity under a universal empire and amounted to the same religious position they had already fought against in the Palestinian Crusades and which they found ruled Andalusia when they dscreetly began settling on the Peninsula. Against the Almoravid intolerance Alfonso the Battler undertook his Córdoba expedition, from which he returned with thousands of persecuted Mozarabs. Ramón Berenger III fought against the Almoravids in his ephemeral conquest of the Balearic Islands. And to defend the holy city of Toledo from Amoravid encroachment, Alfonso VII created a line of defense with Calatrava and his contingent of Templar knights, who were happy to guard a ribat in which the same mystical and military teaching they knew had been imparted.

But it is within those thirty years, the time frame in which these events took place, that a profound change occurred in the religious and political panorama that included Islamic Maghrebs and Andalusians. The transformation came from the hand of Ibn Tumart, Aventumerth of the chronicles,* son of the guardian of the lamps of the mosque

*[It seems that the chronicles give the name Aventumerth to Ibn Tumart. —*Ed.*]

of Córdoba and not only wise but also, according to the thirteenth-century archbishop Jiménez de Rada of Toledo, "versed in astronomy and natural sciences."[19] He was also the preferred disciple of the great Sufi teacher Al-Ghazâlî of Baghdad, whose books had been declared heretical and ordered burned by the Almoravid fundamentalists.[20] It was precisely this act against his teacher that triggered Tumart's messianism. Having returned to the Maghreb, he started to expand the spiritual doctrine of the Sufis and, consequently, to attack without pity the closed-minded orthodoxy of the Almoravids. He soon established himself firmly in the Andalusian soul and his followers, the *al-muwahhidûn*—those who give testimony of the truth—were soon known by the Spanish form of their name, *almohades*.[21]

The sometimes violent protests of the Andalusian leaders who rejected Almoravid fundamentalism spread throughout the Islamic holdings of the Peninsula. Some Almoravids, like Ibn Hamdîn of Córdoba, preferred to abandon their land and seek protection under the jurisdiction of the Christians in the north. Others, like Ibn Mardanîsh of Murcia, opted to rebel and make a desperate plea to the Almohads of the Maghreb, whose spiritual leaders had already accepted the name of *mahdis*—which refers to a figure somewhere between a prophet and a messiah—and who were already disposed to impose their spiritual doctrine over the savage orthodoxy of the Almoravid Bedouins.

Toward 1150 the Almohads already dominated the most important cities and emirates in Andalusian territory, and even though they encountered pockets of opposition in autochthonous Islam, they were about to complete, with enormous military might, the reconquest of the whole peninsular territory.[22] Although its religious underpinnings were entirely different from the fundamentalist Almohavid doctrines, this reconquest continued to be viewed by Christians as an indiscriminate Saracen threat. The Jews, however, like the Templars, did not hold this same view, for they understood the enormous doctrinal differences often distinguishing one Muslim group from another. The experience of the holy war and the more or less secret alliances that the brothers of the Temple forged in the East, where Shiites confronted orthodox

Sunni fundamentalism, could explain why the Order opted to abandon Calatrava and why it withdrew from combat activities in Castile once the Almoravid fundamentalist impulses were defeated. It is even possible that the date to abandon the Calatravan ribat (1157) was chosen because it was impossible to make this decision earlier, perhaps because of undocumented commitments the Castilian Templars had arranged with Alfonso VII, which his son, Sancho III, had virtually no reason to fulfill.

The Dance of Numbers and Dates

Sometimes chronology confronts the researcher with a dance of useless, unreliable, and contradictory numbers—data that make it impossible to establish the order of events. In the case of the Castilian Templars, we can almost—though not totally—begin to grasp why it is so difficult to determine what occurred first as a cause and which events followed as effects. First to consider is the independence of Portugal, which began with the arrival of the Templars on the Peninsula. Second is the circumstantial separation of the kingdom of León from Castile, between 1157 and 1230, during which time the Templars settled in both realms, remaining tremendously active in León mostly under Fernando II, as we soon see, while their activities were somewhat more discreet in Castile. Indeed, with regard to Castile, the search for sufficient, reliable documents to trace the Templars' expansion into the interior of the province, far from the zone of conflict with Islam, has proved fruitless.

Curiously, the under-the-radar nature of the Castilian Templars in the first century of their establishment there, with the exception of the conflict in Calatrava, has resulted in our somewhat "gray" knowledge of concrete, truthful details regarding the Templars' public life and of the exact or even approximate instant when—and how—they came to possess the properties and estates that we have only recently learned belonged to them. (Of course, many of these holdings are pure conjecture, given that the great majority of existing documents record them as belonging to others who came to possess them only after the Order's extinction, when Templar estates were divvied up among individuals or groups who remained faithful to the desires of the monarchs and the Church itself.)

One piece of information is certain far beyond any conjecture: North of the area that might be considered the far reaches of Castile, at the line that would approximately connect Torija with Toledo, instead of Templar fortresses we find protectorates, chapels, houses, oratorios, churches, and the remains of barn-convents. A good part of these possessions are located in the middle stretch of the road to Santiago or its environs and on secondary routes to Compostela.

We may conjecture that the castles and fortresses to the south of this general border were, like Calatrava, royal donations, while the Templar establishments to the north of that line were private gifts (due to their lay status) offered to the Templars for a fixed time of service under the standard of the Order. These were perhaps donations made by the Cistercians, whose Rule inspired the Templars' constitution, or they simply could have been purchases the Templars made in places where they were especially interested in settling.

Naturally, these possessions were not fortified at all or were minimally armed as a means of deterring small-scale plundering or opportunistic robbery. Their ruins show the remnants of small walls—seemingly demarcations that may have existed more to preserve the Templars' privacy than to provide a defense, which, in principle at least, was absolutely unnecessary. The only building that has been popularly declared a castle in this area is Castilejo de Robledo, near the Burgo of Osma (Soria), which can hardly be recognized as such. It looks more like a fortified barn raised on a hill near the hamlet and the church that dominates its immediate environment, though it is surrounded by even greater heights.

Some individuals, such as Father Mariana of Argote de Molina and Campomanes, the foremost scholar of the Templars in Spain, worked to shed light on the nature and location of these possessions and many others in Galicia-León. All of these historians mention places that are impossible to locate today because their names no longer exist or have

Fig. 3.3. The Templar castle of Alba de Aliste, in the ancient kingdom of León

been changed: Canabán, Safines, San Pedro, Neya, and Villapalma. On the other hand, we can find some places that without doubt fell under Templar ownership, though they cannot be found on any document or list.

Today, the reconstruction of a Templar presence on the Peninsula is practically impossible. All attempts have left us with serious doubts and questions that cannot be overcome due to the lack of documentation attesting to the origin of certain possessions as well as the material impossibility of locating the sites that do happen to be mentioned in documents.[23] While I have deep respect for all other efforts to this end, it seems that the most convenient and fruitful method for in-depth investigation of Hispanic Templarism involves studying a sampling of trustworthy documents and traditions. It is true, however, that attempting this kind of exhaustive search could also lend itself to excessive inexactitudes that only increase confusion for readers and scholars.

Among those Castilian Templar possessions, both definite and possible, that were situated north of the border that was not crossed until after the Battle of Navas de Tolosa (1212), we can vouch for the following, though we cannot provide the dates when they became Templar holdings:

- **Villacázar de Sirga,** in the province of Palencia, on the road to Compostela. It was known to have belonged to the Templar order from the first half of the twelfth century, probably since 1158. All that remains is a church, today's town parish, which is of great importance in analyzing the Order's distinctive architecture.
- **San Bartolomé de Ucero,** or San Juan de Otero. This property was probably obtained early on and, according to some documents, abandoned by the Templars a few years before their destruction.
- **La Vera Cruz de Zamarramal,** adjacent to Segovia. This is a Templar property as testified in a brief from Pope Honorius II, when the relic of the True Cross was delivered to the Templars in 1224. It passed into the power of the Knights of St. John of Jerusalem,* who persistently denied their Templar roots. Today it belongs to the Knights of Malta.
- **San Polo,** in Soria's outskirts. This was an early Templar possession and included the sanctuary of the anchorite Saturio, which became a possession of the Sanjuanistas when the Templar goods were divided after the demise of the Order.
- **Toledo.** The Templar order owned the castle of San Servando and some houses in the Jewish quarter, not far from the royal Alcázar. It is impossible to pinpoint the year in which they obtained these properties.
- **Alcanadre,** in the province of Rioja. Nothing remains of this site.
- **Torija,** located in the province of Guadalajara, in Alcarria. Its castle belonged to the Templars, but we are in the dark as to when they obtained it.
- **Santorcaz,** in the province of Madrid. There the Templars had a convent, which became the property of the town council from Alcalá de Henares after the destruction of the Order.

---

*The members of the Knights of St. John came to be known as Sanjuanistas, after St. John [San Juan].

- **Cuenca.** There a Templar parcel was conceded after the conquest of the city. The no longer extant church of San Pantaleón formed part of it in 1176. A well-founded suspicion suggests that the Templars played an active role in the construction of the cathedral.
- **Agreda.** Today this is part of Castile and the province of Soria, but it used to be part of the kingdom of Aragon. It is suspected that it was an early gift that the Templars held on to until the Order was suppressed.

We will revisit some of these sites in chapter 9, when we consider the ideology of the Templars and the singular features of their Spanish monuments.

The Templars Desire a Troubadour King

As is well known, the imperial ideal—the feudal concept of the empire—was an option, with different variables, in which a number of peninsular monarchs of the Middle Ages found shelter and justification. Alfonso II, under whose mandate the Templars settled in the kingdom of Castile-León, was one of these. Emulator of his predecessors—his stepfather, the Battler of Aragon, and a grandfather, the IV of Castile—he was crowned three times: once in Santiago de Compostela as king of Galicia when he was a child (1111); as sovereign of Castile and León in the cathedral of the old capital in 1126; and nine years later as emperor in the cathedral of León, with the assistance of all his theoretical vassals from Navarre, Catalonia, and Aragon. Yet during a long and powerful reign in which his grandiose dreams were more or less fulfilled, he seemed to lose all interest in the future of the imperial ideal. At the time of his death, and seemingly in imitation of what his great-grandfather Fernando I had already attempted, he divided between his two sons the powerful state he had created. To Sancho III, the older, he left Castile and to Fernando he bequeathed a kingdom in León that was full of problems stemming from the Almohavid advance and the factional break up of the Portuguese county, which was on the verge of becoming an independent kingdom.

Certainly, the Templars lived with this division without any worry or suspecting any danger to their existence. In fact, until the dissolution of the Order, there was only one province that took in all three nationalities, and the three often shared masters. The Templars' relations with the rulers of the day were altogether different, however. We should recognize that if, in the early days of the Order in Castile and later in a united Castile and León, they were silent, even about their forced collaboration in campaigns; they acted quite differently in their resolute action in León during the reign of Ferdinand II. This monarch was entangled in family conflicts and internal politics that obligated the Templars to intervene more frequently. While it is true that their Rule did not allow the Order to intervene in conflicts among Christians, it is less evident that by converting themselves into Christian paladins facing the Moors, they took charge of numerous conflicts the soverign engaged in, allowing him to handle with less stress and greater advantages the politico-family questions that assaulted him from either Castile or Portugal.

Following their inveterate custom, historians continue to maintain their silence or, at best, to minimize the importance of the Templars at this moment in medieval history. Archbishop Gelmírez, a significant figure in the history of Galicia and Spain as a whole during his time (1093–1140), would not permit mention of the Order in his chronicle, the *Compostelana,* as if the knights had never entered Galicia.[24] This discounted the Templars' assistance in the building of the province's large cathedrals and avoided acknowledgment of the fact that Templar ships were anchored in the ports of Vigo and Santiago del Burgo.

Oddly, Fernando II (1157–1188) is a monarch seemingly despised by historians who have enthusiastically occupied themselves with these crucial centuries of the Middle Ages. Some, such as Claudio Sánchez Albornoz, do not even mention him in their great work, as if he had been merely one ruler in a long list of Spanish figureheads and sovereigns.[25] Yet few embodied a poetic spirit and the sense of an almost irrational political sensibility as he did. Much like the Japanese samurai, without vengefulness he waged war and conquered half of Extremadura, inspired by the overall poetic work of the troubadour Peire d'Alvernha. Further, he generously ceded municipal government to the conquered Muslims. In addition, he created military orders that were theoretically committed to holy war and that became local rivals of the Templars, who had done their utmost to help recover the forgotten territories of the Ligur region of Portugal, bordering León.

The Templars had barely started their advance on the the lands of Extremadura when they appeared at the monarch's side during the conquest of Trevejo, which was donated to them and over which they built a castle that has remained largely intact to this day. Following this conquest, the Order obtained Portozuelo (1167), Cabeza de Esparragal, and Santibáñez el Alto, all of which are sites that would pass into the hands of the native orders of Alcántara and Santiago during the subsequent reign of Alfonso IX. The castle of Alconétar, however, they kept by deed until the Order's extinction. Today its pentagonal tower, steeped in the Oriental legends of the Moorish princess who was the sister of the brave Fierabrás de Alejandría, rises over the waters of a nearby marsh a short distance from a Roman bridge.

As proof of the unusually divine significance that surrounded a good part of the campaigns in Extremadura, it is worth mentioning that the ups and downs, reversals and victories, fears and euphorias, along with the constant advances and retreats over the frontier bordering Cáceres and the successive defeats in the area, constitute an example that would have been an exception in the Castile of Alfonso VIII. Yet in the ephemeral León of Fernando II, the troubadour king, such events constituted only more reason to sing dead heroes into legend or to make of their exploits a troubadour's poem.

In the campaigns in Extremadura and León, the Templars had to give in once again to the pressures exerted by Alcántara and Santiago. They conquered plazas they would later have to cede to other orders that, as native to the territory, saw themselves as having more legitimacy. Thus the Templars kept only the domain of Coria, over which they actively fought,[26] and perhaps coincidentally Garrovillas and Hervás, both of which had a considerable Jewish population and which the Templars protected until the Order was dissolved.

Creating a State out of Nothing

The notion of the theocratic state came from afar—in fact, it emerged at the very moment when the Cluny Benedictines penetrated the Peninsula and began to haphazardly handle the traditional liturgy of the faithful as well as (which was a measure of their influence) the political decisions of their rulers. In Castile-León, ruled by Alfonso VI, who was married to Constanza of Burgundy, Cluniac reform was born. Nurtured as part of this reform was the first idea of a synarchic Europe strongly ruled by theocratic principles emanating from Rome, to whose authority—not only in religious matters, but also in the the fundamental decisions of high politics—all of Christendom would bow.

No one wanted to question or challenge Cluniac influence. The decision of Alfonso IV to marry two of his daughters to Burgundian counts seems like an arrangement made in the sacristy, unions orchestrated in the monastery to bind the lands of Castile and León and, above all, the peninsular Atlantic border, which had already converted to the theocratic ideology of Cluny. One daughter, Urraca, was destined for Raymond of Burgundy and the bastard Teresa was to marry her cousin Enrique.* A third daughter married Raymond of Toulouse, who became one of the principal leaders of the First Crusade. And a coincidence that verged on religious frivolity was that Sanchuelo, King Alfonso's only son, was engaged to the sister of Al-Motamid of Sevilla, Zaida-Isabel, and died prematurely in the conflict known as the Battle of the Seven Counts, leaving the destiny of his kingdom in the hands of women married to foreigners in Cluny's thrall.

There are still more curious coincidences: After Urraca's and Teresa's respective marriages, Urraca and Raymond were named countess and count of Portugal. The Portuguese bishop of Braga as well as the Galician bishop from Santiago were elected from among Cluny monks, as was Gelmírez, bishop of Compostela beginning in 1093. Gelmírez had no qualms about showing his revulsion for the fickleness of Urraca's policies—especially after her second marriage to Alfonso the Battler of

*Both, in turn, were nephews of St. Hugo, abbot of Cluny.

Aragon—or to her decided favoritism of Alfonso Raimúndez, the future Alfonso VII, whom Urraca crowned king of Galicia in 1111, twenty-five years before Raimúndez received the crown of Castile-León.

Until 1095, Raymond of Burgundy, Urraca's husband, was count of Galicia and Portugal. In that year he became ruler of Galicia alone, when his cousin Enrique married Teresa and consequently received the Portuguese province. This subdividing was accomplished without trauma or protest; an agreement was signed by both cousins before the monk Dalmas Geret, delegate of their uncle Hugo of Cluny, which specified that in the event that Urraca and Raymond became sovereigns of the crown of Castile, Enrique and Teresa would become owners *jure hereditario* (for themselves and their descendants) of Portugal, though they would do so under the sovereignty of the monarchs of Castile. As we can see, it must have been an unofficial order from Cluny to which no one raised the slightest objection.[27]

In fact, all of the sovereigns died within three years of each other: Raymond of Burgundy in 1107; Prince Sancho of Zaida, son of Alfonso VI, at the Battle of Uclés in 1108; and Alfonso VI himself in 1109. Count Enrique of Portugal, who had expanded his territory considerably at the cost of numerous conquests over the Muslims, died five years later, which created a moment of great tension among all the political forces jockeying to dominate the kingdoms of Castile and León. It seemed clear that despite dissension and a state of open civil war, none of the contenders was ready to cede his rights to Portugal, least of all Cluny, which had wielded its peninsular Atlantic influence with a very firm hand. Once a widow, Teresa shunned duties and previously contracted agreements and, with her husband barely deceased, proclaimed herself queen. Although historians have still not agreed on the date, it seems that she summoned the Templars to her side even before the Order was officially recognized in Troyes in 1126.

The Order of the Knights of the Temple, as the inspired product of Cistercian doctrine, formed a monastic warrior collective that Cluny did not look upon with favor. An independent Portuguese county with the capability of becoming a distinct kingdom was a political possibility that was not accepted by the all-powerful Gelmírez, archbishop of Compostela. This religious leader had already provoked the wrath of Count Enrique's subjects when, in 1102, he entered Enrique's territory to loot from Braga the relics of the monk St. Fructoso, an action that was termed *el pío latrocinio* (the pious robbery) by the Portuguese. Under these circumstances, it was not surprising for Queen Teresa to see in the Templars a confirmation of her wishes and a defense of her intentions, or to see in the Cistercian Bernard of Clairvaux the monastic tendency that best suited her interests. The year 1126 is the most likely date for the entrance of the first Templars into Portugal, and it is almost certain that in that very year they received custody of the fortress of Soure and Fonte Arcada. The first grand master of the Order into Portugal was Guillelme (Guillaume) Ricard.

Although they could not serve as a force capable of fighting against the Christians, the Templars' role in the nascent Portuguese state was to give it the tranquillity found in the freedom from dealing with the two battle fronts of Castile and Islam. For its part, the Templars saw the importance of firmly establishing the Order in a country born from nothing, a new kingdom with a young dynasty and a nationalist will over which the Order could exert an influence that would open doors to the Atlantic. Here they could exert more effective influence than they had in Castile and preserve an exclusivity that would have been more problematic in Castile-León. Time would prove them right. Portugal came to allow, as charity, the presence of Spanish military orders, especially those of Santiago and Alcántara, born in neighboring Extremadura, but the Templars always retained their supremacy in Portugal. What that exclusive position meant to the Templar enterprise we will see later. It is enough now to lay out as evidence the quick advances of the Templars' influence over doña Teresa as well as over her son and heir, Alfonso Enríquez, from 1128. As the *Compostelana* confirms, Alfonso Enríquez "did not want to surrender to the domination of the king [Alfonso VII], although he stirred arrogantly after he obtained the lordship."[28]

The Templars had to wait until the year 1137 to act. Before then, they limited themselves to their official role as border guards. In 1137 the Treaty of Tuy was signed, with Alfonso VII recognizing his cousin's sovereignty over all Portuguese territory. The moment had arrived to begin the recovery of the Cantabrian coast. And the Templars were ready to collaborate, as was Bernard of Clairvaux, recently returned from his conflict with Anacleto, the antipope and glorious prophet who announced the conquest of Santarém. For the next nine years, the offensive was unstoppable, as if the Templars were in a hurry to conquer territories before the Almohad machine began advancing like a steamroller. In 1146 the plaza, Santarém, Leiría, and all of the territory surrounding the rivers Mondego and Tajo had been reconquered. In 1149, with the collaboration of English Crusaders (perhaps Templars), Lisbon was conquered. In all of the conquered territories the Templar order accumulated churches, convents, and castles. Portuguese Templar Gualdim Pais distinguished himself as the hero of these military actions, and barely after achieving victory in Portugal, he left for the Holy Land to receive the initiation reserved for the highest eschelons of the Order.

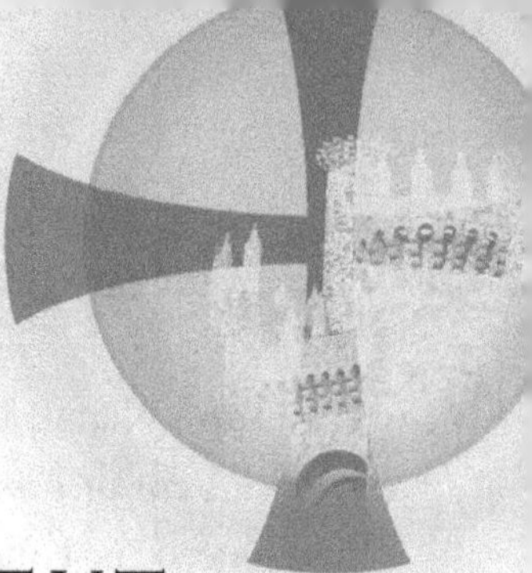

4
The Slow Ascent to the Summit

Strangers in Castile

By the middle of the twelfth century, the Order of the Temple could be found established throughout the Iberian Peninsula, for better or for worse, depending on the state or territory. The Hospitallers (Knights of St. John), and other autochthonous orders born in the Templars' shadow and following its example, were already forming part of the Peninsula's history and sharing formal structures with the Templar order, but were also frequently jockeyed with the Templars in the struggle to influence royal power and religious authority. The Castile-León crown always viewed the Order of the Temple as a foreign institution, no matter how much proof and how many testimonies the Templars provided to illustrate the Order's Hispanic vocation. In additon, the Crown disregarded the fact that the majority of the Order's members were Spaniards, as were most of its leaders. We have only to consider the nature of Templar possessions in Castile and compare the Order's political, territorial, and strategic importance with that of the orders of Calatrava, Santiago, and the Sanjuanistas, or go over the documents, sealed by the grand masters and provincial masters, to affirm that the presence of the Templars in the public life of the kingdom was often no more than an honorific or testimonial act.

Naturally, it is impossible to structure historical circumstances without taking into account the many shades that could transform them and give them their authentic dimension. Thus, it would be risky to outline the Templar presence in Castile without taking note of the enormous importance to the Order of the years between 1157 and 1230. This was a period in which León and Castile remained separate, with monarchs such as Fernando II and Alfonso IX ruling over the western kingdom and leaders such as Sancho III, Alfonso VIII, and Enrique I ruling in Castile's central postion on the Peninsula. During that period, Castile evolved, pleased with what it was given in historic opportunities and circumstances on a day-to-day basis. Meanwhile, León, which included Galicia and Asturias within its territorial boundaries, kept a close connection to older, traditional structures that retained the historical significance and ideology of its rulers and included archaic elements preserved from those times when myth shared its ancient reality with current events. If we remember, during an entire war campaign (Fernando II's war for the territory of Extremadura) that was instigated by the strophes of troubadour Peire D'Alverhna, we can gain awareness of the profound existential and even ideological chasm that separated the state of León from a Castile that was, during the same age, the cradle of such epic, testimonial, and realist poetry as the *Cantar de Mio Cid*.*

During the seventy-three years of Castile and León's independence from one another, the Castilian Templars maintained their ties with the Templars of León and Portugal and formed with them a unique organization with its supreme authority residing in Zamora. Once the Templars had abandoned the plaza of Calatrava—a dishonor that leaders in Castile took their time to forgive, being incapable of understanding the reasons behind it—the Templars established in Toledo their nearest enclave to the border with Andalusia, in their fortress of San Servando and in the houses they occupied in the Jewish neighborhood. We may suspect that their sympathy for partisans on the other side explains why they never asked to be stationed on the front lines of the armies that faced the

**The Song of My Cid* (Lord) is a renowned medieval Spanish poem about the struggles of Rodrigo Díaz del Vivar (El Cid), one of Spain's national heroes.

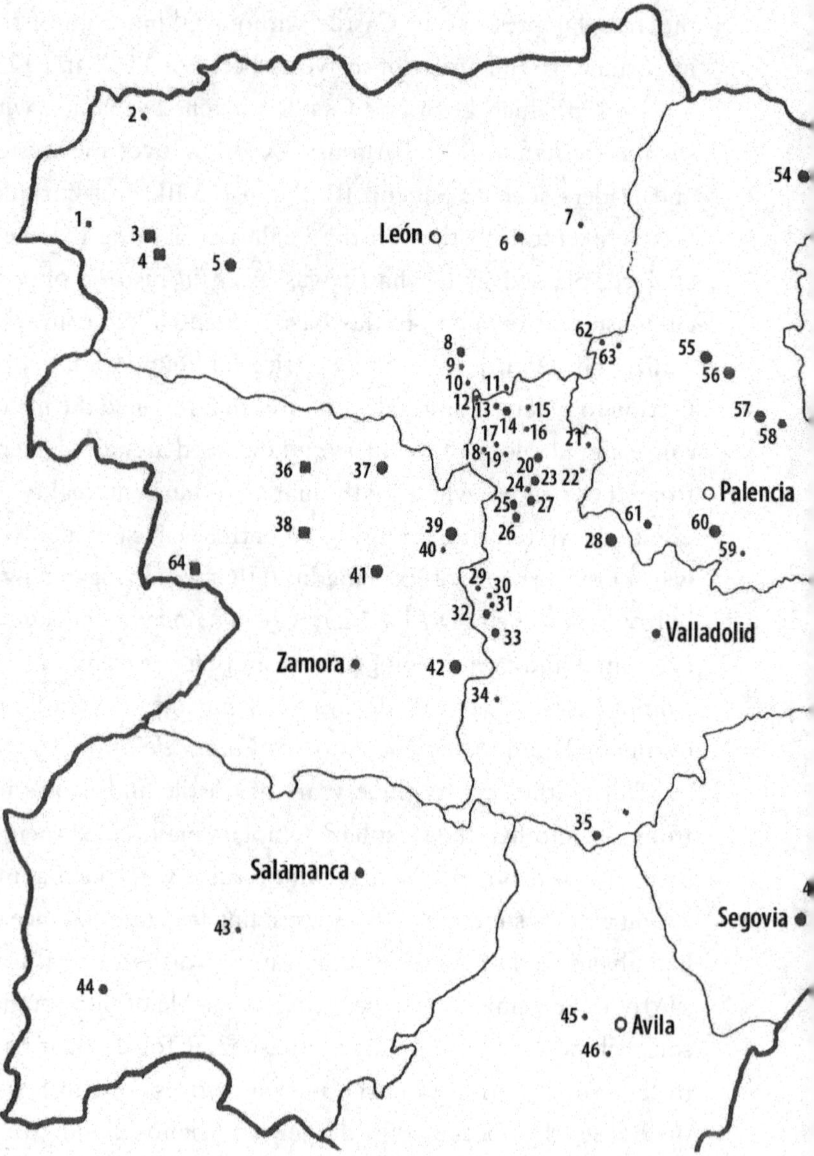

Fig. 4.1. Templar possessions in the kingdom of Castile-León (according to Castán Lanaspa)

1. Corullón
2. Faro
3. Ponferrada
4. Comatel
5. Rabanal del Camino
6. Nava de los Caballeros
7. Almanza
8. Valdesaz de los Oteros
9. Alcuetas
10. Matanza
11. Izagre
12. Valdemorilla
13. Fremosos
14. Mayorga de Campos
15. San Martin del Rio
16. Castroponce
17. Urones de Castroponce
18. Villagrado
19. Becilla
20. Villacid de Campos
21. Herrin de Campos
22. Gaton de Campos
23. Ceinos de Campos
24. Pajares de Campos
25. Zalengas
26. Villafrechos
27. Moral de la Reina
28. Villalba de los Alcores
29. San Pedro de Latarce
30. Villardefrades
31. Griegos
32. Castromembibre
33. Villabarba
34. Cubillas
35. Muriel de Zapardiel
36. Santibañez de Tera
37. Benavente
38. Tabara
39. Villalpando
40. Villardiga
41. Pajares de Lampreana
42. Toro
43. S. Muños del Valle
44. Ciudad Rodrigo
45. Duruelo
46. Aldea del Rey Niño
47. Torrecaballeros
48. Milana
49. Agreda
50. San Pedro Manrique
51. Ucero
52. Villafrandovinez
53. Siones
54. Matalbaniega
55. Carrión de los Condes
56. Villalcazar de Sirga
57. Támara
58. Astudillo
59. Cevico de la Torre
60. Villamuriel de Cerrato
61. Ampudia
62. San Nicolas del Real Camino
63. Terradillos de Templarios
64. Alcañices

Legend

- ○ Provincial capitals
- ■ Fortresses
- ● Churches
- • Churches no longer in existence
- · Provincial capitals

Almohades' aggression and why when they intervened in battles they did so with a small number of brothers and in actions that didn't merit mention in contemporary chronicles. When they looked for settlements for the Order's houses, they did so in isolated enclaves, removed from the aggressive influence of the Castilian rulers, as we can still see in San Polo of Soria and in the Vera Cruz of Segovia-Zamarramala.

In the seventy-three years of independence of Castile and León, only one bellicose intervention of significance can be credited to the Templar monks in Castile: their contribution to the siege and conquest of Cuenca by Alfonso VIII in 1176—and we must suspect that even in this endeavor, the greater part of the brothers who participated could have come from the province of Catalonia-Aragon, accompanying their king, Alfonso II, the Chaste. In any case, through its actions in that campaign, the Order obtained a settlement in the conquered city: the convent of San Pantaleón, near a mosque turned cathedral. It is also more than likely that they participated there in the miraculous encounter and patronage of Our Lady of the Light, which continues even today to be the most important adoration of Mary in the city. Some scholars insist that most ancient cathedral-type structures in San Pantaleón reveal Templar influence.[1]

Even when the Templar order was establishing itself in Cuenca during the conquest of that city, its presence in Castile was discreet. After this campaign, which was the first act of a very young Alfonso VIII, a long period of internal civil conflicts occurred in the province, provoked by the families that intended to increase their areas of power by acceding to the king's tutelage. As was well known, the principal players in the Order of the Temple opposed any intervention in affairs among Christians. Thus, for many years it cut back on its participation in Castile's conquests, reducing its role in the kingdom to helping it defend itself against the Almohades' spurs. It is understandable, then, that in the infrequency of Templar action, any Templar initiative would shine.

The case of the Hospitallers, forever rivals and emulators of the Templars, was quite the opposite: The monks of the Hospital of St. John of Jerusalem, without instigation from any corner, intervened in the conflicts occurring under the rule of the young Alfonso VIII. For instance, they supported the Lara family against the Castro family, whom Fernando II of León, the king's uncle, somewhat directly and openly favored and in whose Extremadura campaigns the Templars had participated.

The Monks' Secret Gold

A year after the conquest of Cuenca, Fernando II of León rewarded the Templars' collaboration in the Extremadura campaigns with the donation of the castle of Ponferrada, in the heart of the Bierzo region, many leagues from the Muslim frontier but on the the pilgimage road of St. James. The very special nature of this enclave and the fame it acquired as it became a Templar site par excellence make it almost a paradigm of the presence of the Order in Spain. Given that the Order's true importance in the area of Bierzo has been suppressed, thanks to the popular success of that old-fashioned novel *El Señor de Bembibre* (The Lord of Bembibre),[2] we must examine more closely the presence of the Templar order. Ponferrada is significant because of the questions it raises regarding the Templars' shift in Iberia from their position as bankers to their prestigous role as exclusive custodians of symbolic reliquaries containing the miraculous Lignum Crucis (one of the most important of which resulted from the *encomienda** of Ponferrada).[3] Today this relic is preserved in the cathedral of Astorga and continues to be the object of the first official show of piety by the bishops of the apostolic see of the Maragatería capital.

As far as I know, no historian or trustworthy document specifies whether the castle of Ponferrada was a gift of the monarch of León or was given in response to an express petition from the Templars. It does seem that it was passed on to them in a calamitous state: The walls of the Roman fortress, known as the Interanium Flavium,† were barely preserved and had been in a state of ruin for centuries. The Templars, however, did not hesitate to make it their own by taking on its reconstruction.

*[The entrusting or granting of land and/or labor. —*Trans.*]

†It is not certain that this Roman site, noted in various itineraries, corresponds with Ponferrada.[4]

In the years after it became theirs, the Order acquired a number of castles, thereby coming to own, or at least control, a good part of the region of Bierzo. Some of these castles were already constructed, while others—Cornatel, Corullón, Pieros, Tremor, Antares, and Balboa (situated on the ascent to the Galician Cerbero)—had to be built. But besides the castles, which were mostly obsolete for purposes of defense and were, for many years, removed from the receding Muslim frontier, they held chapter houses in Bembibre, the Rabanal, Cacabelos, and Villafranca, which made them owners not only of Bierzo, but also of the corresponding stretch of the Road to Santiago, the Maragatería, and that sector in the hills of León that did not belong directly to the Benedictine monks of San Pedro de Montes, proprietors of those inhospitable slopes that surrounded the sites of Peñalba, Valdueza, Foncebadón, Compludo, and the Valle del Silencio (Valley of Silence) on the way to the traditionally sacred summits of Teleno and of the Aquiana.

There has been a generalized tendency among historians to accept, without grounds, the idea that the protection of pilgrims was the primary motive for the Templars settling in Bierzo. This reason, however, can hardly stand. First, the route to the region established by the members of the Cluny order, which came from the coast and passed by Oviedo, was created from the assumption that the difficulties and dangers once threatening the region were in the past and thus did not provide a reason for the imposing complex of Templar fortresses, the first—and only—fortifications that marked the pilgrimage route. The Templars, who had covered the entire route with houses, hospitals, and churches from its starting points in Aragon and Navarre, did not seem overly concerned with establishing themselves in castles here, for the major difficulties once suffered by pilgrims had practically been overcome. This forces us to think that perhaps these impressive fortresses were intended for purposes not mentioned in official documents.

If we examine the history of Bierzo from ancient times to the present, in the midst of long periods of silence we would bump into an element that emerges from the time of Roman antiquity, then nearly disappears for a thousand years, and is now very dear to us: gold.

Fig. 4.2. The Monastery of San Pedro de Montes, from which the Templars of Ponferrada resolved territorial disputes

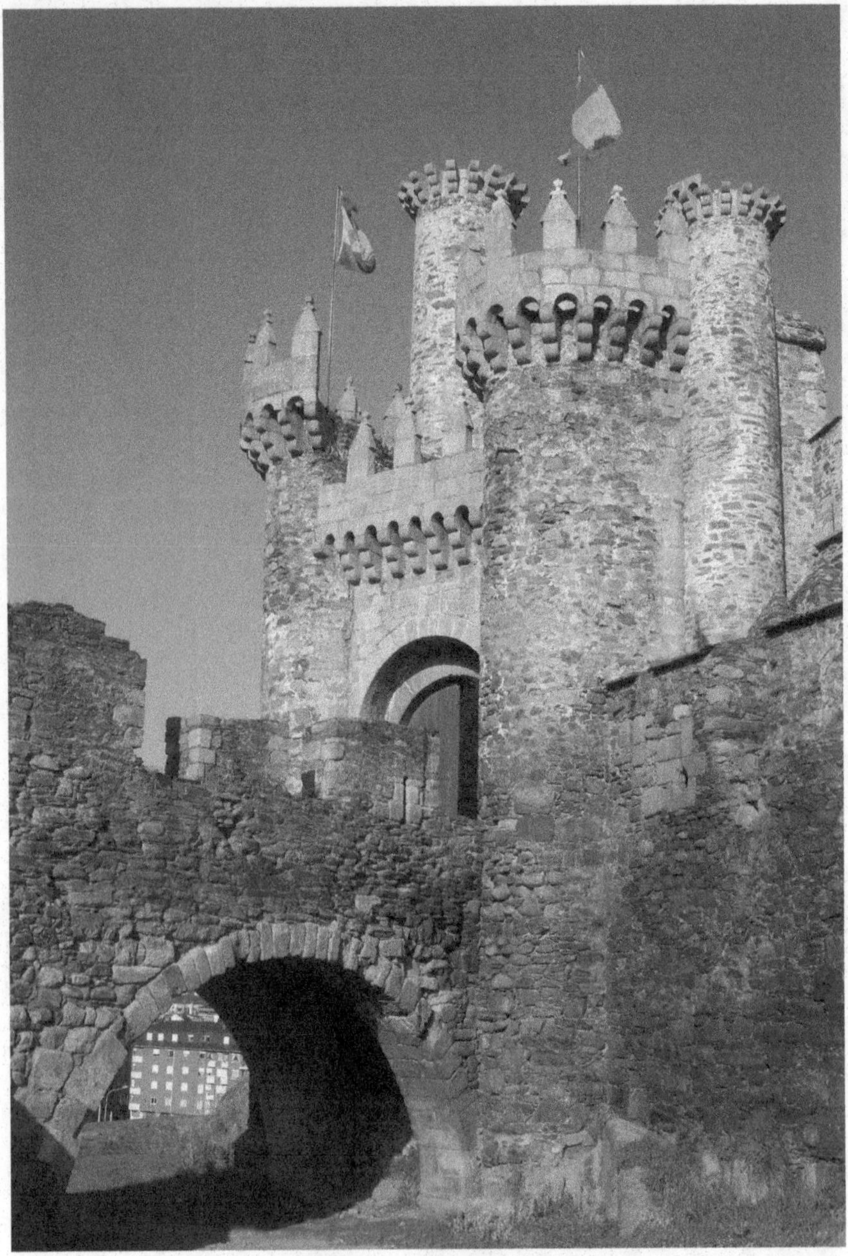

Fig. 4.3. Ponferrada, the paradigmatic Templar fortress in the kingdom of León

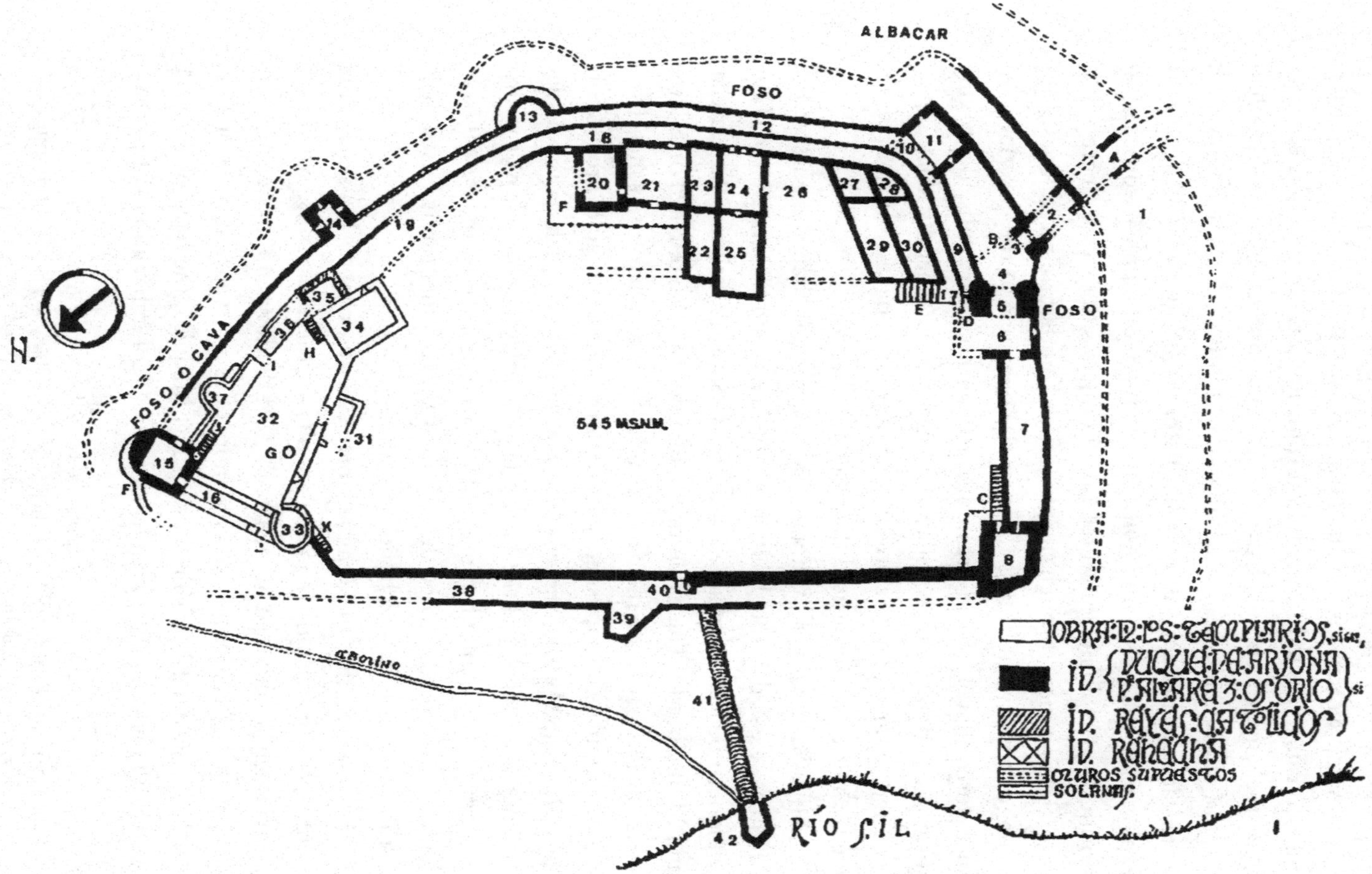

Fig. 4.4. The floor plan of the castle of Ponferrada (according to J. M. Luengo)

Touring Bierzo between Carucedo Lake and the Templar fortress of Cornatel, we can inspect the great site of Las Médulas. The auriferous deposits exploited by the Romans for more than two hundred years filled the empire's coffers. Later, for a reason not revealed by Latin historians, gold mines there were abandoned, although the methods used to extract the mineral can still be discerned. Pliny called this form of exploitation the *ruina montium* (ruin of the mountain): It consisted of storing large volumes of water in containers situated on nearby hills and releasing them through steeply inclined, underground galleries. This strong current would burst through the openings to the galleries with such force that it would crash against the boundary hills, destroying them and provoking their collapse. Mineworkers, generally from Cantabria and Asturias, later removed the masses of detached soil and, washing them, extracted the gold they contained.[5]

Mines of this type, although less spectacular than the ones at Las Médulas, existed throughout much of Bierzo and Maragatería. They could also be found in Santa Colomba de Somoza, Leitosa, Paradaseca, and Montefurado. The exploitation of gold was also pursued on a large scale on the banks of the Sil and Cúa Rivers, where the sands from the alluvium were deposited by the current. Private gold prospectors used this same procedure at various strategic sites, such as the Bridge of Domingo Flores and the Barco de Valderroas, until at least the first quarter of the twentieth century. They were known as the *aureanos* of Bierzo, men who dedicated their lives to a search that rarely raised them out of the misery in which they lived.*

It is curious that the Templar fortresses and chapter houses of Ponferrada are found mostly in the vicinity of those deposits, which had been largely abandoned in the late days of the Roman Empire and more recently have been subject to only more or less private exploitation. The castle of Cornatel is within view of Las Médulas, the barn of Rabanal del Caminois is next to the mines of Santa Colomba, and the fortresses

*In his *Natural History,* Pliny writes that between the years 206 and 168 B.C.E., the Hispania Citerior annually provided the empire with 11,200 pounds of gold. In Augustus's time, close to twenty thousand pounds of gold was exported to Rome. In the time of the Severos, however, an absolute silence surrounded these exploitations.[6]

of Corullón and Pieros, respectively, are downriver from the beds of the Cúa and the Burbia, the two rivers richest in auriferous sands. It is hard to believe that these sites were selected by chance and that the tight line of impregnable fortresses was located there merely for the solace of the St. James pilgrims. In order to reach these fortresses, pilgrims would have had to scale slopes that are almost impossible to climb.

Diverse Riches

There may be an obvious clue here, whispering its presence—one that concerns the Templars' Bercian settlements and has never made its way into any document: The Knights of the Temple of Solomon more than probably exploited the deposits of gold in this area. Do we have proof? There is none. Can we explain as coincidences the factors pointing to this conclusion? There are too many such coincidences, among them the fact that the beginning of the construction of the great cathedrals of León—the ones at Tuy and Astorga—as well as the glorious finishing touch of the cathedral at Santiago all took place after the Templars obtained Ponferrada.

There are, however, other circumstances that likewise sowed the seeds of Templar interest in the areas of Bierzo and Maragatería. Both tradition and archaeology in these territories show that the region was covered with sites considered sacred even before the establishment of Christianity. These include the summits of Teleno and Aquiana. Quite close to the top of Aquiana there is preserved a site called the Campo de las Danzas (Field of the Dances), where pagan festivals were likely held at specific times of the year.

At the end of Roman domination, during the first years of Christianity, the Priscillian heresy spread through this area and all of Galicia as a means of adapting theological concepts developed among the churches of the Orient to pre-Christian rites and devotions that would later be anathematized by St. Martín Dumiense. Together with that development of heretical ideas and practices there emerged during the age of the Visigoths a massive mystic explosion headed by the hermit Fructuosus. This filled the hills of León with seekers of transcendence, individuals whose practices were halfway between those of the anchorites of the Theban desert and the visceral devotion of the first cenobites, led by a guiding abbot who urged them on toward the heavenly paths.

When the Templars acquired their Bercian possessions, the spiritual tones of Fructuosus's cenobites had already been replaced by the perfectly regulated life of the Benedictines who occupied San Pedro de Montes. The properties of that monastery comprised a good part of the mountainside that dominates the Bierzo region on the south. But even under the fundamentalist influence of the monks, in all probability there were found remote followers of the heretic Priscillian as well as people—most probably *maragatos** themselves—who fostered pagan roots in their religious practices. As documents of the monastery of San Pedro de Montes show, occasional accounts are given of the donations made by "pagans" who were converted thanks to the intercession of the Benedictines.[7]

It is beyond all doubt (and it is absurd that a historiography recalcitrant in its rationalism would seek to deny it) that the Templar order structured its theocratic ideology by studying and assuming unorthodox principles. These included those they extracted from Eastern Christian sects and from the traditional structures that had been repeatedly denounced by the Roman Church as abominations. The spiritual world conceived by the Templars was made up of the very practices and ideas that in many cases served their accusers toward the end of the Order's existence. They had laid out the blueprint for a universal theocracy in which many unorthodox Christian sects would have a place, as would a substantial part of the religious ideologies defended by Jews and Muslims. These ideological schemes show up sporadically—and always discreetly—in the Templars' actions, and they undoubtedly were adapted to the environment of traditions and memories that dominated the region of Bierzo and Maragatería. For instance, in the locality of Quintanilla de Somoza there can be found a curious memorial tablet revealing that long ago, gnostic cults also practiced their worship in these remote areas. These groups were severely anathematized by the Church and

*Inhabitants of Maragatería, a county of León.

were never considered in the search for the common roots of the great religions of the Bible and their transcendent relationships to the most profound beliefs that preceded them.*

Gnosis means "knowledge"—the kind of knowledge intended to reveal fundamental truths that religious systems claim appear only as revelations and can be attained exclusively through faith. Gnosis is not really a religion, but rather a form to set out religious fact as something that is spiritually elevated along with all that signifies the search for knowledge. In this search can be found the soul and the mind of humankind and, with them, our ability to penetrate all forms that knowledge adopts. The official Church, as well as official Islam and the most orthodox Judaism, insofar as they stand as established religious, loathe knowledge and break their promise to those who seek both knowledge and truth. But these seekers, whether they operate openly or in secret, emerge in every era, searching so that believers will have the opportunity to reach the light of knowledge in all its facets, even if this means going against the grain of the debilitating devotions established by orthodoxies. Curiously, the hills of León give us an immediate example of this search: a forge. It is unique in design and even in its function. It was built near Compludo in Alcalá de Henares, during the same seventh century in which the teacher Fructuosus recruited hermits for the foundation he established at the foot of an ancient sacred mountain near the location of a cenobium that even then was believed to have vanished long ago. It is here that the forge still gives proof of its vitality, the consummate example of a perfect technology that is almost miraculous, considering the time when it was created. It is a model of what could be an ecological industry in which human beings learn how best to take advantage of what nature offers, for she provides all the energy we need to survive.

The forge of Compludo was not the only one in existence, although it is the only one in perfect working order today and represents a living example of the harmony that could have reigned in that place between science and belief during a time we have always been taught to see as

*Villada y Garcia Bellido comments on the headstone in question, which reads: "They are one Jupiter, Serapis, and Yahweh."

primitive and subject to ignorance. Indeed, in our time, by comparison, we seem destined to a predatory progress that has already put our very survival in danger. If we recall the theory posed by Mircea Eliade, the art of ironworking, like that of alchemy, was a path to perfection in which humans involved themselves during their evolutionary process, a material or technical process through which the foundations of complete knowledge could be reached, allowing individuals to understand the basis of the sacred.[8]

This understanding is what Templar initiates sought, with the idea of attaining through this knowledge the power that would allow them to establish the grand universal theocratic state that was the ideological base of the Order and the very foundation of its existence. The Templars expressed this ideology in Bierzo by establishing a cult that, beyond its devotional values, gave access to an idea the populace had been starting to adopt: the devotion to Mother Earth through the symbol of the Mother of God.

Our Lady of Encina

Historical facts do not exist. Only legends reaches us, steeped in traditional hagiographic details. It is legend that tells us how the image of Our Lady carved by St. Luke, called La Virgen de la Encina, was brought to Astorga from Palestine by St. Toribio and installed in the cathedral until the proximity of Saracen invaders led to hiding it in a place forgotten by parishioners.

We have two versions of what happened next: The first one says that around five hundred years later, while the Knights Templar were rebuilding the castle of Ponferrada, the image was found hidden in a holm oak *(encina)* by Templar carpenters when they were cutting down trees to make beams for the rooms of the fortress. The other version makes the discoverer a wounded brother returning from the defeat of Alarcos in 1184. Lost in the forest, he saw a light in the fog, which, as it turned out, emanated from the image of the Virgin hidden inside the trunk of a tree. Both versions of the encounter are combined in a third act in the drama in which the holy image with a black face was installed by the Templars in a chapel they built in front of the main gate of the castle, where the populace could worship it. They called it Our Lady of Encina, after the place where it was found, and set the date of her feast as September 8, the commemoration of the Nativity of the Mother of God and supposedly the date on which it was found.[9] It is said that around thirty years later, aided by the parishioners' alms, a more grandiose sanctuary was erected on the same site.

The original image (which was lost) and the current one (carved in the sixteenth century) have in common only dark-colored skin. The sanctuary where it is worshipped today was built after the destruction of the Order. It seems that the cult to La Virgen de la Encina was promoted by the Templars, who kept the day of the Nativity of Our Lady as one of their most important liturgies in their monastic life. Article 75 of the Order's constitution sets this date as one "that must be kept in Templar houses."[10]

In the twelfth century the Templars, together with the Cistercians of Bernard of Clairvaux, were the great promoters of a cult to Santa María (the Virgin Mary), a specific worship that the Church had limited or withheld for a number of centuries. Without a doubt, the recovery of this Marian cult was largely a response to a dormant collective consciousness, and the populace embraced it so enthusiastically because it found in it an equivalent to the ancient visceral religion of the Great Mother, which the official Church had tried to negate in order to silence the enormous importance this sacred figure had always held in humanity's religious scheme. Because the Templars responded to an ideology structured on more ecumenical Christian principles, they understood that devotion to the figure of the Mother of the Savior corresponded to that held in Eastern churches far from Rome—churches with which the Templars maintained close contact through their connections to Palestine.

In a certain way, the recovery of the cult of the Mother of God formed part of the Order's great synarchic plan. If we look closely at the Marian cults that emerged in Europe at the end of the eleventh century and throughout the twelfth century, we can conclude that the vast majority grew in areas directly influenced by either the Cistercians or the Templars.

There are certainly those who believe these matters have little or nothing to do with the strict history of the Templar order. I don't see it that way just as I refuse to accept that European expansion did not correspond to some intentions that began to manifest from the very moment the Council of Troyes approved the Order, for at that time the Order immediately to grow throughout the states of the Christian Occident and, fundamentally, throughout the kingdoms of the Iberian Peninsula. The intentions of those who make history do not appear in documents; and surely they are not exposed if they reveal a projection of power that could alarm those who might lose their control should an up-and-coming ideology materialize. In such cases it is advisable not to discount any statements as sticky or unworkable, as they might appear in a first approach, for behind these seemingly nontranscendental notions lie many more profound intentions, forming part of an ideology that, for the moment, might be manifested only partially or incompletely.

Regarding the Templars, because the Order was extinguished some time before it was able to mature, we must consider the existence of a planned venture that never became concrete reality. Before the Templars' demise, few circumstances had occurred to allow a decisive step toward the realization of its ideology. The Templar order as an unfinished ideology has lent itself to many fantasies, but even more, it has suffered from a vast indifference stemming from researchers' unwillingness to interpret the more or less important or nontranscendent events in which the Templars were direct or indirect protagonists or even merely extras.

The introduction of Marian cults into popular devotion is such event. In fact, there are many testimonials to the birth of this devotion. Those scholars who simply throw together their history have been inconvenienced by these accounts, while others too lazy to face all the facts fail utterly to see their importance. Only a few historians have taken the time to delve into what these testimonies reveal. Some believe they are manifestations of a much more substantial plan that began with the creation of a new kind of thought: Return to the populace a devotional element that could transform people's consciousness and later, after the structures beneath it had reached maturity, could shape people's attitudes when they were confronted by other political, social, and religious phenomena.

Gualdim Pais, Model of the Portuguese Templar

Herculanus, father of Portuguese historiography, tells us that in the campaign that ended with the conquest of Santarém (1147), 250 knights "and many Templars" accompanied the king don Alfonso Emriquez. This suggests that the number of Templar brothers was at least as great as that of the nobles who participated in the first significant act of war of the newly formed state. Great or small, the numbers matter less than the fact that they corroborate evidence that the Order was solidly rooted in Portugal and, especially at the beginning of the kingdom's particular Reconquista, already constituted a military force of substance capable of measuring up to the Almoravid forces of King Badajoz.

That same year, before launching the assault on Lisbon, the sovereign extended a deed of donation to the Order of the Temple in which he affirmed the fulfillment of the vow "to give to the knights and other religious members of the Temple of Solomon who reside in Jerusalem in defense of the Holy Sepulchre all ecclesiastical rights over Santarém."[11] This gift called for the Templars to become owners, in fact, of an extensive territory that, shared with the Cistercians (who would in turn receive the site where the monastery of Alcobaça would be built), represented the greater part of the northern basin of the Tajo River in Portuguese lands.

At that time, the grand master of the Portuguese Templars and second to hold that position was Hugo Martins. Both Martins and the Templar brother Gualdim Pais distinguished themselves in the Portuguese Reconquista. Pais was born in Amarâes in 1118 or 1119 and was knighted by the king after the battle of Ourique, when he was merely twenty or twenty-one years old. With the offensive resulting in the capture of

Santarém barely completed, he was summoned by the Order to join the head house in Jerusalem, where he remained for just more than six years, alongside Grand Masters Robert de Craon and Evérard de Barres. He surely wasn't the first Portuguese Templar to join the central power of the Order; there are reliable suggestions that one of the nine knights constituting the founding group, the one the French call Arnaud de Roche, could have been named Rocha and could have been a native of the land that would later become Portugal. In any case, a Templar invited to dwell in the Holy Land could theoretically have access to the most profound private affairs of the Order and without a doubt a leg up on positions of greater responsibility within the hierarchy of the Templars.

We can assume that Gualdim Pais's garrison in the Holy Land took part in the military operations in which the Templars distinguished themselves. We can also infer that the garrison was located close to Grand Master Barres, surely one of the strongest spiritual personalities of the Order's beginnings.* In all probability, Pais was deployed in Gaza and was present at the capture of Ascalón, where death found Bernard de Tremelay, the fourth grand master of the entire Templar order. Likewise, it is almost certain that before his return to Portugal, Pais met André de Monbart (St. Bernard's uncle), who would eventually participate in the drafting of the statutes of the Order, which were published when Bernard de Blanquefort was grand master. Thus Gualdim Pais's deployment to Jerusalem probably coincided with one of the Order's most intense periods, a time in which Templar ideology was finally structured and the Order was defined as a multinational power capable of actively influencing the politics of Christian Europe.

Pais's presence can be detected in Portugal around 1155, coinciding with the Templar letter of protection dispensed by King Alfonso. It seems Gualdim brought a precious relic from Palestine, one that was highly symbolic, as the majority of original relics were: the hand of St. Gregory of Nazianzus in a sumptuous silver case. In this instance, as in many others, we can discover the special merit of Gregory, a holy father

*Éverard de Barres resigned his command in 1149, after which he retired to Citeaux, where he died in 1173 under the aura of sainthood.[12]

of the Church: He was the son of a bishop connected with the Ipsistarian heresy* and a companion to the cenobites Basil and Gregory of Nyssa in their spiritual campaign to establish Oriental monachism. It was from Basil and Gregory that the Templars and many separate churches took so many teachings and codicils of knowledge.

Major events had begun to take shape in the newborn kingdom of Portugal at the time of Gualdim Pais's return. The dispute for ecclesiastical rights over Santarém, instigated by the English bishop of Lisbon, don Gilberto, during Gualdim's stay in the Holy Land, began to calm down and was resolved just as Gualdim Pais was named fourth grand master of Portugal after the death of the third Portuguese grand master, Pedro Arnaldo, during the conquest of Alcácer do Sal. A very astute political arrangement had been concluded that implied the ceding of the churches of Santarém, with all their tithes, to Lisbon's bishopric in exchange for the king's confirmation of the Templars as absolute owners of the territories of the northern slope of the Tajo River and the basin of the Zêzere River: Pombal, Tomar, Ces, Almourol, Idanha, and Monsanto. The Order immediately started to repopulate these deserted lands, converting the wilderness into places of *nullius diocesis*—"nobody's dioceses"—in which the only recognized religious authority would be the pope, to whom the Templars offered an honorary bishopric first in the person of Adrian IV and later to Alexander III (1159–1181), both of whom accepted and confirmed these dioceses and reaffirmed them as exclusive properties of the Templars in which no one might intervene.

There is no doubt as to the strategic importance of those territories over which the Templars had acquired such firm rights. In fact, the knights eliminated the possibility of any future surprise invasions, given that all the throughways and fords allowing penetration of Portuguese territory from the south passed through these lands. They also held the country's most traditionally important sacred site, full of the kinds of associations and ancestral connections that could potentially transform it into an Axis Mundi from which messianic action could be solidly realized.

*This heresy distinguised itself by its syncretism of the Jewish and the pagan worlds. In it, God, like Jupiter, was called Ipsistos, the Highest.

The Key to the West

The European Atlantic coast and its most fundamental occidental reaches that border the unknown sea—Cornwall, Normandy, Ireland, Galicia, and Portugal—have always enjoyed a particular magical prestige based on their traditional definitions as places were the world ends and their associations with the mythical dawns of knowledge. The most academic historiography cares very little for the improbable reality held in these beliefs that have so often been usurped by those who study esotericism and traditional knowledge. No one, however, could deny that countries and ideologies have frequently been propelled by ancestral beliefs firmly embedded in the collective consciousness, waiting to emerge at the slightest provocation.

In this way, the westernmost extreme, as the end of one world and the door to another, remained a constant in the mental framework of the ancient and medieval worlds, from the Road of the Dead traced by Egyptian priests to the Amenti, or Egyptian abode of the dead, to the innumerable migrations and invasions throughout history that almost without exception follow an east–west route. The West and what lay beyond together served as the nucleus of the traditional Atlantic legend in Plato's *Critias,* and, curiously, in many key periods of the past the structures that create cultures have arrived from the Occident in the hands of peoples who had traveled the road to *finis terrae* (the ends of the earth) and come back presumably steeped in knowledge. Thus, the way to the West was the path for an ancestral homing instinct that had its most definitive expression in the Road to Santiago. Joined to the motivation for this pilgrimage was the sum of needs that have moved humanity and its nations from their origins toward the edge of the unknown, the undefined point where, traditionally, the end merged with the beginning, death became one with life, and ignorance was replaced with knowledge.

In a way, possession of that Portuguese territory comprising everything from Cape Carvoeiro—this westernmost point on continental Europe differed by a few yards from the Galician Fisterra—to the Zézere

River presumed ownership of the principal group of ancestral traditions and beliefs in this territory (which was a place where, more than in almost any other, the mythic memory of a past survived by becoming legend, faith, or fantasy).

Without a doubt, this situation allowed for the quick repopulation of this inhospitable area, for Christians arrived from the north and Muslims preferred to rest there before migrating farther south. Other advantages in the area piqued Templar interest: for example, the possession of strategic ports that could serve as stopovers for a Templar fleet that would soon become the largest in Europe and true competition for the squadrons from Pisa and Genoa, which had always officially split between them the commerical maritime dominion of the Mediterranean. The Templars also practically possessed—though not by right—the port of La Rochela, where they crafted a jetty in Burgo, near La Coruña. They controlled the Portuguese coast between Nazaré (very near Alcobaça) and Peniche, next to Obidos, a city that was then much closer to the sea than it is in our day. On that vast stretch of coastline, at least four key spots existed where Templar ports could be built, protected, and controlled from the network of fortresses that bordered the Tajo and surrounded prized inland Templar enclaves.

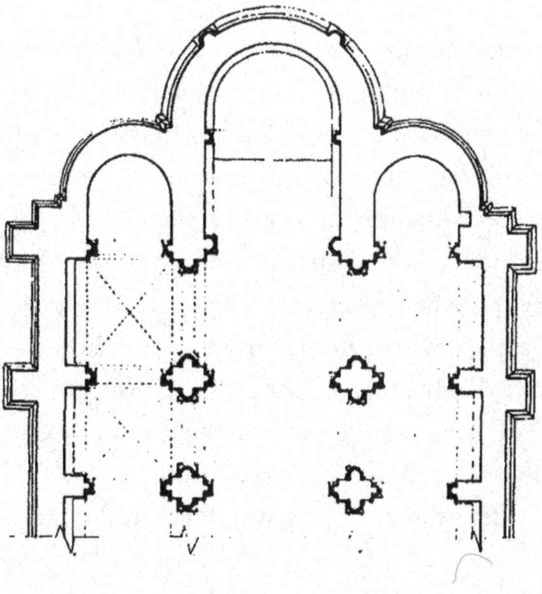

Fig. 4.6. The floor plan of the Templar church of Burgo del Faro in La Coruña (courtesy of the College of Architects of Galicia)

Fig. 4.7. The Templar fortress of Obidos, in Portugal

The center of this dense Templar nucleus of power was the castle of Tomar, built under the leadership of Master Gualdim Pais in 1160. Members of the Order immediately settled there and formed the governing council of the Order in the kingdom even before the foundations of the castle were laid. The council's first project was the complex that surrounded the chapel of Santa María de Olival, situated at the foot of the hill where the fortress was to be built. In time, the chapel became the place where all the Order's grand masters from this kingdom were buried, while the knights themselves were buried in the cemetery next to it, in the Huerto de la Orden (Order's Garden), now known as the Huerto del Rey (King's Garden).

Before the fortress was finished, Grand Master Pais, indisputable

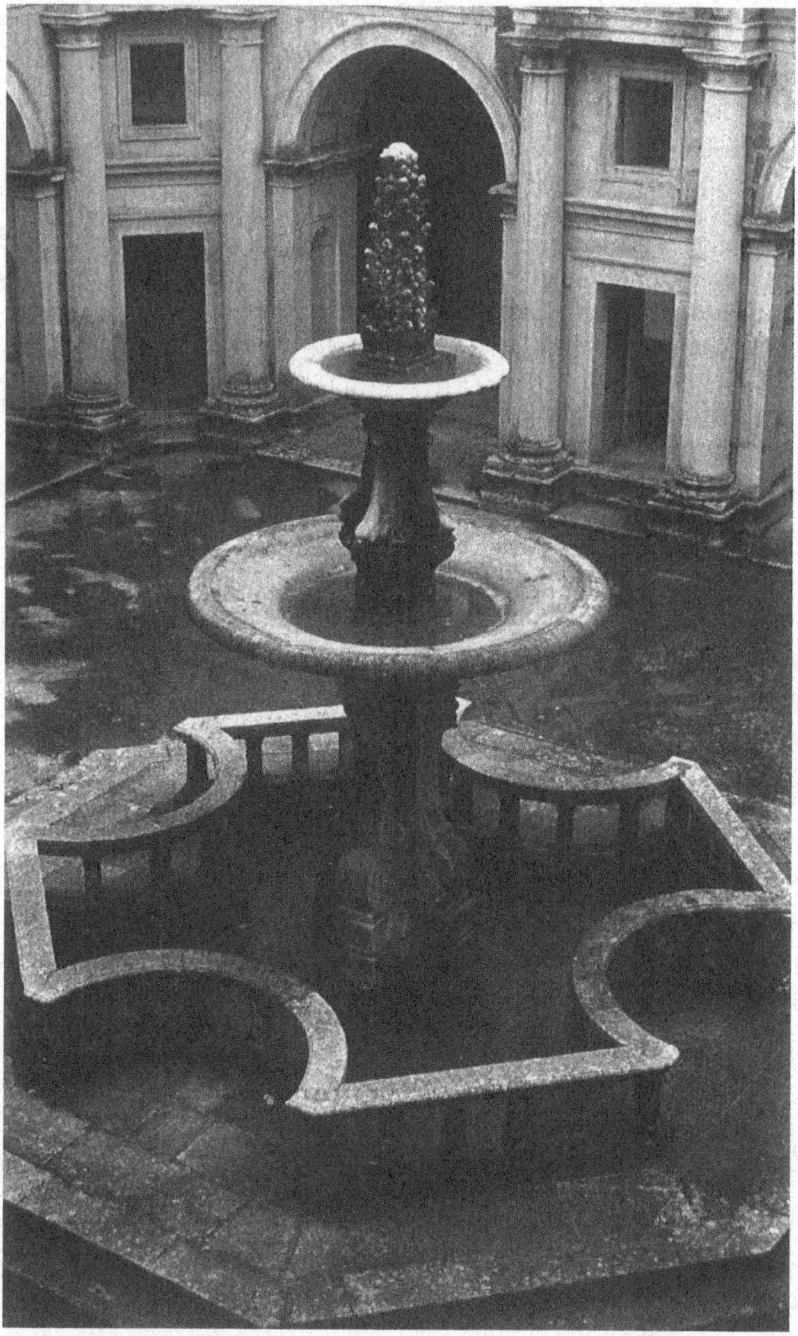

Fig. 4.8. The cloister's fountain in Tomar adopts the shape of the Templar cross.

owner and lord of the territory, established up to three different codes of law among the populace. In these statutes the Order refers to itself as "the lord." The first begins with a unique declaration: "I, Grand Master Gualdim Pais, with my brothers, to all inhabitants large and small of Tomar, of any class that you might be, and to your children and to your generations, it behooves us, brothers of the Temple, integrated in the faith of Salomon, to confer to you a letter affirming the right over your inheritances . . ."

In the third code, passed in 1174, the Templar order revealed itself as an authentic feudal force that required the inhabitants of Templar land to contribute taxes amounting to a quarter of their goods and harvests—a heavy load for people who could barely survive in such an inhospitable area of the kingdom.[13] According to the Templars, the view of this obligation as heavy was due to the fact that the people of these lands had never before had a tax imposed on them. The farmers attempted to protest on more than one occasion, but the Templar prepotency and their influence over the Portuguese monarchy ensured that all complaints would be judged in favor of the Order. Protesting continued until the dissolution of the militia by the Council of Vienne, in 1312. In the seven years that passed between the disappearance of the Templar order and the rise of its substitute, the Order of Christ, the citizens of Tomar managed to erase from the code the six lines that decreed their dependence on the brothers, who in this case had acted harshly and out of a greed that coincided with the most absolute principles of feudalism.[14]

The Templars in Portugal

Grand Master Gualdim Pais died on October 13, 1195, after having resisted a difficult siege by the Almohads in 1190, and was the first to receive burial in Santa María do Olival. His grave marker can still be seen in the second chapel behind the entrance to the temple, next to those belonging to all of the other Portuguese masters of the Order. Thanks to these markers and to the information provided by the Order of Christ's eighteenth-century chronicler, Friar Bernardo da Costa, we have a fairly

Fig. 4.9. An outline drawing of the castle of Tomar

clear idea of the Portuguese Templars' history. Friar Bernardo had set out to write a history of his order, but managed to complete only the first volume, which he dedicated specifically to the Templars. This chronicle is mostly a summary, but it provides us with a guide to the power held by the Templars throughout the history of the young kingdom.

In 1195, Gualdim Pais was succeeded by the fifth grand master of Portugal, Lopo Fernandes, who, despite the precepts of the Order forbidding brothers to intervene in struggles among Christians, died in 1199 during the siege of Ciudad Rodrigo, fighting against the king of León, Alfonso IX.

The sixth grand master of Portugal was Fernando Dias, whose enemies were nature's forces. First, a great famine spread through Portugal in 1202. Later, in 1206, a plague that devastated Tomar and its surrounding countryside took the life of this grand master.

The seventh Portuguese grand master, Gomes Ramires, had been a Templar in León and Castile since 1210. At that time, the commander of Tomar was the banker and close friend of Sancho I, and so the Crown's goods, or at least a major part of the kingdom's treasure, some twenty thousand *maravedíes,* were kept in the custody of the Tomar castle. While master to the Castile-León Templars, Gomes Ramires actively took part in the Battle of the Navas de Tolosa (1212) and died fighting the Almohads eight days after the battle in the assault of Úbeda.

The eighth grand master of Portugal, Pedro de Alvito, was grand master of three kingdoms. He had received for the Templar order the possession of the Castelo Branco (White Castle) and gave it a code of law. Through Innocent III in 1216, he also confirmed the attachment of the Templar Portuguese dominions to the Holy See. He gathered the Templars of the three kingdoms—Castile, León, and Portugal—and other European Templars for the conquest of Alcácer do Sol (in 1217) and was a personal adviser to and great favorite of King Pedro Anes, who ruled from 1223 to 1224.

The next Templar leader, Martim Sanches, also grand master in these three kingdoms, ruled until stepping down in 1229. Esteban Belmonte succeeded him from 1229 to 1237. He also became a favorite of Alfonso II after leading the military operations that conquered the plazas of Jeromenha, Aljustel, Serpa, and Aroches (or Arronches). Pero Nunes succeeded Belmonte, though he died shortly after he became grand master, in 1239. Nunes was succeeded by Guilhelme Fulcon, who was possibly French and who governed in the three kingdoms until his death in 1242.

The youngest grand master of the Castilian-Portuguese Templars was its fourteenth leader, Martim Martins, who assumed his command at barely twenty-five years of age and was linked through his family line to the oldest nobility of the Portuguese kingdom. Together with the Portuguese king Sancho II, he managed to join forces with the Knights of Santiago, which up to then had intervened only sporadically in Portugal. With them he ventured out on the Reconquista of the Algarve.* During his mastership, King Sancho II was forced into exile in Toledo (in 1247). That same year the grand master resigned his position and found a place in the service of Fernando III, king of Castile and León. He died during the conquest of Seville in 1248.

*At this time they called the Algarve the area of the county that extends to the left bank of the Guardiana River, officially the territory of Castile-León.

Gomes Ramires, fifteenth Portuguese grand master, grand master of the Templars of Castile-León, and subject of Alfonso III, entered Sevilla with his forces and obtained from Alfonso III the donation of the Alquería de Rastiñana. He died in 1251.

Paio Gomes continued the grand mastership of the three kingdoms and, although he had a main residence in Zamora, convoked a chapter of the Templars at Tomar in 1251. That same year, Emperor Friedrich II Staufen (a figure who should not be overlooked and who will appear again in subsequent chapters of this book) died in Sicily. Master Paio Gomes always remained very close to King Alfonso III, acting in a military capacity and as an adviser. Yet he did great honor to Templar tradition by resigning his command when he was presented with the obligation of joining his Portuguese Templars to the resistance against Castile. His successor, the sixteenth grand master, Martín Nunes, acted as an intermediary in resolving the matter of the partitioning of the Algarve between the two kingdoms of Portugal and Castile. Pope Urban IV personally addressed him in the papal bull *Glorious Deus in Sanctis suis,* in which he gave indulgences to the members of the brotherhood of Santa María do Olival, founded under the auspices of the Templars. During the leadership of Nunes, the Portuguese conquest, one of the attempts by Castile to absorb Portugal, ended thanks to his mediation. This allowed him subsequently to join his Castilian Templars and fight on the side of Alfonso III of Castile in the king's Andalusian campaigns. In 1265 he returned to die in Portugal.

Later, we will look more closely at the last grand masters of the Portuguese Templars, for they play parts in the fall of the Order; all their actions were undoubtedly tied up with their demise, an end for which, some believe, the seeds had already been planted.

The Templars of Navarre: An Ambiguous Presence

The most recent studies of both the presence of the Templars in the kingdom of Navarre since the restoration of the Order under García Ramírez and the possible importance they could have had in this kingdom's historical development have sought to demonstrate, perhaps unsuccessfully, that the Templars confined themselves to the administration of only a few possessions. Most of these were presumably rural properties that held no relevance whatsoever to Navarre's politics, which were becoming increasingly entangled with those of France. The brothers were likely limited to contributing their farm products to meet the needs of the Order in the Holy Land.[15] The evidence presented to support this thesis is based on documents found in national archives and read to the letter, with the consequent rejection of anything that does not figure in these parchments that have been preserved. In this way, uncomfortable archaeological evidence—and even, in some cases, the possibility to interpret or to state facts that are available only between the lines in existing archive material—has been swept away by academic historiography. Evidence of this can be found through both studying the national archive documents and rejecting anything that does not appear in the parchments that have been preserved.

It is not my intention to belie the documentation, but to try to open the minds of those who, in their close reading of it, confine themselves to an allegedly wholesome, pure, and simple reporting of reality while discarding everything that does not fit in with their preconceived notions. The so-called exhaustive works of these scholars are usually based on ideological structures already established in these researchers' minds; documents are thus cited without having been previously subjected to analysis or questioning, which—who knows?—might shake previously constructed schemes. These researchers avoid the whys that might remain unanswered or that could be answered differently. In the end, what is left is taken as all there is of evidence, without considering the possibility—however conjectural—that what might have been sacrificed or hidden to preserve vested interests could well form the heart of the matter.

Everyone knows the irascible heterodoxy that has enveloped the Templars since their inception. This has led to historical investigation of the Order by the majority of conservative academic researchers who make up the unmovable support of official learning to avoid—indeed haughtily to ignore—the reality of the Templars or to free the Order from all suspicion and reduce it to the original official character it assumed when it was established and which it kept, despite errors about its establishment in its documents (which led to its disolution) and its public and political statements.

For the moment, let us continue with these postures, which have been assumed in Spain since the time of Campomanes. As needed, we can immerse ourselves in doubts based on the clues of very different certainties. Above all, let us abandon the fear of questioning ourselves or of thinking less of ourselves if many of our questions lack reasonable answers.

Concerning Navarre, the national, local, diocesan, and provincial archives offer no fewer than two hundred relevant documents, most of them related to donations, purchases, exchanges, concessions, disputes, and codes of law. The dates of these frequently indicate an establishment of the Templars immediately after the approval of the Order, which coincided with the controversial will and testament of Alfonso the Battler and the emancipation of Navarre under García Ramírez.

Between 1128 and 1136, seven important donations to the Templars are recorded. The first are private offerings, which are followed by a royal one. All are on the Navarrese shore of the Ebro, south of Tudela. Of these donations, the one that stands out is that of Lope Kaisal, given in 1134. It was made shortly before the death of the donor in the battle of Fraga, in which he fought on the side of Alfonso the Battler. The first royal donation is the village and castle of Novillas, given to the Templars in 1135, in one of the first official acts of the Restorer King. The donations in question—before the grand master of Provence Pedro Rovira (known as Rovera in Navarre) appears as their recipient—seem to have been made quietly. As the Aragonese historian Paulino Usón y Sese points out, they are all agrarian in nature, corroborating the Templars' clear preference for fertile territories over strategic ones.[16]

Naturally, this preference seemed logical in Navarre. After its emancipation from the crown of Aragon, it had been left without land to conquer from the Moors. No valid reasons existed to ask for or to accept places on the border, nor could the Templars offer counter grants of such sites in Navarrese lands. It is significant, however, that this situation is echoed in royal donations. There were six donations during the reign of García Ramírez (1134–50), which were reduced to five during the reign of Sancho the Wise (1150–94), and one in that of both Sancho the Strong (1194–1234)—despite the Navarrese Templars' intervention in the Battle of Navas de Tolosa—and Teobald II (1253–70). In any case, these donations are different from those received in the same period by the brothers of St. John, whose holdings allowed them to build a Navarrese priory for their order while the Templars could barely put together a couple of commissions to administer territories that were distributed throughout three single areas of the kingdom. These areas were:

- The land that stretched between Tudela and the left bank of the Ebro, with Ribaforada as this territory's vital economic center
- The land of Rioja, located to the west of Tudela and reaching to Alcandre, Yanguas, and Arenzana, with Funes as its center
- The land in the district of Estella, enclosing an area of the Road to Santiago

This last was perhaps the most significant regarding the firm establishment of the Templar order. They had quarters in Estella—perhaps in what is today the sanctuary of Rocamador—Artajona, Sagües, Legarda, Aberín (which was donated in 1177), Allo, and Obanos (all properties in the district of Estella). According to every indication, the nucleus of this property could be found in Puente la Reina, ceded by King García Ramírez to the Templars in 1142 and called by him *illam meam villam veteram* (my veteran villa).

The relationships among existing documents referring to the Order of the Temple offer a series of significant facts at the margins of the concrete nature of each one of these documents. First, there was a marked progressive reduction of donations to the Templars from 1200 to 1250: During this time, the Order received barely anything and was limited to buying or exchanging properties in an early attempt to concentrate its landholdings. Second, there is a progressive scarcity of documents throughout the time of the Order's presence here, dropping to practically nothing in the last years of the Order's existence. Third, there are no papers referring to any participation by the Navarrese Templars in the military campaigns begun by their monarchs, not even in the well-known campaign of the Navas under Sancho the Strong. Fourth, there are no documented references to the Holy Land, where we would be likely to find the benefits obtained by the Templars from their Navarre possessions. Nor do we find reference to the location or existence of houses, monasteries, or residences where the brothers would be concentrated. Documents refer only to land, vineyards, groves, windmills, irrigation ditches, and the like. There do exist four charter letters given by the Templars to places under their direct jurisdiction between 1234 and 1247.

Concealed Evidence

All these circumstances lead to the conjecture that there must have been a deliberate intent—although we will never know by whom or when—to suppress all evidence of the Templar enclaves in Navarre. Further research should be devoted to clues supporting this hypothesis. Two such clues are Puente la Reina and Eunate. Academic historiographers argue that we do not know who built the Church of the Crucifix (and the so-called funerary chapel). Yet, clear evidence exists indicating the Templar origins of these structures. As for the chapel at Eunate, whose Templar roots have been repeatedly denied by historians maintaining that the land was not owned by the Order, there is a document on record that specifies that the Templars exchanged agricultural land in Novillas on February 28, 1175, for other properties located between Obanos and Poyo, which today is known as El Pueyo.[17] Perhaps it is merely coincidence, but the chapel of Eunate and the small church of Olcoz—whose portal echoes the north portal of the chapel—are located in the fields and hills situated exactly between the localities mentioned in the document outlining this exchange.

In the same compilation from the Congressional Committee on Military Orders that I quoted earlier,[18] there is one from don Luis Romero Iruela that refers to the foundation of the Monastery of the Crucifix in Puente la Reina. The researcher, citing this after confessing, for unknown reasons, his reluctance to confront "unsettling" documentation, refers to the discovery of a document from the collection of Juan de Lastics, grand master of the Order of St. John of Jerusalem. In 1414, Juan de Lastics wrote to his ensign in Navarre, Pedro del Bosco, charging him with finding an ideal location to build a hospital for pilgrims to Compostela, a task that the queen, doña Blanca, had indicated was close to her heart. Facing the possibility of converting an establishment they already possessed in Bargota, which was run, as he put it, by "four idiots and an ignorant monk," they decided to build this establishment in Puente la Reina, where, from what can be gathered from the text, they had no previous construction. Beginning at this point, the existing documents are an authentic mishmash of dates: The creation of a confraternity promoted by a pontiff who ruled forty years later is confirmed; churches that the brothers of St. John already owned for many years are cited as being purchased; a convent already in existence for more than a hundred years is listed as being newly built. From this vantage point the documentation looks like the result of scheming—a creation of improvised and falsified information. Sadly, those who have committed themselves to studying it note merely that any discrepancies—especially involving dates—can be interpreted as mistakes of the copyist.

The reality is much simpler and, at the same time, intentionally ambiguous. As we have seen, there exist documents that testify to the donation of Puente la Reina to the Templar order in 1142 and to the transfer of Templar properties to the brothers of St. John per the express order of Clement V in 1313. There is also evidence of the close family relation of the Navarrese monarchs to the French royal house. Puente la Reina was not the first Templar possession the brothers of St. John made their own after the Order's destruction.* What is more, today the

---

*See chapter 9 for the historical details relating to the Church of the Vera Cruz in Segovia.

Church of the Crucifix still displays Romanesque architecture, including its doorway opening under the arch that served as a passage for pilgrims. It goes without saying that a building designed and constructed in the middle of the fifteenth century (on the site where the Sanjuanistas are said to have built a hospital that had already existed for many years before they decided to take it over) could not possibly have been built in the Romanesque style.

These examples, whose circumstances we will have the opportunity to explore in more depth later on, confirm a firm suspicion: In this region there was a deliberate attempt to erase any sign of the Templar presence. Although this occurred not only in Navarre, it is possible that here we can find and combine the exact factors necessary to provide evidence of this cover-up. As we have seen, one such factor is the progressive lack of documentation; another is the progressive decrease of donations to the Order. Should we consider the possibility that the most recent documents are the ones most likely to have been destroyed or distorted by those who, in their own interests, wanted to erase any trail of inheritance that might imply actual theft of those properties?

Facing this possible manipulation (from which history, unfortunately, has never been able to free itself), we need to take into account other evidence that has been systematically forgotten—evidence directly concerning medieval Navarre. The kingdom's role in the Reconquista ended early, which allowed numerous members of its noblity to join the subsequent expeditions to the Holy Land, where they could immerse themselves in that crusading spirit that Cluny had sown and eagerly follow the early example of García Ramírez's father, Prince Ramiro. The most important of these expeditions was undoubtedly the one carried out by King Teobald I between 1239 and 1243, on which he was accompanied by both Crusaders from Navarre and Navarrese Templars. Those exploring the Order's path in Navarre have not taken into consideration this event.[19] King Teobald's expedition, affiliated with the Crusade of Louis IX, was surely the spark that started the decline of the Templar order in Navarre. What we know for certain is that actions in Gaza mounted by Teobald I were frowned upon by the Templars, leading to a subdued response from the soldier-monks, who were regarded by the Navarrese monarch as being partially to blame for the famous defeat he suffered there.[20]

Historical events never occur in a vacuum. It is not possible to explore a specific circumstance without taking into account all others, even if they seem unrelated. The result is a subtle meshing of facts that demonstrates that none of them could have occurred without the concurrence of the rest. Any apparently unrelated circumstances might actually have been the triggers for the rest. Despite our relative ignorance of the Templars' true significance in European history, evidence consistantly supports the claim that without the Order's influence, events of history undoubtedly would have turned out quite differently. This raises the question of whether the Templars were the cause or the effect of such events, and also necessarily increases our dedication to an investigation that requires, first and foremost, a conscientious revision of a good part of the history of humanity—which established interests absolutely refuse to understand.

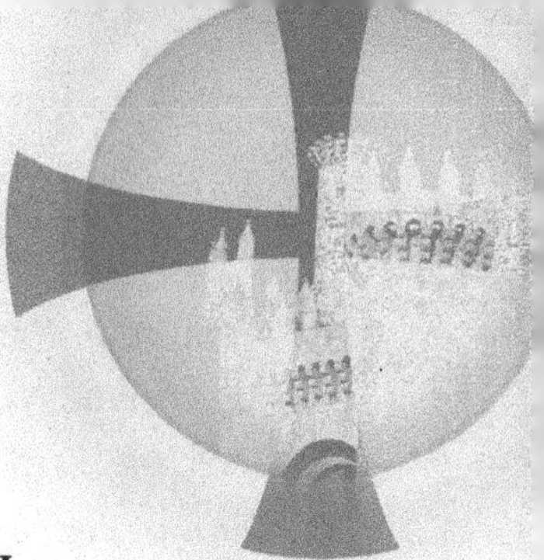

5
The Catalan-Aragonese Crown: A Templar Objective

Upon the death of his father, Ramón Berenger IV inherited both the royal Aragonese crown as Alfonso II and, as Alfonso I, the county of Barcelona with all its annexes. In him, as the common descendant of the governing families, the two states were united under the same title, which has been either the crown of Aragon or the Catalan-Aragonese crown, depending upon the origins given to it by historians based on their particular ideological posture. As a historical reality, it hardly matters which title is adopted; there is no need for the stubborn insistence on preserving varying monarchical nomenclature. The subsequent confusion of what is included and what is foreign gets in the way when we attempt to locate precise historical moments, events, and individuals. Here I will assume the designation of Alfonso II only to avoid confusion when the same monarchical name and number are ascribed to Alfonso the Battler—who continues to be the secret protagonist of this strange story—and to his nephew-grandson, Alfonso the Chaste, who gathered in a single state the Catalan counties and the kingdoms of Aragon (which the will and testament of the Battler had left as inheritance to the military orders formed in the Holy Land) and Barcelona, whose counts had openly proclaimed themselves to be lay members of the Order of the Temple.

Impossible Renunciations

Historiography continues to silence realities and evidence. Even today, many historians avoid speaking of the Templar order, much as chronicles have. Yet the shadow of the Templars glides among historical events, configuring seemingly impossible legends that are denied or overlooked by all but that rare scholar who takes the time to stop and scrutinize the possible motives behind such traditions. At the least, historians could make a simple note of the evidence presented by some phenomenon or synchronicity rather than shooing it away like an annoying guest.

The political treaty that the Templars and Ramón Berenger IV provisionally agreed upon resolved the problems of the rights conferred in the will and testament of Alfonso the Battler. The Order agreed to exchange these rights for a sizable legacy of middle- and long-term donations and obtained the dependence of Ramón on the participation of its soldier-monks in the kingdom's plans of conquest. Politically, the Tem-

Fig. 5.1. Alfonso II of Aragon (also Alfonso I of Catalonia), according to the Liber Feudorum Maior. *At the bottom we can see the king's sign, reminiscent of the Templars' insignia.*

plar order was to acquire an influence in the state as decisive and substantial as those rights it had formally surrendered. This only strengthened the influence it had exercised from the very time the Templars were given official status in the counties on the other side of the Pyrenees. Barns, homes, hospitals, and other donations transformed the Order of the Temple and its members into arbiters of the politics of their rulers and, in fact, turned them into unofficial guardians of the population's behavior, thanks to their control over a good part of the means of subsistence: ovens, mills, hospitals, docks, and even working fields.

Researchers have been doing nothing less than hiding their heads in the sand with their persistence in deliberately ignoring the influence the Templars exerted through their well-paid relinquishing of a few castles and some ethereal promises. The Templars were aware that what they had renounced opened the way to a venture of greater magnitude, which, from the moment of their official entry to the recently constituted kingdom, Catalonia-Aragon, began to evolve silently, waiting for the precise moment when its true dimensions could be revealed.

When Ramón Berenger IV died, his son, barely ten years old, inherited the throne. His name, also Ramón, was changed on his mother's insistence to Alfonso,[1] affirming his direct link to Alfonso the Battler, whose memory had not dimmed in spite of the years that had passed since his death. Queen Petronila, still too young herself to assume the role of mother and queen, spent a couple of years supervising matters of state, but prepared her son to fulfill his functions by putting him under the guidance of those whom she thought would best help him. These individuals, who formed a type of small state council, were Guillermo IV, lord of Montpellier; Lord High Chamberlain Guillén Ramón de Montcada; and the bishop of Tarragona, Guillem de Torroja, who was linked to the Templars through his brother Arnau de Torroja, who was grand master of Provence, Catalonia, and Aragon between 1167 and 1180. In fact, in 1180 he was named grand master of the entire Templar order after Eudes de Saint Amand was taken prisoner by the Muslims in the disaster at Peneas and, in accordance with Templar precepts, was never rescued.

The young sovereign was watched closely as he took his first steps in

Obano
HUESCA
Cinca River
Alchabez
Novallas
Novillas
Alberite
Ambel
Gallego River
Castellón C.
Monzon
Marlofa
Jalon River
ZARAGOZA
Ebro River
Chalavera
Belver
Corbins
Gardeny
Remolins
Serós
Gebut
Rici A
Encinacorba
Monaspe
Algars
Flix
Ascó
Batea
Gandesa
Corbera
Miravet
Pinell
Horta
Rasquera
Guadalupe River
Castellote
Santolea
Villarluengo
La Zuda
Buriacenia
Orrios
Alfambra
Cantavieja
La Iglesuela
Ares
TERUEL
Villel
Villastar
Corbo
Benasal
Albocacer
Pulpis
Peñíscola
Bot
Culla
Vinrobí
Cuevas de Vinromá
Chivert
Abzaneta
Libros
Albeniosa
Turia River
CASTELLON
Burriana
Moncada
VALENCIA
Barbazachar

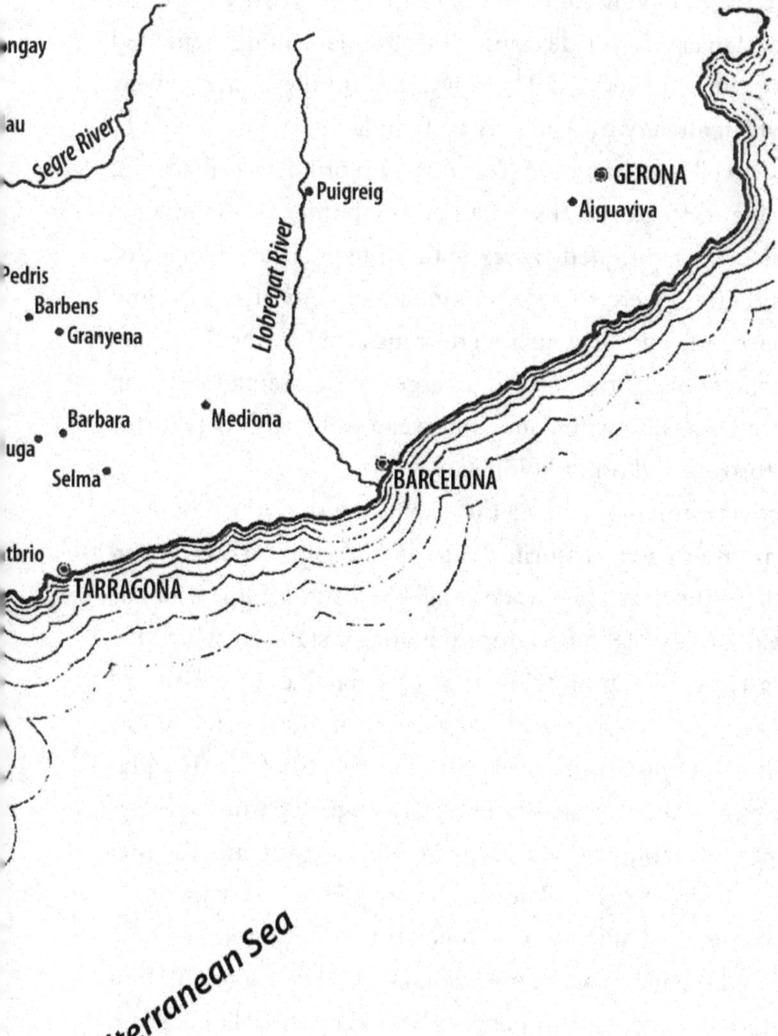

Fig. 5.2. Templar fortifications in the Catalan-Aragonese kingdom

government and the politics of war. As a minor, he fulfilled the established treaties to the letter, launching offensives in the lands of the Aragonese *maestrazgo* (grand master's jurisdiction), which fundamentally benefited Templar interests. In 1168 and 1169 he conquered for the Order Chivert and Oropesa, which already formed part of Templar claims in the established treaties, as well as Alfambra, Castellote, Escorihuela, Villarubio, and the whole line of fortresses that guarded the border of the Moors' kingdom of Valencia. He signed truces with Aragon: In exchange for peace, the royal coffers were to receive annually twenty-five thousand *morabetinos,* one thousand of which were transferred to the Templars in payment for their role as the force in charge of overseeing the truce[2] and as insurance that they would not intervene militarily to take for themselves the fortress and other holdings.

While it actively collaborated in the expansionist politics of Aragon, the Templar order had transformed into an authentic territorial and economic power of the first magnitude in all the counties north of the Pyrenees and was calmly planning a future union of states in which the principle of a vast confederation, the bud of its synarchic dream, would be established. For this they had laid out their own internal hierarchy, establishing that a sole provincial master was in charge of the Templar properties in Provence, the Languedoc, Foix, Cominges, Bearn, Toulouse, Bigorra, Catalonia, Aragon, and Navarre. We have already met the first of these masters, Pedro Rovira. The second was Hugo of Barcelona, under whose command an alliance was forged between Ramón Berenger IV and Henry II of England in an attempt to take over the county of Toulouse. The mastermind behind this contract was the chancellor Becket, archbishop of Canterbury, who was predisposed to the Templar ideology. After Henry II had Becket assassinated in 1170, the Templar brothers made him a saint before his official beatification.

The third provincial master was Hughes Geoffrey, who in his time at the helm experienced the death of the Catalonian realm. Arnau de Torroja, whom we have already mentioned, was the fourth master of these provinces and became grand master of the Order itself. Without a doubt, he was the chief architect of the plan that, in theory, would bring about a great concentration of territories controlled by the Templar order toward their reconfiguration as the foundations of its universalistic enterprise.

When the King Turned into a Frog

If we consider historical events as signs of a widespread global plan (as is too often the case) rather than as events that have an intrinsic value on their own, we would do well to look at the many phases such a plan undergoes. We can start with a look at the triumphal tour made through Provence by Alfonso II, who was still a child, on the insistence of his mentors after the death of his lord, Ramón Berenger III. Ramón had been shot by an arrow while laying siege to the port of Nice, which had sided with the naval influence of the Pisans against the count's open support of the the Genoese. The voyage of the Catalan-Aragonese king, Alfonso II, was financed by a banker from Montpellier, Guillén Latric, who took as the guarantee for his loan the taxes that were charged to the Moors of Valencia,[3] which the Templars took care to collect from their border fortresses in the maestrazgo. The boy-king's trip was, politically speaking, the tacit demonstration of the authority of the peninsular kingdom over those lands sharing a common culture and language. These territories were joined as a kind of macro-state that was being developed under the authority of a monarch who, at barely sixteen years of age, appeared—or was made to appear—to represent their union as an enterprise that could institute an occidental political force capable of confronting royal French authority, which had been the official owner of those territories since the times of Charlemagne.

The Templar order, which was the ally of Genoa while it structured its own naval power, was the owner of numerous goods and lands throughout the Occident and, from the sidelines and through third parties, controlled the prestige of the boy-king. This ruler was presented as a unifier and, above all, as heir to Alfonso the Battler's mythic, carefully promoted fame. By giving him the mantle of lord of the land of the Grail and of a missing-though-not-dead hero (the Battler) who was always capable of emerging from behind these isolated events, they sought to weave a sense of unified destiny among those small states north of the Pyrenees and bring about their immediate dependence on the predestined monarch, the supposed light of a glorious future.

Yet Alfonso II, who had barely reached his majority, began acting on his own, ruling as a sovereign without heeding the interests—whether right or wrong—of those seeking to use him. The first well-known opportunity for Alfonso to act independently came about on July 4, 1172, when, as Count Gérard II of Roussillon lay dying, he declared Alfonso to be his heir—despite the fact that the king of Aragon had no formal right over the count's small fiefdom, which officially belonged to the king of France, nor rights over the counties of Perelda and Ampúries.[4] The Aragonese sovereign presented himself in Perpignan twelve days later to take charge of his inheritance, and upon arriving at his estate found that the county was indeed his. But the Templars, who, we may suspect, inspired this will, had received, among other trifles, all the rights of the territory concerning weights and measures, all the ovens in a capital that had more than twelve thousand inhabitants, and all the windmills that surrounded it. Meanwhile, the count's testament granted the Hospitallers the leper hospital at Perpignan.

It was not very much later when the king, although still demonstrating his friendship to the Templar order, started to act on his own behalf. Because he seemed chronically short of the income necessary to fund the relatively luxurious court life he had adopted, he found himself in financial straits, which were complicated by the Templars' denying him credit. The king then took advantage of a visit to Perpignan to woo the Hospitallers, whose see was on the nearby Mount of Lepers, on the remote outskirts of the city. A few days later he made public a decision that fell like a bombshell on the population of the region: Given the difficulty of defending the city, built on a barren plain, the king decided to move it to the foot of the Mount of Lepers and fortify it sufficiently for the defense of the citizen district.

This decision upset the Templar order, which had no knowledge of it until its publication, for the Order had very much ignored the yeomanry of Perpignan. The citizens of the city now saw the continuity of their comfortable existence threatened by the great expense that such an arbritary move would entail. Those closest to the king revealed their willingness to negotiate an arrangement that would rid them of this dilemma. The answer came surprisingly fast: The king had spent a great deal on the project, and he had to be compensated in some way. The citizens of the region of Rousillon, who were people of means, thus offered to collect monies that would pay for anticipated expenditures. The amount gathered translated into six thousand Montpellierian salaries,* which ended up in the hands of the king in exchange for the promise of postponing a project that never came to completion.

Although this royal scam was of minor importance, an incident that not even the citizens of Perpignan found objectionable, it does reveal in the king signs of a personality that would not conform to the schemes and plans of the Templar order. In addition, it occurred in tandem with events that could have made conditions worse for the Templars: for instance, the rapid Aragonese expansion of the militia of Monsfragüe, or, as they came to be known, Montgaudí, the Order of the Holy Redeemer of Alfambra.

The Order of Monsfragüe was a monastic-military creation of a noble Galician, don Rodrigo de Sarria, who likely established it as the Order of Montgaudio in the Holy Land, where it was deployed during the reign of Baldwin III. Around 1171, it was revived in Extremadura by St. Julian of Pereiro, later known as Julian of Santiago.†[5] Meanwhile, the Order of Monsfragüe became entrenched in Extremadura, where it established its see in the castle (converted into a sanctuary) that took its name from an image of Our Lady that don Rodrigo allegedly brought from Palestine. The great difficulty Rodrigo met with in competing with the Spanish orders recently established in Castile-León forced him to seek recourse before the pontifical legate Cardinal Jacinto, whom he met

*Approximately twenty-five hundred of today's *pesetas,* according to the calculations of Mazières, "Une curieuse affaire du XIIe siecle: celled u 'Puig del Lepreux' à Perpignan."

†St. James; its members came to be known as *santiaguistas.*

in Zaragoza during the betrothal of Alfonso II and Sancha, the daughter of Alfonso VIII of Castile.

On this occasion the count of Sarria killed two birds with one stone. Upon obtaining a promise of intercession from Pope Alexander III, he met with the king of Aragon, who wasted no time in granting the Order of Monsfragüe the territory and castle of Alfambra, which belonged to the Templar order, and in quick succession granted him a whole series of fortresses that had been in Templar custody or that had been firmly promised to the Templars: Castellote, Villel, Libros, La Peña del Cid, and Villaruego. These donations took place between 1174 and 1177, all of them in the territory of Teruel, and were complemented by the donation of the hospital of Santo Redentor, also recently established in the city of Teruel.

A Missing Person's Return

Almost immediately after the donation of Alfambra to the Order of Monsfragüe (renamed the Order of Montgaudí) as its first settlement in the kingdom, and the blow this represented to the Templar Order, which had taken possession of the Alfambra four years earlier, something happened in the kingdom. Zurita y Castro recounts this, though, oddly, he is mistaken regarding the dates of these events:*

> In these circumstances, a certain novelty occurred which was like a representation of a very memorable and remarkable spectacle in the eyes of the whole populace . . . that caused great consternation and scandal in the land, especially among the common folk, who are naturally more open to new things, which they casually receive and approve. So it was that almost suddenly a rumor spread throughout the kingdom that the emperor don Alonso, king of Aragon, who was killed by the Moors in the battle of Fraga twenty-eight† years before, was alive. Following this rumor, a man appeared who

*These errors always seem to be hidden, but in this case, several documents leave no doubt.

†In reality, forty years before, given the chronicler's obvious mistake.

> claimed to be him; and once this thing was divulged, it was given great credit by the common folk . . . and there was a shortage of those who would take him in and give him shelter and help him so that he might return to his original position and rank. With his artifice he did persuade many, representing in his person and semblance the seriousness of authority in such a way that people gave him reverence and understood that he was deserving of the rank he claimed . . . He helped those of advanced age, who were usually favored by all. Yet though he placed himself under the judgment of rich men and of the court, as was the custom, there could be no just cause for him to have left the kingdom when it most needed his favor and support, none for leaving without protection his loyal vassals and subjects, who so well and faithfully served him in the wars that he had . . .[6]

According to Zurita y Castro, to those who would listen to him—not few in number—he explained that, overwhelmed by the defeat at Fraga, "he, who had always been a victor, went to Asia as a pilgrim, were he found himself in many battles waged by the Christians against the Turks." Among his interlocutors were those who had personally known the lost king, and it appears he provided numerous signs and details that only the late king and his interlocutors could have known: "[H]e gave each one reason of who he was and the origin of the lineage and houses of the kingdoms and of the succession of these and of the accomplishments of its progenitors, remembering many deeds which they had done in their time in past wars."

The so-called *Annals of Turuel* explain the fraud was a blacksmith by profession, adding that it all began as an event of mostly popular interest, which seemed to affect only dreamers. It started to take on an alarming aspect the moment part of the Aragonese nobility gave credit to the plot and pronounced itself willing to recast history from the moment at which the Battler disappeared and left as heirs to his kingdoms the military orders that had emerged from the Crusade to the Holy Land. Indeed, the story had attained such life that Alfonso II was forced to travel to the monastery of Montearagón to confirm, in the company of his brother, Berenger, and a trustworthy, hand-picked retinue, that his granduncle was indeed rotting in the tomb in which he had been buried. Yet once a snowball has been pushed down a slope, it is very difficult to stop it in its path, and it keeps growing. The presence of the impostor was beginning to pose a very real danger that could not be rebutted, even by the obvious reason that if Alfonso I was alive, he would be more than one hundred years old. What was at stake was the legitimacy that affected three states: Aragon, Catalonia, and Navarre, kingdoms that could actually be destroyed with the same relative equilibrium that had presided over their establishment when their nobility, who refused to become subjects of some foreign master, agreed to a pact with their rulers to reestablish a dynasty that was in fact extinguished.

Within two years of gathering followers and finding believers and supporters among the Aragon nobility, the aged blacksmith was forced by royal harassment to flee to Louis VII's France. But even from there

Fig. 5.3. The abbey of Montearagón, where Alfonso I, the Battler, is said to have been buried in secret

he must have let his voice be heard, because in 1178 Bishop Berenger of Lérida, the brother of Alfonso II, came before the French king with a letter urging him to put the impostor behind bars and do "justice of his body." It is not really known how the following events transpired, but it seems that in 1181, the false king was captured in Barcelona and was hanged almost immediately in front of the city's walls. Certain unconfirmed accounts complement the story, saying that after royal justice dealt with the blacksmith who wanted to be king, his body was secretly taken to the abbey at Montearagón and given a Christian burial in the same tomb that held the mortal remains of Alfonso the Battler.[7]

The Genesis of and Reasons for a Myth

Stories such as this sporadically appear throughout the historical evolution of human consciousness, from the tale concerning Paçu-Rama—who came from the Agartha to bring peace and harmony to humankind and was later secretly taken to Mount Mahendra, from whence he would return when his presence was once again required—to Emperor Frederick Barbarossa, who disappeared while wading through a river on his way to the Holy Land. Tales were told of Alexander the Great and of King Arthur, and in the modern age of peninsular history, there is the story of the Pastry Maker of Madrigal, the false king, don Sebastián, who returned supposedly to recapture from Felipe II his rights to the Portuguese crown. If we look closely, we find in this a story analogous to the Second Coming of Christ, which opens the door to the end of time. On its own, the theme of the Awaited King constitutes a universal myth that various traditions have used to their advantage to structure a synarchic ideology. Fundamentalist groups of many stripes have also latched on to it as a means of giving themselves legitimacy. For example, on more than one occasion, current neo-Nazis have managed to launch the rumor that Adolf Hitler survived the bunker attack in Berlin and is hiding somewhere in South America, waiting for a new opportunity to conquer the world.

The years that brought the last quarter of the twelfth century to a close are the same ones that kindled the development of the Grail legend. This is the time when Robert of Boron and Chrétien de Troyes deployed their art and ideology in the configuration of a transcendental myth that ultimately spread throughout Europe in an epidemic of traditionalism that had its maximum expression in *Parsifal,* from the Templar Wolfram von Eschenbach. In many ways, the Templars are seen as custodians of the Grail miracle, thanks to the development of its subtle propaganda in relation to the Order. And it is no coincidence that in real life Alfonso I was not only the guardian king of the Grail of St. John of the Rock, but also the sovereign who dared write his will in favor of the Templars so that the Order would assume responsibility for his legacy.

The Templar order had followed the rules of the game of history: It had renounced its inheritance but had buttressed itself as the strongest force and an undisputed authority in the the Catalan-Aragonese territory. This was perhaps accomplished with the firm intention of starting their synarchic enterprise there, for the kingdom's structure made it very eligible as a candidate for a new Axis Mundi, the New Jerusalem intended to guide the destinies of humanity.

There was, then, justification for the Templars to "plant" a myth of the return of a monarch who would return things to their rightful place—for they had been displaced by a sovereign who displayed personal qualities that were not exactly those the Templars saw as appropriate for the leader whom they would place at the helm of their plan, the king who was to rule the world. The false Alfonso the Battler was in no way an anecdotal fraud. Rather, he represented a call to attention that all could understand so that the destiny outlined in the Templar blueprint could be fulfilled either in the person of Alfonso II, whom the Templars surely would have rejected as a candidate to head their venture, or through the maintenance of the structures that would make such a plan viable in the future, based in part on the constant ascent of the Order's influence over the political and social structures of those territories under their watch.

The inventor of this histrionic adventure is likely to have been Grand Master Arnau de Torroja, who at that moment was the highest authority among the Templars of the Catalan-Aragonese territory. He held this post until 1180, when he marched to the Holy Land to assume the great mastery of the Order because Eudes de Saint-Armand had been made a prisoner. His promotion to the highest rank among the Templars could not have been merely a product of circumstance, but was surely a consequence of having collaborated on the most important tasks within the Order. A member of an important family from Lérida with ties to the Temple, Arnaldus de Turre Rubea, as his name appears in several documents, remained very close to the king throughout his extensive provincial mandate.[8] In fact, his name is mentioned with those involved in the better-known events of the reign between 1166 and 1180,[9] among them the wedding of Alfonso II and the daughter of Alfonso VII of Castile in 1174 and, in 1179, the signing of the Treaty of Cazola, in which were marked the borders of both Catalan and Aragon and the limits of their future expansion through Muslim territories that had yet to be conquered.

It is not difficult to assume that the Templars' synarchic plan was too significant a historical operation to be ignored or forgotten in official documentation. Of course, any leaks could have doomed it. Yet it does not make sense that under the guise of objectivity, research has been limited to merely exposing the most obvious reality of the time. This imperfect objectivity is generally content simply to expose events without troubling to penetrate into their possible causes. As I recall, only Professor Antonio Ubieto has attempted to go beyond disconnected facts and pure documents. When studying some events no one else wanted to research,[10] this was how he established that the Aragonese representatives who had accepted the impossible reality of the reappearance of the Battler were, in many cases, the same—or at least their names were the same—as those involved in the legend of the Bell of Huesca, attributed to Ramiro II. There they appear as instruments of the falsified operation that the monk-king allegedly organized to punish rebellious noblemen and impose his authority and legitimacy in the kingdom.

Many events during these years appear as a product of history—as spurious occurrences that the conscientious, objective historian would have to reject so that truth can shine, free from any additions that might contribute to a false interpretation of the historical moment. No one, however, seems to have the energy to propose that these false events often surpass the supposed inventiveness of those who first consigned them to the pages of chronicles. Thus, the records of these happenings become documents that should be not only transcribed, but translated and interpreted so that their reality may emerge from the cryptic and symbolic language used to record them. They are not lies or even anecdotes; rather, more often than not they are messages that notify us of evidence that, for some reason, could not be openly shared. Precisely the same phenomenon occurs in the Romanesque art of the era, which transmits ideas and principles deliberately camouflaged by pious images that cry out to be interpreted authentically in order to be understood.

History is the constant object of synchronicity, which, for some reason, we persist in ignoring, for we usually study history in fragments, without reflecting that different types of events could be the consequence—or indeed, the cause—of a certain situation or some other incident that appears to have nothing to do with them. Thus, there is no way to separate the whim of Alfonso II—that is, his wish to offer his protection to the Order of Alfambra to the detriment of the Templars (whom he would eventually join around 1190)—from the ghostly and impossible appearance of a false Battler, who, oddly enough, was accepted by an incredible majority of the kingdom's citizens. But we cannot reduce this fact to a single cause or effect. Every time the Catalan-Aragonese state was involved in some problematic consolidation or expansion involving the Templars' synarchic ideology, they could use the Order's unifying assistance.

This is where things stood when the problem of the Cathars became a significant influence on the politics of the region. The Cathar question was to be a major one in these realms for the next century. Aragon, Catalonia, and Navarre were almost drawn into war with France because of the Cathars and the issue of Occitan independence. Until this time, the Cathars had not awakened jealousies or excessive reservations in a Roman Church that felt an unavoidable obligation to control all that occurred in the Christian Europe over which it exerted it authority.

The Unstoppable Ascent of a Heresy

Let us pause and examine the synchronicity of some events that might seem to have occurred independent of each other. In the year 1167, Arnau de Torroja became grand master of the Templar order in the Catalan-Aragonese province. That very year, after much silence and extreme discretion, a council was convened at St. Felix of Caraman in which the Occidental Cathars received Nikita, a Bogomil from Albania. With his Eastern speech—undoubtedly familiar to the Templars from their relationship to the various sects in Palestine and Lebanon—he managed to unify into one coherent doctrine the vague religious ideals that had been put forward by the Cathar Perfects and which, for the first time, gave structure to the two basic principles of Manichean gnosis. The Church said nothing about that gathering (perhaps it was unaware of it), but from that moment on, Catharism gained strength as a parallel religious force that could cause in orthodox Christianity an absolute, categorical schism.

This doctrinal phenomenon of Catharism initially occurred in territories that had always been dependencies of the Catalan-Aragonese crown. It also took hold in lands where the greatest concentration of Templar properties existed and thus fell under Templar influence.

After some years of Cathar expansion and doctrinal affirmation—including a structured church and hierarchy and a great number of followers and sympathizers in Occitania—the first encounter between Cathar theologians and Catholic bishops (all called themselves Christians) was celebrated in Lombiers in 1176. Along with the theological arguments contributed by each side, there appeared here for the first time Nikita's austerity as opposed to the ostentation and luxury exhibited by the Catholics. What is more, while the Catholics expressed themselves in a Latin that very few understood, the Cathars spoke the language of all: the *langue d'oc.*

Registered in the Vatican archives is a letter from Prester John,* written jointly to the pope, Emperor Frederick Barbarossa, and three

*[Prester John was the supposed Christian king of an African territory near Ethiopia. —*Trans.*]

other European Christian kings, which the *Catholic Encyclopedia* does not mention (although it alludes to them in an answer to Alexander III, sent by the intermediary of his personal physician, Master Fillipo, who, it seems, did not return from his trip[11]). Of course, we keep overlooking the names of the kings to whom the letter is directed. We can guess fairly certainly at some possible identities. Their remembrance is colored by mythical events associated with them. One of these rulers was Emperor Frederick I (Barbarossa), who some years later would become another "mythic king" after disappearing beneath the waves on his way to the Holy Land. Another was surely Alfonso II, the proprietor of the Grail, in whose kingdom, precisely around the latter half of the twelfth century, the strange adventure of Anfortas-Alfonso I took place. In a poetical composition, an Occitan troubadour, Bertrand de Born, would call him the one who *feu penjar al seu antecessor* (had his ancestor hanged). He was also the king of all the territories in which the Cathar heresy was gathering momentum, the one who took from the Albanian viscount of Béziers and Carcasona, Roger II Trencavel, and of Nîmes, Bernard Ató, not only their vassals, but also custody and guardianship of their properties, in case they were attacked by the defender of the Church in that area, Raymond V of Toulouse, who denounced the most distinguished individuals of his land to the Cistercians by declaring they allowed themselves to be corrupted.[12] And in the midst of this silent and discreet accumulation of beliefs, interests, devotions, hopes, and threats, the Templars and their master, Torroja, tried to deal with all the players as if moving pieces in a game of chess in which were at stake—however early in the competition—the destiny of the Church and the political future of the Europe whose likeness the Order was trying to alter to match its synarchic plan.

At the time when Alfonso II received the vassalage from the Cathar viscounts, the Church called the Third Council of Lateran (1179), which, for the first time, pronounced open, even violent, opposition to the Cathar danger. In its twenty-seventh canon it announced:

> For this reason, because in Gascoyne and the regions of Albi and Toulouse and in other places, the loathsome heresy of those that

> are called the Cathars or the Patarenes or the Publicani or by different names has grown so strong that they no longer practice their wickedness in secret . . . but proclaim their error publicly and draw the simple and weak to join them, we declare that they and their defenders and those who receive them are under anathema and we forbid, under pain of anathema, that anyone should keep or support them in their houses or lands or should trade with them. . . . We enjoin all the faithful, for the remission of sins, that they oppose this scourge with all their might and by arms protect the Christian people against them. Their [Cathar] goods are to be confiscated and princes free to subject them in to slavery. . . . Those who in true sorrow for their sins die in such a conflict should not doubt that they will receive forgiveness for their sins and the fruit of an eternal reward. We . . . grant to the faithful Christians who take up arms against them, and who on the advice of bishops or other prelates seek to drive them out, a remission for two years of penance imposed on them.*

Perhaps it was not yet formally a crusade, but it was nearly so. In the midst of all these circumstances, certain events took place in the Catalan-Aragonese kingdom as well as in a small strip of territory north of the Pyrenees that fundamentally depended on the kingdom. What occurred were events that tend to be silenced in the scope of European history, as if they were an unimportant adventure in which sovereigns of states hardly participated and people still counted for very little in the development of the European idea. Yet all the elements that would form the structures of a new Europe some years later were involved in open, existential foment: the Grail; the great Cathar crusade; the great confrontation between the papacy, under Innocent III, and the Empire, under Frederick II; the Europe of knightly culture, in which the myth of the Grail and the search for a transcendental, heretical, essential identity was ubiquitous—complete

---

*We must remember that only one representative of the Catalan-Aragonese kingdom attended that council alongside the three hundred European delegates, bishops, abbots, and theologians: Berenger, bishop of Lérida.

with those who proclaimed Christianity to the death, like the dreamer in a spiritual adventure who searched for the traditional knowledge granted by the symbol of the Holy Cup, which was later deposited at the feet of Prester John by Parsifal's son, Titurel.

A Compendium to Concurring Aims

In the wake of Roger II Trencavel revealing his intimate friendship with confessed Cathars* and the pope's stalking of him for his lack of collaboration in the annihilation of these heretics, as urged by the councils on heresy—an annihilation the Templars also opposed—Alfonso II decided, in the last year of his life, to make the pilgrimage to Compostela. As Ventura admirably sums up, with this journey, Alfonso II completed a plan that, on the one hand, would reconcile him with Rome, burnishing his image as a reverent pilgrim, and, on the other, would give him the opportunity to speak to the other peninsular Christian kings with the purpose of getting all of them to commit to engaging in a crusade against not the Cathars but instead the Almohads.[13] With this crusade he might be able to deflect the attention of the Church, which was urging him to take steps that he was in no way willing to take—that is, through the Council of Lateran, demanding that Christian monarchs crush the heresy of Provence's Catharism.

This last year in the life of Alfonso II (who died on April 25, 1196, at the age of thirty-nine) serves as a compendium of all the intentions that would definitively configure the kingdom and monarchs as the nucleus of the future synarchic state conceived by the Templars—a state ruled by a dynasty capable of a complex kingdom, one territory in which beliefs could coexist peacefully and harmoniously and consciences and creeds might be unified. The meeting that took place in Lérida a month before the death of the king[14] was significant. To gauge just how important it was, we need to consider who attended it: Gilbert Erail,† grand master

*He died two years before Alfonso II, on March 20, 1194.

†Gilbert Erail, or Erall, was master of Provence, Aragon, and Catalonia between 1184 and 1190. He probably came from Catalonia or Provence.

of the Templar order overseas; Ponç Rigaud, grand master of France; Arnau de Claremont, grand master of Provence, Aragon, and Catalonia; Pere de Calonge, commander of Tortosa; Bernardo Serón, commander of Gardeny; Ramón Gorob and Ponç Menescal, commander and prior, respectively, of the castle of Monzón; Ramón Ferradella, commander of Corbins; and Friar Folch, commander of Ascó. These were the cream of the crop in the kingdom. Officially, what was addressed at Lérida was the definitive union of the Order of Montgaudí (or Alfambra) and the Templars and the recovery of the sites the Order of Montgaudí had taken, which would complement the Templars' custody of the maestrazgo still under Muslim authority. Interestingly, acquiring this area was a goal of the Templars throughout their Hispanic tenure[15] and eventually became the preferred refuge of the fugitive Cathars when, years later, the Inquisition made it impossible for them to live in Occitania. To these donations by the king were added a considerable increase in rents conceded to the Templars.

According to Zurita y Castro, "[T]his was around the month of April. From there the king departed for Barcelona and passed Perpignan, where he was aggravated by a long affliction from which he died the twenty-fifth of April of the same year."

In fulfillment of his will and testament, Alfonso II (it is not well known why he was called the Chaste) was immediately succeeded by his oldest son, Pedro the Catholic (we do not know why he was called the Catholic). Pedro's seventeen-year reign (1196–1213) was not long enough for the completion of any long-term plan. Nevertheless, his years of rule were spent carefully preparing the most important attempt at creating the synarchic state conceived by the Templars.

Pedro II (as he was known to the Catalans) always seemed to be more a robot fulfilling designs than a monarch wholly conscious of his own function and his own destiny. Every one of his steps—at least, those decisive ones that can could have changed the course of life or history—seemed contradictory and even involuntary. He married against his desire, and both his union and that of his sister were designed to unite the states of heretical Occitania and Navarre and Roussillon until

Fig. 5.4. Pedro II, the Catholic, from the Liber Feudorum Ceritaniae *(thirteenth century)*

they formed that inconclusive "empire of the d'oc tongue," as Higounet defined it.[16] Pedro felt an irresistible attraction to the heterodox ideas of the lands just north of the Pyrenees, which he held in his custody and of which he steadfastly insisted on being crowned ruler by Pope Innocent III in Rome (which occurred in 1204). Pedro bragged about his role as a Crusader; he participated in the Navas de Tolosa (in 1212) and was in fact killed by the Crusaders launched by the pope against the Cathar heretics of the Languedoc in the most cruel and brutal campaign of the many promoted by the Church.

For some historians, these evident contradictions in King Pedro were due to the fact that his character had not matured; he did not have the opportunity to become a full, stable adult, which translated into his predilection to reach toward whatever he craved at the moment and made him an inconsistent and indecisive figure. Yet we might want to look at him from another angle, which can allow us both to comprehend and to justify his actions. If the monarch did nothing but fulfill the policy set by Templar ideology, and if the Templars continued forward with their plan to build a synarchic state starting with the Occitan nucleus joined to the crown of Aragon, he had to avoid at all costs France's action in the problem triggered by the Cathars. The way to contain the impulse of the Capetian monarchs to intervene in the internal affairs of Occitania was to show at the kingdom's helm a tough Catholic sovereign who was capable, when necessary, of containing the presumed danger posed by the expansion or intensification of the heresy.[17]

The first years of the reign of Pedro II were distinguished by a relative calm in Occitania, a territory that was crisscrossed by monks striving to convert the Cathars but which had no political difficulties or war that required military intervention. Once the differences were settled with his mother, Queen Sancha (a settlement tht occurred with the help of the Templars as well as the provincial Templar master Pedro de Montagut, who played the role of the "good guy" in the dispute over Ariza), Pedro arranged increased activity in the peninsular campaigns against the Moors. The kingdoms of Valencia and the south of Turuel, poor and mountainous lands, were the object of conquests in the vicinity of

Ademuz, which, although carried out principally by Templar knights, were attributed to royal initiative that was merely aided by the Order. Of course, the Templars were always the principal beneficiaries of the campaigns. Echoing the words of Zurita, Campomanes gives an account of the conquests of Ademuz, Castelfabib, and Sertella on the one hand and of Cantavieja on the other, and confirms that they not only precipitated a number of donations to the already considerable holdings of the Order, but also prompted the admiration of many Aragonese knights, who asked to be admitted to the Order after witnessing the enthusiasm of the soldier-monks in battle. One example is don Atorellas Ortiz, lord of Quinto, who took the Templar vows right on the battlefield. In 1210, immediately after these military conquests and as a complementary compensation for them (undoubtedly by arrangement), the Templars received the whole city of Tortosa, which this time was taken from those who had served King Alfonso: don Guillén and don Ramón de Cervera.

But the Cathar situation was slowly and inexorably worsening. In 1203, while the Templars were taking hold of the maestrazgo of the fortress of Albentosa, Innocent III sent his legate Pierre de Castelnau to the Languedoc with instructions to convert heretics at any cost. He was accompanied by the abbot of Cîteaux, Pierre Amaury. "These two resplendent candelabra of the Lord inflicted a servile fear in those servile weapons, threatening them with the loss of their goods and causing the thunderous indignation of kings and princes. They invited these rulers to throw aside the heresy and the heretics and obliged them to leave sin not for love of virtue, but, as the poet says, for fear of the punishment."[18]

Since his terrible decree was promulgated in 1198 against the heretics "of any sects they might be," to which no one paid attention, Pedro II had barely shown up in the Midi. On one occasion he came to Carcassonne to preside over a gathering of both the papal legates and the Cathar ministers, which ended with a dialogue of the deaf, to which all involved were accustomed. At the end of 1203, with the Languedoc stirred up by the comings and goings of Pierre de Castelnau, the solemn ceremony of coronation and the enfiefing of the kingdom to the Holy See took place in Rome, which, curiously, did not displease the

Catalans but served momentarily to contain the French threat, although King Pedro formally committed himself to fighting the heretical perversity of Catharism. Later, the royal compromise of the anointed—that is, Catholics—resulted in the bloodless takeover of the castle of the Cathar knights in Lescura, which was also enfiefed to the Holy See.

In 1206, barely two years later, the papal legate in the Languedoc fought the heresy by force of anathema. His assistants were two Spanish clerics, the bishop of Osma and his assistant Domingo de Guzmán, plus twelve Cistercian abbots from diverse French monasteries, with their corresponding monks.

We might easily count conversions on the fingers of one hand. And in that great sea of restlessness and more or less veiled threats, only the Templars kept silent, barely seen or heard. As landholders in Occitania, their activities were discreet exercises in doing what no one else could.

A Propitiatory Victim

The events preceding the death of Pedro II in the Battle of Muret give a clear example of the unstable and capricious character that many historians have attributed to a king who very probably had his flaws but was moved to dance to the beat of a different drummer.

When the papal legate Castlenau was assassinated in Occitania in 1208 and Pope Innocent III immediately convened the Cathar crusade, Pedro and his Templars were "crusading" far away in the lands of Cuenca, Valencia, and Turuel. Because they were involved in those skirmishes, they could not act in defense of the Occitans, who were being indiscriminately annihilated by the crusading armies of the north, whose members were anxious for the loot that could be obtained in holy wars. Defending the Cathars, however, would have earned the Templars and the king immediate condemnation from the Holy See; thus these small battles for a Moorish castle allowed them to fulfill their duties as Crusaders in the strict meaning the word retained since its origins and the only one officially recognized by the Templar order. Before the events in Occitania and in direct opposition to the pontiff's call to arms in that region, Grand Master Guillaume de Chartres proclaimed that there was but one Crusade: the one against the Saracens. The Templars would not fight against Christians, however heretical they might be. They would also not fight against the disparate Christians in the Middle East. Of course, being a monastic order, they could not declare themselves party to heresy—although it is suspected that they themselves may have practiced it—on pain of condemnation and risk of their one-hundred-year existence and their reputation as staunch defenders of the Cross.

The problem, at that moment, was to take care of appearances and wait for circumstances to make it viable to move forward with the great plan they had conceived. If they had to sacrifice a king who had been inserted in their plans, they would do so and look for another they could substitute when possible and necessary.

Between 1208 and 1213, the Order of the Temple vainly attempted to ensure that Pedro II would survive unscathed the serious dilemma in which he found himself. Did the Order prompt the king to accept the vassalage of Simon of Montfort as a way of gaining recognition for the self-titled viscount of Béziers after the horrible massacre he instigated in Béziers? We may never know for certain. We also do not know who came up with the idea of arranging the marriage of Pedro's son and heir—the future James I—to the daughter of this Crusader, which essentially made the child, still in her swaddling clothes, a hostage who would guarantee Catalan-Aragonese neutrality during the bloody conflict that decimated the Languedoc. We do know that Innocent III urged everyone to finish off the Cathars, who, as a result of their terrible extermination, were beginning to awaken the sympathy of a good part of Europe. We also know that in the face of the pope's urgency to eliminate the Cathars, Alfonso VIII's call for a Crusade against the Almohads provided an authentic breather from the tension in the Languedoc, one the Templars as well as Pedro II acted on at once with an enthusiasm worthy of a better cause. This Christian jihad culminated in the victory of the Navas de Tolosa, thought by many to be as significant as the seizure of Jerusalem by Godfrey of Bouillon.

Out of pure ancestral patriotism, every peninsular kingdom except

León attributed to himself the victory of Las Navas. In that heroic conquest the Catalan-Aragonese saw the prestige of their sovereign reach the summits of glory; he needed no further evidence to prove to the world his devotion to the Church, a devotion the pope recognized when he crowned him. If he now intervened in defense of the territory north of the Pyrenees, his gesture could not be considered a show of sympathy for the heretics, but rather a perfectly justified intervention in favor of relatives and allies from whom Simon of Monfort had stolen patrimony while sheltering himself behind the so-called Statutes of Pamies, which merely provided a cover for his thirst for power.

The Statutes of Pamies were a compendium of legal codes prepared by the chief of the crusaders, Simon of Montfort, to justify his tacit ownership of the Languedoc. To publish the codes, Simon convoked an assembly that, at the same time, elected twelve men who theoretically would represent all sectors of society: four clerics (two bishops, a Templar, and a Hospitaller), four French crusader barons, and four representatives of the autochthonous society (two knights and two members of the bourgeoisie). Naturally, the chosen individuals were those who, without the least discussion, would approve the already drafted text. The statutes did not mention the Cathars (because, plainly and simply, they were people to be eliminated); nor did they mention the king of Aragon. Only the lord of Montfort was cited—he who proclaimed himself viscount of Béziers by the grace of God, "desirous of maintaining this land in peace and calm and keeping it for the glory of God and the Holy Roman Church and the king of France."[19]

Through its representative, the Templars signed this document giving Simon absolute control over the lives of the Occitans. They could not do otherwise; to oppose the statutes was tantamount to officially declaring the Order a supporter of the heresy, risking the survival of the almost eighty encomiendas the Templars possessed throughout the entire Languedoc and facing the Crusaders the Holy See had launched against the Cathar rebels in that land. From within, the Templar work could continue, though in secret and with maximum discretion. Being forced to become public with their work would have meant the extinction of the Order and, above all, the abandonment of their synarchic plan. This would require sacrificing the monarch by pushing him to extreme solutions to defeat *ab foc et sanc* (by blood and fire) anyone who intended to rob him of his rights: bishops, crusaders, or pope. Leave it to the troubadours to glorify King Pedro I.

The situation during the first half of the year 1213 was one of increasing tension between Rome and the Aragonese king, which could be resolved only by giving in to the crusade of Innocent III or answering the hopes of the populace, Cathar or Catholic, who only wanted to be free of pressures and killings committed in the name of the Faith, which felled citizens indiscriminately. There were no mediators; everyone had chosen his option or, as in the case of the Templars, they kept quiet. Finally, the great option of King Pedro was to face the will of the pope and risk his proclaimed catholicity, which kept on his side the populace, the Cathars (with whom he was allied), and his other sympathizers, and, *in pectore* if not actively, the Templars and all those who controlled their vast territories. Before throwing himself into war, he made donations to the Templars in Toulouse and signed acts in their favor, in an attempt to show that the Order was the only ecclesiastical establishment he still trusted. On September 13, he threw himself into the attack before the moats of Muret and met death at the hands of the Crusaders. Despite his defeat, his death allowed the Templar order to breathe more easily.

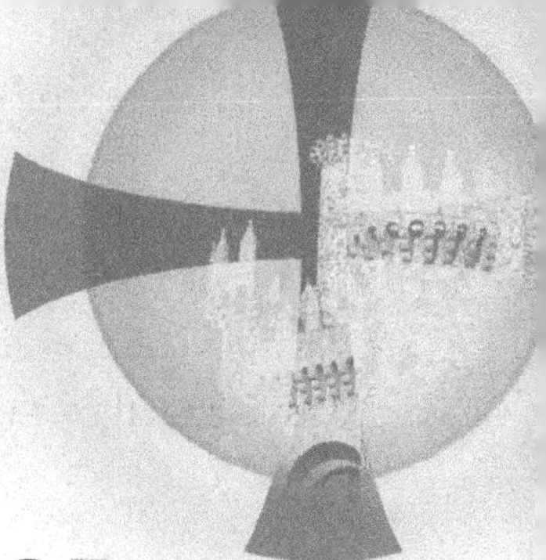

6

The Search for the King of the World

Riding both historical reality and myth, between popular saying and the daily supernatural, at the time he recorded the story of his life,[1] James I, known as the Conqueror, revealed himself as a being touched by Providence, someone for whom circumstances coincided in a way that is very different from the way things work out for common mortals. There is a whole group of previously established premises for recognizing an exceptional individual. A person deemed as such should also be designated the visible head of a superior enterprise that only a *chosen one* like him could realize. Miracles, as events that caress the limits of the supernatural, are a prerequisite for those supposedly destined to do great things. The same characteristics could also have been amassed by this individual's progenitors; the average medieval man would find it difficult to harbor doubts when facing a superior being capable of leading him not only to heights of glory, but also to the threshold of the kind of well-being that is always seen as a wellspring of possibility.

In James I we can immediately see the Templars' influence without a word being said; its presence is understood more by what it evades than by what it manifests. If the king's actions, thoughts, writings, and decisions throughout his prolonged life conform to Templar ideology, what does it matter if the Templars are rarely mentioned in the chronicle written for his kingdom? The very fact that he titled it *Libre dels Feyts* (Book of Deeds) seems to indicate that he was deliberately narrating what had happened, and that all the whys and hows were to be deduced and supplied by the reader or listener.

The Wonders of a Birth

At his conception, James I already possessed the first requirement for a monarch destined to be the protagonist of the synarchic ideal of the Templars. Through his father he received the blood of a monarchy considered to be descended from the Grail: the blood of Alfonso I, the Battler. From his mother, María of Montpellier, he received the blood of the emperors of the Eastern Empire. María was a granddaughter of the Byzantine emperor Manuel Commeno, who had sent his daughter Eudoxia to contract nuptials with Alfonso II of Aragon. When the princess arrived at Montpellier, however, she found that her husband-to-be had already married the daughter of Alfonso VII of Castile. Faced with the prospect of returning to her land unwed, she then accepted the proposal of Count Guillermo IV of Montpellier. From that union came María, who married Pedro II in 1204, in a ceremony that took place in the house of the Templars in Montpellier.

When James I ordered his chronicle to be written, he was careful to conceal the circumstances of his birth—though they had already been published sufficiently for other Catalan chroniclers such as Desclot and Ramón Muntaner[2] to record all the details. Muntaner tells us—and it was widely documented—the marriage of Pedro II and María was a disaster from the beginning. After three years and a newborn daughter, the countess asked her protector, Pope Innocent III, to annul the marriage without the king doing anything to prevent it, for he had designs on another marriage, this time to María de Monferrato, heir to the kingdom of Jerusalem. In this union he could maintain his firm but unspecified intention to give the kings of the Latin states in the East the support of the crown of Aragon. Letting things run their course didn't seem to please Pedro II's subjects. They wanted an heir.

Then, as the chronicles tell and as Occitania's poets sang, the noblest hierarchies of Montpellier participated in a conspiracy that depended on the secret acquiescence of the city's citizens. After a week of devotions to the image of Our Lady of Vallvert, including fasting, singing countless Masses, and intoning the Seven Holy Mysteries, the officials and notables of Montpellier fooled the sovereign, who was spending a long holiday there (by and large ignoring his wife). They led Pedro II to believe they were facilitating his access to a fickle damsel with whom he was then infatuated. In truth, in darkened quarters they introduced him instead to his wife. And while the king of Aragon unwittingly pleased himself with his wife, twenty good men of Montpellier, accompanied by twelve ladies and twelve damsels, notaries, abbots, and a representative of the bishop, were gathering in the antechamber. "And equally, that night all the churches in Montpellier were open, and all the populace was in them praying to God."[3] At dawn, the conspirators entered the chamber with lights and candles and showed the king the identity of the woman with whom he had spent the night, so that he could have no grounds for doubts in the future. The king was furious; he mounted his horse and left the city, but the miracle was accomplished, and in nine months, on February 18, 1208, the eve of the Purification of Our Lady, James I was born in Montpellier and was subsequently entirely ignored by his father. Coincidentally, February 18 was also the beginning of the feast of the Candelaria, a celebration cherished by the Templars.

Light often plays an important part in myth, consecrating it. In the *Libre dels Feyts,* James I records that while still a baby, he was taken to the cathedral, where, precisely as he was making his entrance and the *chantres* were singing matins, they sang the verse *Te Deum laudamus*. Later, he was taken to the temple of San Fermín and, by miraculous coincidence, entered as the *Benedictus Dominus Deus Israel* was sung. But the seeming prophecies did not end there. "Upon returning home, my mother was elated by such good forecasts. She immediately had twelve candles made of equal size and weight and," after assigning to each candle the name of one of the apostles, "promised God, Our Lord, that I would be christened with the name of the candle that would last the longest . . . St. James's lasted approximately the height of three fingers longer than the rest. Because of that and by the grace of God we call ourselves James."

It is certain that King Pedro ignored both the name of his son and his very existence. When he decided to meet him two years after the infant's birth, it was only to take him away from Montpellier and hand him over to the Cathar scourge of Occitania, Simon de Montfort. Simon was given charge of the future monarch by a pact (confirmed two years later) in which the crusader's lordship over Béziers and Carcassonne was recognized and there was arranged a marriage between Pedro's infant heir and Simon's daughter. Also, the pact specified that until the future king turned eighteen, Montfort would govern as lord of Montpellier, and at that date the projected wedding would be celebrated. Pedro II, in this way, would rid himself of a son whom he did not love and, at the same time, would achieve a political action he deemed to be an intelligent move. His hopes were futile, however, as he was unable to avoid the violence of a war, which, despite all his efforts to prevent it, took his life.

Those writing a historical narrative have an obligation to take into account the slights directed by one person toward another. Yet James I does not acknowledge the slights he suffered from his father and instead politely praises Pedro: "[H]e was the most generous, courteous, and affable monarch that ever was in Spain . . ." However brief his words were regarding his father, he did not run short of words in describing his mother, Queen María, who left for Rome as the authorities took away her child, with the intention of obtaining a separation from her husband via the intercession of Pope Innocent III. The queen eventually died in Rome and her fame as a saint spread throughout Christendom, as James I relates:

> Our Lord loved her so and gave her such grace that she is called the Holy Queen, not only in Rome, where she died, but all over the world. Many sick are to this day cured by drinking in water or wine the dust scraped from her tombstone in the church of Saint Peter in

Rome, near that of Saint Petronilla,the daughter of Saint Peter. And look ye, who peruse this writing: Is it not a miraculous thing?

The Rescue of a Monarch: The Magical Stage

Queen María of Montpellier lay dying in Rome a few short months after the death of her husband in Muret. She specifically requested in her testament: "*Volu ut Templum recipiat filius meum et custodiat donec et illum reddat*" [I will that the Templars receive my son and take custody of him until he has reached the age of majority]. But the boy-king was still in the custody of Simon de Montfort in Carcassonne. The crusader was not so eager to fulfill the queen's will. It was at this point that the joint courts of Catalonia and Aragon gathered at Lérida agreed to seek the mediation of the pope in reclaiming the boy. They already considered him to be their king despite the fact that since the death of Pedro II in Muret, the regency was being disputed by Count Sancho, son of Ramón Berenger IV and granduncle of the king, and don Fernando, abbot of Montearagón and brother of Pedro II. Interestingly, there are well-founded suspicions of Count Sancho's Cathar sympathies.

Confronted by pressure from Pope Innocent III, who turned to the court of the bishop Ispán of Santa María de Albarracín as his legate, Simon de Montfort was forced to concede. A papal bull, more persuasive than any demand, was given to him at Carcassonne by Pedro de Benevento, a direct messenger from the pope, and compelled the crusader to return the monarch, now a little more than six years old. According to the memoir of James I:

> The French took us [Simon and James] as far as Narbonne, whither many of the noblemen and citizens of Catalonia went and received us. When they got to Catalonia, a consultation was held as to who should bring us up. All agreed that the master of the Temple should bring us up at Monzon. The name of that master was En Guillem de Montredón. He was a native of Osona and master of the Temple in Catalonia and Aragon.

We know very little about Guillem de Montredón before he joined the Templar militia. He was born around 1170, the second child of a powerful Vic (Osona) family, and he probably entered the Order while still very young.[4] When he accompanied Pedro II to the Navas, he was already provincial master. Seven months after Pedro II's death in Muret, he was in Toulouse, where he witnessed the city's inhabitants swearing to abide by the law condemning the Cathar heresy. The wishes expessed in Queen María's will, in which she entrusted the education of her child to the Templars, were already known when Guillem formed part of the commission called on to pick up the boy James I in Narbonne. That appointment was followed by another, given by the pope in the same bull delivered to Simon in Carcassonne and approved by the courts of Lérida: The Templar order, known for its financial abilities, was also to be responsible for repairing the economy of the kingdom through the administration of the very scarce rents to which the kingdom could lay claim, "which did not yield enough . . . to maintain ourselves for one day, our legacy being so wasted and mortgaged," as the king wrote in his chronicle.

The place chosen by the Templars to house the young monarch was the castle of Monzón. The reasons for this choice were obvious: The castle was in good living condition and was in a safe location, very close to the border between Catalonia and Aragon and quite far from any threat of Muslim attack. In addition, the Templars who formed part of its barracks were native to both states of the Crown, which could alleviate any nationalistic reservations that might emerge between the Catalans and the Aragonese during the young monarch's education.

But if we examine another circumstance, one not usually considered in the narration of historical events, we can confirm that Monzón meant something more, something decisive and significant for the future of the boy-monarch.

Up until the death of Alfonso I in 1134, the lord of Monzón had been Prince García Ramírez, whom the Navarrese claimed as the Restorer when the Battler's will was not honored. García Ramírez, grandson of

El Cid Campeador*—his father, the crusader prince Ramiro, was married to one of El Cid's daughters—is said to have inherited La Tizona, the sword that belonged to the Campeador. Deep-rooted traditions in Monzón indicate he left it there when the Navarrese offered him the throne and that there it remained, a significant relic of the world of chivalry when the castle was handed over to the Templars in 1143 by Ramón Berenger IV, almost grandson of Rodrigo Díaz del Vivar. As would any other tradition, La Tizona came to play an important role in the parallel history that tradition structured around the stay of James I at Monzón: the legend of the miraculous discovery of La Virgen de la Alegría (Virgin of Joy). As we know, devotion to this icon was shaped by the Catalan-Aragonese monarch's fondness for the cult to Our Lady, which characterized his religious life.

According to the legend, as he walked one day near the surroundings of the chapel of La Virgen de la Alegría, accompanied by his Templar mentors, the young James I encountered a hermit who predicted he would attain heights of glory if he took the Tizona sword, which Master Montredón carried on his belt, and tempered it the backwaters of the river that ran at the foot of the sanctuary.[5] There is no doubt that on the sidelines of a game played against historical reality, legend holds a significant symbol: a triumphant and victorious monarch predestined to the loftiest ends, whose rightful station and glory are announced by the wise hermit. Significantly, we can continue to detect the apparently supernatural element in the story of James I. This king belonged to an existential context in which the past—with its constant and necessary attribute of magic—was rejected and from which the supernatural had almost completely disappeared. In this case, although the veracity of the legend could be called into question, it is certain that many years later, when the king was fencing in Borriana on the way to Valencia, he wrote to the Templars soliciting the sword "that was named Tizona and that was very good and lucky to he who carried it." The sword still exists,

---

*The name Cid comes from the Arabic word *sayyid*, meaning "lord" or "master," while Campeador means "battler" or "victor."

having passed from the Real Armería (Royal Armory) to the Museo del Ejercito (Army Museum).

I have always had the conviction—which the study of history confirms—that one of the reasons, perhaps the main one, allowing academic historians to avoid esoteric thought and magical attitudes is the essential incommunicability of these principles. Esoteric behavior based on internal experiences produces a manifestation that is not explicit, because it employs clues instead of direct expression and because it is directed at the co-participants of an initiative ideology that serves only those who follow it. It has no value to those for whom its particular language is foreign. Ancestral traditions teach that these kinds of experiences and lore cannot be transmitted in writing, as if they were some school text to be learned and repeated by rote. Instead, they can be conveyed only from the mouth of the teacher to the ear of the catechumen. This is how it was with the Druids, in the mystery cults, among the Islamic Sufis and the Hebrew Kabbalists, and in the mute alchemy books. In the rare instances when such experience has been expressed in writing, those who have access and used the medium have done so through a hermetic language that is incomprehensible to the uninitiated. Part of this language includes parables or seemingly insignificant stories, embedded with clues that cannot be understood by the uninitiated.

The Rescue of a Monarch: The Facts

During the last years of James I, very special praise was given him by Pope Clement IV confirming this sense of initiation: "Certainly, among the rest of the princes of the world whom literary science did not instruct, the Lord excellently endowed you with natural ingeniousness, and you have learned through much experience and heard to good degree the pronouncements of the wise, which you entrusted to your tenacious memory."[6] To listen and to entrust to memory are the first two directives to initiates, to which we may add a third: to be silent.

In my opinion, these suggest that the *Libre dels Feyts*, written by

King James I probably between the years 1244 and 1274 (or written under his direct supervision in two stages during this time), is far too superficial. We can find very little in it about his life with the brothers of the Temple during the few years he spent at Monzón. Likewise, nothing in the chronicle confirms the semi-kidnapping alluded to by various historians, and apart from telling of the obligatory teachings of the devoted life, including reading and fencing, which were proper knowledge for the knight that he was by birth, we learn no specifics of the type of teaching he received at Monzón. There is no mention of teaching regarding manners and the proper ways of his rank, or what notions of politics he learned and how much of it was naturally part of his own personality and perspectives. Only a few phrases in the few pages dedicated to that era suggest the impatience of a young king who already desires to be the protagonist of his own destiny. "Great was our desire to be away from that place," he says, referring to the stay of his cousin Ramón Berenger V of Provence, son of Count Alfonso II, brother to his father. Perhaps this spontaneous admission alludes not merely to the boredom of living in an undesired place, but also to the anxiety of publicly revealing what he learned and incorporated as a vital ideology.

Memories in the chronicle are limited to daily worship ceremonies, to learning the arts of war, and to the assumed vision of his own dominions, which are almost always observed from the battlements of the fortress. According to the chronicle, James's exit from Monzón coincided with a sudden and almost incomprehensible manifestation of maturity that was unnatural in a boy barely nine and a half years old. This is how James I compels any reader of his chronicle to guess his age based on the text. His definitive entrance into public life took effect at precisely the right moment, when "the master of the Temple resolved with the rest to let us be free." All the set objectives had been reviewed: the establishment of an effective unification of the Catalan-Aragonese crown under the hegemony of a predestined sovereign who was touched by the celestial grace of that Providence in which they all devotedly believed—the Providence that turns its chosen ones into great leaders of humanity.

Of course, when these superhuman objectives emerge, they do so not in the person of an obedient boy or man, but rather in a rebel. The rebelliousness of James I was in fact an indispensable condition of the Chosen One who is recognized as such precisely because of his nonconformity—whether open or secret. He demonstrated this nonconformity throughout his life through acts that seem to be mere anecdotes that would go unnoticed were it not for the profound meaning they imparted. James I, who likely was not truly aware of his actions because of his young age, left Monzón in June 1217. After a gathering of the courts, which took place in the very Templar fortress that approved his leave-taking, his first official act as a monarch was to visit the tomb of his father, who was buried in the neighboring convent of the nuns of St. John of Sigena.

This visit could not have had any sentimental motivation. Pedro II had ignored his son, in fact barely glancing at him when the infant was handed over to Simon de Montfort. Yet Pedro symbolized the king who, under compromised conditions, fought in favor of an ideology anathematized by the Church, an ideology that had become the object of millenarian martyrdom for a substantial number of the subjects of the Catalan-Aragonese crown. As if these associations were not enough, the visit concluded with a ceremony (suspicious, to say the least) in which the abbess of Sigena solemnly handed over to the boy the sword his father had used when he met his death at the hands of the Crusaders blessed by the pope. This ceremony—the apparent coincidence is doubtful—coincided with the gathering of a force that immediately targeted Toulouse, which was defended by Ramundo VI against Montfort's followers. The contingent, fundamentally formed by Occitans and Catalans, crossed the Pyrenees and defeated the Crusaders in Salvetat. On September 13, 1217, coinciding with the fourth anniversary of Pedro's death in Muret, the contingent freed Cathar Toulouse, which immediately provoked a bull from Honorius III (the successor to Innocent III, who had proclaimed the Crusade) in which he attacked those who promoted the expedition. Perhaps because he was still a child, James I seriously threatened his tutor, Count Sancho, advising him that if actions like this were to occur again, "the Roman church could not ignore so much injury to

God and herself, and maybe would weigh the hand in such a way against this kingdom that its punishment would be an example to others."

Perhaps this threat was the reason behind the fabrication of an urgent antidote that imparted a new hint of supernatural manipulation to the predestined king under Templar tutelage. In the middle of the year following the king's departure from Monzón, a legend was created that James I never mentioned in his chronicle: the alleged joint apparition of the Virgin presenting herself to James, Pedro Nolasco, and Ramón de Penyafort, which served as the pretext for the immediate creation of the Order of Mercy to redeem captives and to obtain all available benefits and sinecures. The Order of Mercy was introduced to the Catalan-Aragonese crown at once in a solemn ceremony that took place at the Cathedral of Barcelona on August 10, 1218. Almost as a pragmatic mark of the beginning of his reign, James also introduced his white habit and its insignia: a footed cross of silver over a red field, above a gold quarter bearing four red stripes. Once the race to reconquer territories began, the new order gradually but firmly established itself in all those lands it had newly acquired.

We must consider that the direct intervention of an illustrious member of the Dominican order in the genesis of the cult of La Virgen de la Merced (Virgin of Mercy) speaks of the possibility of direct Templar inspiration. There is no doubt, however, that the Templars, like the Cistercians who gave it their support during its early days, were a determined promoter of the cult of the Great Mother under the image of Our Lady, Mother of God. The Virgin was not so much a pious object of the cult as it was a great syncretic symbol of a broad, universal religious vision, as it was in the gnosticism still practiced in the Holy Land. It is also significant that, having a Dominican among the founders of the Order of Mercy, the emblem of which was the Latin sacrificial cross that would very soon become the symbol of the Inquisition's tribunals, the members of the Order of Mercy adopted the Greek cross worn by the Templars. As for the Templars and the Fatimite warriors who were closely related to the Templars, white with the red of the Catalan bars were the colors and insignia of the mercenaries.

The Conquest of the Magic Islands

Some of the early years in the reign of James I (when he was still a child) have been defined as an effort to leave unified the Catalan-Aragonese kingdom and to forget the grave difficulties north of the French-Spanish Pyrenean border that had tragically brought his father's reign to a close. Almost as a sign of that sudden forgetting of the extraterritorial preoccupations of the kingdom, from the beginning of the reign of James, the currency of Roussillon stops circulating south of the Pyrenees and is replaced by the Barcelonan *sueldo*. The Templar transactions were the only exception; for its transactions the Order used the golden *morabetino* of Muslim origin and approximately seven times higher in value than the common coin.

Once the years of interior unification had passed, there emerged the king's desire to reconquer. This spontaneous need, which marked his life and name, found a parallel in the Castilian push to reconquering, executed by Fernando III in Andalusia. This desire, in fact, evolved from a preexisting scheme that required only a vocal component to set it in motion. From their place at the margins of James I's profound sense of military and political strategy—which is not to be underappreciated—the reconquering campaigns make up a mission that, from an accumulation of signals, impart a sense of transcendence. Apparently these signals indicated to the king what needed doing at every moment and confirmed his desire to take up the task ordered by Providence.

The adventure of the Balearic conquest, seen through the autobiographical tale of the *Libre dels Feyts,* does not hold many surprises for the scholar capable of remaining in the traditional context. The first of these nonsurprises is that the king arrives at the concrete idea of this conquest not as a consequence of long reflection but from a sudden inspiration. Finding himself in Tarragona at less than twenty years old, he was invited to a dinner "by a merchant very experienced in matters of the sea," Pere Martell. The merchant spoke to him of the islands, and the nobles who accompanied the monarch to the banquet started to spur him to take on their conquest, making him see "that the will of

God cannot be twisted," despite the fact that nothing in the merchant's words showed that God was involved. This scene makes us think that there was confirmed some type of subliminal message already written in the subconscious of the monarch and in those who accompanied him. Was this message a subtle Templar suggestion? Since the Templars approval by the Council of Troyes, the Balearic Islands—which two counts of Barcelona with Templar affiliation had already tried to conquer—figured into the provincial division established for Europe.

From the remotest antiquity, a time when history was still confused with myth, this Mediterranean archipelago had posed a curious identity problem. Ibiza has been frequently identified with the land of Scheria that Homer speaks of in the *Odyssey.* If we remember the epic of Ulysses, we can recall that near the end of his journey the hero travels from Ogygia for twenty days, accosted by storms, and arrives exhausted on the beaches of Scheria, the land of the Phaeacians *(phaiakés)*. He

Fig. 6.1. The banquet of Pere Martell, where Providence decided the conquest of the Balearic Islands

awakens to find himself surrounded by girls, who flee when they see that he has recovered. Only Nausicaa, daughter of Alcinous, the king of that insular territory, remains by his side. In the Homeric poem there is a flavor that we should remember, one that hovers at the edge of an amorous adventure forming the meat of the story: The poet insists the Phaeacians are not warlike, which makes them citizens of a singular country of committed pacifists, very different from the fierce Balearic slingers we have come to know through the Latin historians. Is there a way to explain this discrepancy?

The excavations made on Ibiza seem to show that the island remained uninhabited until the arrival of first the Phoenicians of Tyre and later the Punic inhabitants of Carthage. The opposite phenomenon is produced on the island of Minorca. There archaeologists have found no Punic remains. Yet there exist there samples of megalithic cultures that seem to indicate that the island, just like sectors of Mallorca, was surely considered a magical space, a mansion of the gods rather than of men, who would go there only to render homage to the divine.

Already during the Roman era the investigations of Blázquez and Tovar have concluded that the abundance of sacrificial sanctuaries was nothing more than an extension of the cults to the Great Mother and demonstrated a Phoenician presence with their depictions of Tanit and of Astarte. We will have to remember that the sacrificial mysteries chose preferential cult places that had already been specially sanctified by previous religious traditions, those configured by apparently prodigious events—as occurred in Lusitania—by mystical heroes who lent their memory to creating a feeling of independence that would characterize the inhabitants of those territories.

This sense of freedom, the consequence of the paradigm of a people convinced of being in possession of a sacred place at the Center of the World, has been present in the Balearics since they became part of our historic knowledge. It could be found on its summits and in the slingers that temporarily detained the Roman conquest; it is also found in the warrior Fatih Ellah, whose sting greatly irritated the conquering troops of James I. In any case, within certain set parameters, it is not difficult to understand that the conquest of the Balearics planned by James I and inspired by the Templars contained magical-religious elements of the first magnitude. These transformed this adventure from one with merely political implications into a kind of transcendent goal in which no less important factors intervened, which, explicitly or implicitly, greatly surpassed the strict meanings of holy war or Christian Crusade.

Strangers in the Conquest

Barely had the conquest of the Balearics been raised as a possibility when the courts of the kingdom gathered in Barcelona. In what could be called an opening statement, this still almost beardless king clearly proclaimed himself supernatural: "[A]s you know, our birth was a miracle of God." By employing these terms he also announced the no less supernatural magnitude of the enterprise that he proposed to undertake, which made it deserving of all means of support. Indeed, the Catalan populace—much more than the Aragonese—enthusiastically entered into this enterprise, and on September 6, 1229, "one hundred fifty big barks, without counting the small ships," departed from Salou, Tarragona, and Cambrils. The king was among the last to set sail in the galley of Montpellier, his native city. But let us not throw this circumstance into the torn bag of coincidence. James I would leave it clear that Occitania was not foreign to him: He was Occitan by birth and his direct and immediate avoidance of the problems affecting that land did not mean he had absolutely forgotten its citizens. In fact, that gesture surpassed what it could have symbolized: A respectable number of people from the Midi, including numerous Cathars or those seriously involved with Catharism, formed part of the conquering expedition to the Balearics.[7]

The study carried out by Alomar Esteve, the results of which were not understood even in its day, reveals not only that there was a very clear Occitan presence in the forces from the very moment the Balearic conquest was proposed, but also that the king encouraged it. Occitan natives sailed in his galley, and he was accompanied by significant figures such as the brothers Gausbert and Guilhem de Servian, members of a known Occitan family from which numerous Cathar Perfects were prosecuted by Inquisition tribunals. Previously, in the *Libre del Repartiment* (Book of the Division of Lands), we detected an abundance of surnames that indicate a Cathar relationship and their direct intervention in the conquest of the islands. There we can find the Mosset, the Corsaví, the Jordá, the Ferriol, and the Termes.

Only by paying attention to lineage and personalities can we detect the presence of a Berenger Dufort, a relative of troubadours and Perfects who figured as general *batlle* of Mallorca in 1239; and a Berenger Martí, a relative of the Albigensian bishop Bernat Martí, burned by the Inquisition in 1240, who was included in the army of the count of Béarn (a sympathizer of the Cathars). James I awarded Martí the lands in the zone of Sóller. The king himself cited on one occasion Dalmau de Barberá, who formed part of his Christian vanguard, and Bernat Desclot. In his chronicle[8] he tells us of men such as Jaspert and Pere Arnau de Barberá, who would later return to Occitania to take part in the Albigensian cause during the second stage of the crusade. The king must have had a great deal of trust in Jaspert's tactical sense, for the monarch cites him in the *Libre* paying homage to his value as a strategist: *"Pus en Jaspert hi va, iré i jo"* (If Jaspert goes, I go too).

In Laurac there was a Cathar family named Caramany. One of its members had received the *consolamentum* and one of its female members, Cirauda, was among those immolated at Montségur. In addition, some of its members appear as representatives of the ephemeral kingdom of Mallorca ruled by the son of the Conquerer.

What should most interest us is the relationship between these families suspected or "convicted" of Catharism and the Templar order. Therefore, when the *Libre del Repartiment* confirms the location of properties and the how they were awarded, we might show that the Occitans were spread throughout the whole island of Mallorca. Those that smelled of Cathaism looked for their settlements in the zones that were left under the direct and immediate influence of the Order of the Temple: the area of Pollensa and the territory that surrounds the mountain of Randa. A number of these families appear directly involved in matters concerning the Order, which could corroborate the close relationship of the Templar order to the Cathar heresy. Some history of the islands can also be used to corroborate this relationship:

The surname Escafré is documented in the area of Artá from the thirteenth century. Following Alomar's record, we find the name Bernat d'Escafré, who was procurator for the Templars of Béziers in 1180.

Pere Fenollet VI, from an Occitan family that settled in Mallorca at the time of the conquest of the Balearic Islands, was the first viscount of Illa by appointment of King Sancho in 1314. He was a direct descendant of another Pere Fenollet (1209–43), whom the Inquisitors persecuted for being a Cathar in 1229 and who found refuge in the Templar *encomienda* of Mas Deu, together with Ponç de Vernet, who participated in the conquest of Mallorca. The Vernets were also beneficiaries of the division of the island among those who contributed to its conquest.

Three members of the Riusech family took oaths before Alfonso III of Aragon in 1285. An ancestor of theirs, Amiel de Riusech, was stripped of his lands and goods by Simon de Montfort and joined the Templar order. Pere Serra, a relative of the first Templar commander in Mallorca, Ramón Serra, also figures in the Repartiment* and his record as a Cathar can be followed in the Midi.

There indeed was an intimate relationship among the Templar order, Catharism, and the (ephemeral) dynasty of Mallorca that enjoyed substantial popular support in the last years of the thirteenth century, when the islands briefly separated from the Catalan-Aragonese crown. We should also mention the Mallorcan Cathar saints, San Cabrit and Santa Bassa.

Curious Wonders and Strange Avocations

James I and a host of Occitans were about to set sail for the islands aboard his flagship *Montpellier* (perhaps to a chorus of Cathar prayers).

*[The *repartiment* refers to the reallocation of Balearic territory after the conquest of these islands by James I. —*Trans.*]

In the monarch's Mallorcan history, just like the later narrative of Bernat Desclot, the miraculous emerges as a regular element, part of daily events that reveal a king who assumes the supernatural is one with his person and historical circumstances.

Let us try to dig a little deeper into those miraculous cases that could be considered especially significant. First there is the instance of the strong southeast wind from land that reached twenty miles off the coast and caused the boatswain to recommend to the king that he turn around and return to shore. The monarch's response was immediate: "If in His name we march, it is just that in Him we deposit all of our trust so that He can guide us." The wind ceased at dawn and the Mallorcan coast could be seen.

Desclot writes in his chronicle of another event that borders on the marvelous: the appearance out of nowhere of an apparition of a Moorish youngster who climbs the king's galley and confesses to the monarch that his own mother had predicted the monarch's arrival—and that his men would be the liberators of the island. The phantasmagorical Moor Alí is a prophetic—and Muslim—apparition that seems to come from another world.

The chronicle cites even more wonders at the walls of the island's capitol, and the king who has ordered this written history accepts these miracles with the absolute conviction that he is under divine protection.

On one occasion, the Christian armies attack the walls with catapults. In order to protect themselves, the besieged place prisoners on the battlements. Undeterred, the Catalan-Aragonese continue their attack without one single prisoner being hurt.

A notable island Moor named Ben Abeet comes to the aid of the Christians with provisions at a time when they are experiencing grave supply difficulties. In his chronicle, James I describes this Muslim as an "angel of God" and specifies: "When I write angel I mean to say Saracen, but with what he brought us, such was the good that it did us that as an angel we took him then and we call him now." Needless to say, in the thirteenth century a word such as *angel* could not be taken simply as an affectionate or pet name.

But the greatest wonder accepted as a matter of course by a king who views himself nearly as a predestined messiah—a good solar king—was produced during the definitive assault against the walls of the city. Let us listen to the story in the Conqueror's own words: "As the very Saracens told us afterward, the first one they saw who attacked them on horse was a knight dressed in white and carrying all his white weapons, by which we are firm in our belief that it must have been St. George, who, the stories tell us, has appeared repeatedly in many other battles between Christians and Saracens."

This same St. George became the declared patron saint of Catalonia in the courts of Monzón in 1436 and, curiously, presides on his feast day over the country's most representative cultural manifestations. These are reminiscent of the Georgic feasts of which Virgil sang, those celebrating spring. In addition, St. George is an autochthonous substitution for the figure of St. Michael-Hermes, who, as messenger of Glory and measurer of souls, was the saint of warrior devotions throughout the high Middle Ages.

Curiously, although he is always represented as armed and engaged in the warrior's act of defeating the dragon, in Catalonia St. George has always been a fundamentally agrarian saint, as spelled out in the refrain "Sant Jordi kills the spider": He blesses white mulberry trees and the *missa dels cucs,* which is celebrated in the fertile plains region of Plana de Vic. It is precisely in this apparent dichotomy of the joyful agrarian tradition and the warlike image of the saint that St. George to his enigma resides. His presence is generally linked to traditions that mostly predate Christianity, as can be demonstrated by many local myths similar or parallel to that of the *pastoreta* of Vic, who raised the dolmen of Puigseslloses all by herself in an act of supreme devotion to the saint. This saint also has a chapel dedicated to him in the surrounding area.[9]

St. George entered the West with the Crusaders. The Templars were advocates of his expansive labor. In fact, his feast was a precept in Templar houses.[10] Jacobus Voraginus recounts that St. George extended his celestial favors upon the Crusaders who reached the lands of Georgia.[11] As proof of the evident messianic intention of those who exalted the supposed Christian martyr, his passion as recounted in *The Golden Legend or Life of the Saints* lasted no less than seven years, during which time he was resurrected three times, as witnessed by seventy kings.[12] Eventually, the account of his martyrdom turned out to be suspicious—most probably because of its obvious initiatory content—and in the fifth century a council was assembled during the papacy of Gelasio declaring that his passion had been written "by a heretic's hand."

St. George is also especially prolific in relics and genealogies. The Merovingian kings declared themselves his descendants and from approximately the sixth century there was talk, although not at popular levels, that his remains were in the Galias. During this medieval period, a time in which the venerated remains of saints had become the primary objects of fervor and cult status, relics of St. George appeared everywhere, and kings as well as large abbeys, cathedrals, and collegiate churches fought among themselves for the right to preserve and own them. In 1355, Pedro IV reclaimed the supposed head of the saint from the city of Lydia, in Neopatria. In the following year, the royal chapel of Barcelona possessed "a bone of the shoulder of the arm" of St. George; Valencia received a finger in 1373.

The constant wondrous aura that turned the conquest of the Balearics into an authentic heroic deed with supernatural overtones points to the enormous political importance that this achievement had for the Temple and its goals and for the king for whom the Templars had gone out of their way with all their might and influence. James I was the most immediate and viable candidate for the solar epic that would pave the way for the Templar synarchy.

Let us not forget a fact that many have ignored: The Mallorcan adventure started precisely the same year that Emperor Frederick II was excommunicated for his reluctance to participate in the Crusades convoked by Pope Gregory IX and meant to free the Holy Sites once and for all. Eventually, the emperor decided to join this Crusade. That very year a secret pact among the great military orders was signed in the East, with the goal of proclaiming the emperor as king of Jerusalem—and king of the world—upon the conquest of the Holy City, which was to be the axis or center of the universal synarchic project. But that glorious result could come to pass only through an accord with the Muslim Fatimites—with whom the Templars kept significant though discreet relations—and the destruction of the Sunni Muslims of Egypt. In fact, it was reached without glory through an understanding established between the emperor and the sultan of Egypt: Muslims would be the effective owners of the Holy City and Christians would be able to access their sacred places there. Though the sovereign did declare himself king of Jerusalem, despite the solemn coronation ceremony in the Holy Sepulchre, it was only an honorific title. The Knights Templar refused to attend, for their original see was taken from them with impunity because of the demands the Muslims had made of the emperor.

Templar Mallorca

With the unappreciated help of the Templars, James I took control of Mallorca in 1228. Approximately one hundred knights of the Order entered the Mallorcan campaign and worked hard as shock troops in the siege of the capital and as the implacable pursuers of the Muslim guerrillas who tried to organize resistance movements in the interior of the island. This was the same year that marked the Order's centennial of recognition by the Council of Troyes. Even without having proclaimed it to the four winds as a key event, that centenary was decisive in the Templars' ideological scheme, which, though it suffered failure in the Holy Land thanks to Emperor Frederick II, achieved tremendous success in the conquest of Mallorca. The Conqueror barely cites this victory in his chronicle, but we could consider it transcendental when examining the proportion of territory obtained by the Templars when the island was divided among those who collaborated in its conquest.

The Templar' prizes included an area of considerable magnitude on the northeastern part of the island, including Pollença and Alcúdia and running below the sanctuary of Lluch. Our Lady became the patroness of the archipelago, a veneration that was probably instituted by the knights of the Order, who promoted her miracles until they transformed their see into the preferred place of pilgrimage and the nucleus of the devotions of the new Christian inhabitants. The power of the Templars in those territories was omnipresent, depending on neither the authority of bishops nor of kings. There they established an eminently feudal regime, charging tithes from their numerous renters and even administering justice in places such as the peak of Les Forques, which is known today as the Peak of the Templars in recognition of the great center of knighthood it had become. The name of the Templars is also preserved in the Castell dels Templers, though it was not a Templar castle. It was a prehistoric *talayot* located under the Order's jurisdiction in proximity to Alcúdia and was probably used as a watchtower to control the wide coastal zone.[13]

The first commander of the Templars in Mallorca, Brother Arnau de Cursalvel, did not reside in the house of Pollença, still preserved near the Templar church of Santa María de los Ángeles, but rather in the capitol of the newly conquered kingdom. After the occupation, the city was divided into *barrios;* the Jewish quarter, located in the northeastern zone of the city, which had been quite large during the Muslim era, was squeezed into an ample plot that came to be called the Partita Templi. Here the knights built their house and church against the Muslim wall. We can guess that the same thing happened in other places where the Order came to settle. The desire to situate in Jewish synagogues formed part of the Templar plan. In the case of Palma de Mallorca, the *buxolers,* or Jewish cartographers, installed themselves near the Templars. They had already gained a well-deserved reputation for the quality of their maps and added to it long after the Order had disappeared, many of them moving on to lend their services to the nautical school of Sagres, established in Portugal by the Order of Christ, which took the possessions and place of the Templar order after it was abolished by the Council of Vienne.

According to documentation, this was a period focused on disputes and donations that conferred on the Majorcan conquest a value quite a bit greater than what some have wanted to give it. In fact, the Templars' influence in the islands constituted a separate kingdom under the

Fig. 6.2. La Casa de la Ploma, in the proximity of Pollença, formed part of the Templar properties.

government initiated by the Conqueror's son, James II. Their influence remained until long after the death of the Conqueror and continued to grow during the brief period in which the Balearics were considered a bridgehead of the first degree, which led to the possession of the Middle East for which the Templars emphatically fought until they had to confront the very process of history. We might even suspect that Pollença and the port of Palma became important maritime bases for the Order. The Templar vessel *Falcó* (Hawk), based in the Bay of Palma, and the graffiti found along with ships in the Templar location of the Font de S'Horta undoubtedly speak to the importance to the Templars of these island refuges.[14]

Ciotat de Mallorques, a Templar encomienda, was the nerve center of island life, as is testified to by the enormous quantity of documents that were signed and stored there. In the first of these, the *Libre del Repartiment,* are consigned the donations made to all those taking part in the conquest, and it ends by saying that "In that very house of the Templars the documents of the very short run of the feudal kingdom of Mallorca will be kept and the riches that constituted the part of the bounty that belonged to the king will be stored."

The conquest did not end with the occupation of Mallorca. Although James I did not intervene directly in the campaign, the fight continued with the capture of Minorca, in which the Knights Templar once again actively participated under the leadership of Commander Ramón de Serra.

Meanwhile, as if obeying an uncontainable urge to conquer (for which the Aragones clamored, after the kingdom's relatively minor participation in the Belearic Islands campaign), James I rushed to organize the campaign that led him to conquer Valencia. Structured in part by Templar strategic thinking, he began to prepare the campaign's plans in Teruel, after taking the fortress of Morella in 1232.

The Road to the Synarchic Enterprise

The conquest of Valencia implied, on the one hand and from a fundamentally political perspective, the complete possession of the territories that, fifty years before (in 1179), had been divvied up by the kingdoms of Aragon and Castile. On the other hand, it signified an urgent need to counteract the growing power of the Castilian kingdom, which in 1230 united with León once again under the august figure of a monarch predestined for sainthood: Fernando III. At this time, James I was being pressured to join a Navarre that was already largely lost. He met with Sancho the Strong and agreed vaguely to join his kingdom of Aragon and Navarre after the death of the Navarrese king, who had years of advantage over the young Aragonese monarch. All indications are that the fundamental desire of James I was to expand his power at the expense of Islam. This was not prompted solely by a hunger for territory, although he felt it was important to enlarge his kingdom, but also because, as is shown in diverse episodes of his life, he had a very special interest, which was also attributed to Fernando III: to achieve an effective, spiritual union between the fundamental religions of that Mediterranean world and Templar ideology.

Of course, this point of view has not been seriously considered. Many scholars have fallen into the trap of judging appearances and supposed evidence and, as a result, have declared these as having little to do with the profound reality of that intrahistory that has never been expressed in official documents. Here I reproduce some paragraphs I wrote some years ago in which I express a point of view that has not substantially changed and which, to my way of thinking, goes a long way toward clarifying the real meaning of James I's historical task:

> Let us remember that James I, like his son-in-law, Alfonso X, the Wise, of Castile, never felt a visceral enmity against Jews and Muslims. Political circumstances and, surely, his transcendent mission, drove him to a series of territorial conquests, but his sympathy for these groups is evident: We could say he *gets along* with Moors and Hebrews. We need only remember the mediating effects that some eminent Jews, such as Azac, had on his policies, and his good relations with Muslims throughout his reign. Let us think, too, of Ben Afleet, the angel of the conquest of Mallorca, or of the Muslim chivalry well demonstrated in the capture of Peñíscola: When the king arrived with an escort of only seven knights to personally take charge of the surrender of the plaza and, because he arrived late in the day, tired, and unarmed, the Muslims sent him provisions for his dinner. James I always responded with the same gentlemanly behavior and the same profound respect toward members of other religions.[15]

In this respect, I believe it is worth recounting an event of profound and unusual significance that took place in Barcelona in 1263 and was repeated in 1265. The protagonists were James I, the great Kabbalist Moíses ben Nahmán (Nahmánides) of Gerona, the converted Dominican Pau Chrestía, and St. Ramón de Penyafort.

It was then that the mendicant friars of the Dominican order, which was already defined as a confirmed persecutor of nonbelievers —wherever they came from—and whose war against the Cathars was characterized by baths of blood and fire, turned their attention toward the Jews, who up until then had been tolerated and who lived in relative peace in the Christian kingdoms. (We must not forget the clear role the Templars and their protection played in this peace.) Friar Pau Christiá, connoisseur of Jewish books thanks to his background, proposed the celebration of a public debate with Rabbi Nahmánides in which they would discuss the greatest matters differentiating the Jews from the Christians: essentially the divine essence and the coming of the Messiah. The king himself, profoundly interested in the development of the controversy, gave the rabbi all the guarantees of security and freedom of expression and personally attended the discussions, which took place on July 20, 27, 30, and 31 in 1263 and which had to be interrupted for fear of the riots they came close to inciting. This did not impede the king from unstintingly praising the participation of the Kabbalist wise man, personally participating in the polemic, and making a gift of three hundred *sueldos* to Nahmánides. Successive royal decrees allowed the Jews to free themselves from the obligation imposed on them of listening to the sermons that the Dominicans delivered in their own synagogues and forbade the custom of stoning the Jews of Xátiva's homes on Good Friday. Ultimately, the bishop of Gerona himself pressured the rabbi to write the points of view that he offered in the debate (and which, of course, were later distorted in the summaries published by the friars of Saint Domingo).

In 1265, the controversy that had been interrupted two years before was renewed in the royal palace of Barcelona in the form of a false trial during which Nahmánides, as the accused, came out better than could have been expected. The Dominicans, however, went before Clement IV and presented their claims, and almost immediately the pope published his *turbato corde* bull and sent it as a letter to King James, demanding the immediate punishment of the rabbi for having expressed himself—obviously these were not precisely his words—according to his conscience and beliefs. The king had to give in to the papal order, and Nahmánides went into exile in the Holy Land, where he eventually died.[16]

"Certainly, James I was far from feeling the free-thinking inclinations that men of his generation attributed, for example, to Emperor Frederick II. All his life he cooperated with the popes of his time, persecuted the heretics of his kingdom, and fought against Islam as one of the authentic Crusaders of the Faith, even years after the dispute over projected a crusade to the Holy Land, which he ultimately did not carry out for reasons beyond his control." These words, written by the Jewish historian Baer about the controversy in Barcelona, are a common example of how academic investigation at times seems to limit analysis to outward appearances, dispensing with a deeper analysis of the facts and of personalities who played the main roles in them. Calling Frederick II a freethinker naturally associates him with some attitudes that his messianism could have never adopted. But to strictly limit James I to the typical mold of medieval monarch—scourge of heretics, orthodox conqueror, and faithful servant of the papacy—is to understand only a personality or a vital attitude that had been programmed for quite ambitious goals. James I managed to materially carry out these goals despite the religious conditioning that dominated his world and directly influences all, from kings on down.

Just as the quarrymen of the Gothic cathedral and the humble architects of the Romanesque era had to adapt their transcendental intentions to symbols and forms that, in appearance at least, faithfully fulfilled the canons imposed by the powerful ecclesiastical authority ruling all aspects of the life of their faithful, so rulers, although they might hold ideas that went beyond the function authorized by the omnipotent papal see, had to officially proclaim their obedience and play the game of submission in order to realize their ideal. Each act and each word must at least seem orthodox and loyal, or such rulers would soon find themselves anathematized, made prey to all those who, hoisting the sign of the cross, might want to exploit them and destroy them with the excuse of faithfully fulfilling the precepts that emanated from the legitimate and irreplaceable representatives of God on earth.

Divine Conquest

Some continue to insist, perhaps overmuch, on the strong Aragonese character of the campaign that ended with the conquest of the kingdom of Valencia. Surely this insistence is a compensation for the strong Catalan character that was stressed in the conquest of the Balearics by King James. In reality, if we follow the development of both campaigns, we will realize, above all the nationalist conveniences of the territories that made up the crown of Aragon, that both characters contributed equally to the warrior prestige of the monarch and that both supposed the fulfillment of moral compromises that chained James I to the Templars. If the Balearic province formed part of the Order's vision from the moment of its creation, then Valencia, a long strip of Mediterranean territory, also had been in the Templar sights ever since the Order acquired the promise, on behalf of the grandfather and great-grandfather of the Conqueror, Alfonso II and Ramón Berenger IV, respectively, that certain territories and fortressed plazas would be handed over to them.

Dispensing with precise details, we can say that the conquest of Valencia was a campaign that went like a song. It was realized by each concrete group of combatants—royal forces, noble armies, and troops ascribed to military orders—according to the settlement promises previously established, with the exception of the capture of the capital. For that step, the forces combined in a sacred place that served as propitiatory center for launching the definitive attack: the ancient Puig de Ceba, later called Puig de Santa María because of a miraculous apparition of Our Lady, which the king did not mention in his chronicle. Perhaps he felt the apparition was far from what should be told in a narration in which the event and not its circumstances is significant, or maybe the king considered himself above events that seemed intended only to move believers and stimulate their sensibilities.

More so than in the tale of the conquest of Mallorca, James I highlighted in his chronicle the profoundly chivalrous and respectful character that surrounded the different stages of the Valencian campaign, as if the relations between Christians and Moors—and, above all, the monarch's relations with Islam—were matters between rivals rather

Fig. 6.3. The castles of Xivert (above) and Pulpis (below), obtained by the Templars during the campaign for the Moorish kingdom of Valencia

than sworn enemies. Here we can read how the king rides through unconquered territory with practically no escort, how he receives provisions from the Moors when he is in need of them, how a strange understanding exists when it comes time to arrange surrenders and truces, and how there prevail respect and an interest in understanding and accepting the stakes.

An example of this existential posture related in the conquests of Mallorca and Valencia is the likely promise made by the conqueror king to the defenders of these plazas to include the image of the bat in the city's banner if it was handed over without bloodshed. It is significant that the proposal facilitated the end to hostilities, as if that apparently banal promise implied a meaning much more profound than what its simple enunciation seemed to proclaim.

As Robert Graves reveals to us, the king undoubtedly knew about certain symbols that the Knights Templar adopted from the Muslim sects of the Ishmaelite Sufis. Graves posed to the Sufi philosopher Idries Shah the possibility that this bat had a deeper meaning—one hidden from the eyes of the populace—than the one it was given in the legend. This is Shah's explanation: "'Bat,' in Arabic, is KHuFFaSH, a word derived from the root KH.F.SH, which means 'to overthrow,' 'to subjugate.' Bats usually inhabit ruined edifications. This meaning could give us the first answer to the choice of the conqueror king: The bat would be, in a certain way, the hieroglyphic of his own condition as Vanquisher."[17]

But there is another, more profound meaning by which Sufis identify the bat. The root KH.F.SH also means "weak vision," "pupil which sees only at night." The blind man—and this is a symbol that has existed in all cultures since time immemorial—is equivalent to the disciple, the visionary. The follower has done without the vision of other men, the contemplation of the exterior world, the attention toward all that takes place during the day—that is to say, preoccupation with the mere human struggle—to watch instead those things that take place when the rest are asleep. According to the transcendent syncretism of traditional forms, we find that many initiates of the ancient world whose physical characters have been transmitted through myth or legend have been blind men: Homer and Tyresias in the Greek world and Samson in the Hebrew world were all blind. Oedipus acquired his knowledge after blinding himself. St. Paul reached Christian illumination when the light momentarily blinded him, and St. Lucía, who in many Hispanic sanctuaries occupies the place in Christendom reserved for the Lusine divinity, is the beatific patroness of the blind.

The suspicion confirmed here is that, despite the view of some historians who insist James I had no intellectual education and was probably illiterate, the Aragonese monarch almost certainly received an education—presumably from the Templars—which allowed him to understand Islamic ideology. More than understanding it, he could profoundly communicate with a world which, for the greater part of Christendom that fought it (including the Castilian kings), was no more than a diabolic force that must be vanquished so Rome's Faith could triumph.

James I's vital attitude intimately confronted strict orthodoxy and ran parallel to the one the Templar order had adopted since its origins: It embraced non-Christian creeds and sought ideological coincidences before anathematizing the differences that would make others irreconcilable enemies. We have seen the monarch's tendency to delve deeply into Christian-Hebrew polemic; here we see his attempt to ideologically deal face-to-face with the Moslems. But a synarchic vision, as vague as it might still have been and as poorly structured in the minds of the Templars as it was in the mind of James I, comprised an approach to Christians separated from the Orient and, above all, included the perceptive and definitive conquest of the essential Holy Sites of the Mediterranean world, starting with Jerusalem.

The Failed Overseas Enterprise

If we read closely the *Libre dels Feyt* and dispense with what was both written by and inspired by the king, we can easily discern the king's actual desire for and the semi-reality of leaving for the Holy Land in a Crusade. By contrast, other sources documenting events involving the Crusade to the Orient seem to skillfully ignore these desires, as if they didn't fit with the soverign's intentions.

Yet Engracia Alsina points out this certainty: "We cannot overlook the infancy and youth of the Conqueror, who was educated by the Templar order. He would have been perfectly familiar with the history of successive Crusades in which so many kings, magnates, and knights fought for the conquest of Jerusalem."[18] No doubt the young king was very directly shaped by the Templar—surely by Guillén de Montredó, who was his mentor—regarding his understanding of the importance of Jerusalem. He surely would have comprehended the fundamental importance of that center of the world.

Yet the sovereign maintains his silence concerning concrete facts about Jerusalem. In 1224, Juan de Brena, king of Jerusalem, arrived on the Peninsula as an official pilgrim to Santiago de Compostela, and probably with a petition for assistance from the sovereigns of the peninsular kingdoms. It is known he stopped at Toledo, where he had an interview with Fernando III, and it is more than likely that he spoke with James I, who by then was sixteen years old and fully involved in a struggle against the feudal lords of his territories. The king's chronicle, however, guards its silence on this subject.

On January 25, 1245, the conquest of Valencia ended, although it was not yet a place of peace, requiring that James retain forces their to ensure his victory—forces Pope Innocent IV asked the monarch to send to the Holy Land to assist in the defense of the sacred sites.

This was in may ways a crucial moment. Some years before, the Turks had taken Jerusalem, and the Templar grand master Armand de Périgord had died fighting in Gaza. The Castilian Templars had received the castle of Caravaca and in Occitania the Cathar fortress of Montségur had fallen. Yet James I's chronicle ignores these events. He apparently marched to his own drummer when he prepared ships, attempted sail to the Holy Land, and, after "seventeen days and seventeen nights" of resisting winds from Provence, gave up.

In 1267, when the king was fifty-nine years old and a few months shy of the conquest of Murcia, an ambassador named Abaga from the khan of Tatary asked his assistance in the reconquest of the Holy Land, which at this time was almost entirely under the control of the Seleucid Turks. The king once again mentions this event only superficially: ". . . an embassy from the Tartars had arrived, with a very friendly and brotherly letter from their king . . ." That is all. He does, however, report news of a visit from the Catalan ambassador Jaume Alarig to confirm this petition, as well as the 1269 return of the Tartars' messengers, accompanied by the emperor of Byzantium, Miguel Paleólogo, to secure the help they were thinking of lending the enterprise to wrest control of the Holy Land from the Seleucid Turks: the Tartars, men; the Byzantines, war machines.

Finally, by the time James I was seventy-one years old, the moment of his involvement arrived. His enthusiasm seems to reveal that, after a long period of digestion and planning, he very conscientiously and intentionally assumed his role at this time. The fact that his son-in-law, Alfonso X, offered little help did not intimidate him, nor did the lack of enthusiasm demonstrated by the Templars, who no doubt suggested his involvement long ago. Nor was he deterred by a slap on the wrist from Pope Clement IV when the hour came to declare his Crusade. The pope refused to affirm the sacredness of James's expedition due to the love relationship of James I and Berenguela Alonso, whom the king intended to marry: "the Crucified does not accept the service of he who crucifies him again by maintaining an incestuous bond."

Although indifference circled him, the old king threw all his might into his Crusade, gathering "between one thousand three hundred or more knights and men on horses." With a limited squadron and a more determined spirit than circumstances should allow, the king took to the sea, though storms once again forced him to return to land. A pair of barks did manage to arrive at St. John of Acre (the last Western holding in the Middle East) and remained there, assisting the few Franks who were left and creating on their own a useless and senseless war the king could not see but the Templars had surely foreseen.

If we analyze the king's attitude at this moment, we are given the impression of a man who felt rushed, who was afraid of arriving too late to participate in an effort and ideal about which he dreamed his whole life and which he was about to lose. In that same year, 1269, the pope convened a council in Lyon. The king attended and fought for his ideal, imploring European believers to throw themselves into the adventure of his conquest of the Holy Land—and no doubt that the enterprise be under his command. When the attendees were invited to express their opinion, the Templars excused themselves, having little faith in the success of the king's venture; the nobles in attendance stepped back, frightened, for they did not believe they could gather enough forces to recover what at that point everyone felt was lost. En Artal de Balari articulated what was surely the feeling of all but James I: "[T]he enemies have possessed that land for a long time and now it would not be the easiest thing to recover. Let us not be the small dog that barks at the mastiff, who pays it no attention; because even though a king or any other character goes overseas, it will not be as easy as some seem to think to win the land. Because of this, I understand the opinion of the master of the Templars as being good."

For James I, the Conqueror, the Holy Land was the grand, unattainable dream, the goal of all his synarchic plans. In his old age, he glimpsed the possibility of achieving his dream and had to yield to it, however unrealistic. Something of his remained in the Holy Land: the body of his daughter Sancha, who was buried in Acre after having spent her life since 1255 humbly serving the pilgrims. But though this fact is recorded in Prince Juan Manuel's account, *Libro de las Armas,* the king does not mention it in his chronicle. It is as if he deliberately ignored what he believed was a failure. He knew very well that a royal chronicle, *Libre dels Feyts,* could not be a chronicle of failures, but instead must be of the glory and miracles the Templars had shown him his life should be.

The Secret Knowledge of a King of the World

As we have learned, some historians say the Templars taught the young King James I little in the way of letters, and that consequently the monarch would never been capable of writing his own chronicle. Some even doubt that he dictated it.

Yet there exists a text, the *Libre de la Saviessa* (Book of Knowledge or Book of Wisdom) that could prove the opposite.[19] King James appears to attribute this text to himself in the first few lines of its prologue: "And I, King James of Aragon, made the effort to do and learn of those things, which are precious, that Salomon willed me." The book itself is composed of a series of maxims and thoughts put in the mouths of Greek philosophers and Persian wise men. Some are familiar and others are fabrications, but all show the paths to be followed by the man of goodwill who aspires to wisdom.

The more skeptical critics continued to proclaim the impossibility that this *Libro de la Saviessa* could be the work of the Catalan-Aragonese monarch. In 1876, however, in a long article published in the *Revue des Langues Romanes,* the baron of Tourtoulon pointed out a fact that could be significant, if we accept the importance of the role the Knights Templar played in the formation of the king's conscience. Tourtoulon affirms that one of the philosophers quoted in the *Libra de la Saviessa,* Joanici (see maxim 167, below), is actually Ioanicci de Isach, or Honain ben Isahq, a Nestorian Arab of the ninth century who wrote a work, *Apophtegmata Philosophorum,* whose spirit can be found in the small treatise attributed to James I. Honain was part of a family of important and distinguished translators of classical Arabic philosophy. Curiously, the libraries of the Dar al-Hiqma (Houses of Wisdom), the first of which was founded by the caliph Al-Ma'mun in Baghdad in 829, started to nourish themselves from their literary holdings, and the Templars of Palestine certainly had access to these libraries.

The teachings of the *Libre de Saviessa* form part of the texts that were known by the most representative dignitaries of the Order* and, in their entirety, form an authentic framework for conduct. They support an indisputably "solar"† outlook, giving to those who read these teachings the impression that such guidelines were not meant to be used in the pursuit of knowledge that leads to power.

---

*Llabres already proposed this idea in the first edition of the *Libre* (1908) and noted that at least the first eight chapters must have been part of a collection of Greek works collected in the lower empire and brought back by the Templars.

†[In Paul's "creation" of the Christian religion he confers on the Christ a "solar" or Hellenic status, thereby breaking with Judaism, which did and still does view as heresy the notion that Jesus was the messiah. —*Ed.*]

Because it falls outside of the scope of this book, it would be difficult to complete here a comparative study of sources to establish the number and character of gnostic teachings, however fragmented, contained in the *Libre de Saviessa.* But it would be illuminating to look more closely at some of the book's maxims to affirm that Templar solar mysticism (like that of Catharism and Gnosticism) had much to do with the genesis of the treatise, just as it had been transmitted to a king barely eight years in Templar custody:

86. The second one [philosopher] said: If God's wisdom could know the destiny of men, wouldn't it have then fulfilled its own destiny?
87. The third one said: It is advisable to begin knowing where we are before we attempt to climb to where the others are.
137. The senses are God's; the teaching is what everyone must gain by himself.

Maxim 167, ascribed to the presumed translator Joanici (Honain), tells us he went from temple to temple looking for the books of the wise, and that a learned hermit allowed him to search until he found the answer to a question posed by Alexander to his teacher Aristotle. (It is advisable to note that throughout the *Libre de Saviessa,* Aristotle and Plato are presented not as philosophers, but as masters of kings: Aristotle is master of Alexander; Plato is master of one Nitaforius, son of Rafusca, *"rey dels grechs"* (king of the Greeks). The supposed answer of the philosopher to the solar king (Alexander) merits translation here (though I have taken some liberties):

168. To you, honorable son and recognized King of Justice: I read your letter in which you manifested the sorrows of your thinking because I could not see you, or go with you or give you counsel. And you begged me to make a book that would guide you with its counsels as I would guide you myself. But you know that I stopped accompanying you because I find myself old and sick. What you now ask me is so large that it could not fit in

> living bodies, much less on parchment, that is a mortal thing; but because of the debt that I have with you, I shall fulfill your will. And it is advisable that you not desire that I uncover these secrets that I will recount in the book, as I say so much in it that I trust only in God and in your understanding so that you are able to comprehend it conveniently; think of my words and all that you know about myself, and you will immediately comprehend how much I want to say. I do not show so clearly my secrets [for fear] that my book fall into the hands of men of bad faith and excessiveness who may know of these matters what they must not nor God forbid should they understand, as it would be a great treason to uncover secrets that God does not show.

Aristotle continues to describe secrets to Alexander and announces that the book contains eight treatises, the first of which deals with kings and the second "the state that kings must show." Reading these treatises does not clear up the many mysteries that even today the long reign of James the Conqueror holds, but aside from the certain participation of James in this eminently solar treatise, we can glimpse something of the messianism that the Templar friars injected into the young king. It is quite possible that James I was another sovereign trained to share the Templars' dream of a universal empire. If this objective was not reached, it was in large part because the alleged king of the world would rule over a populace in which each citizen would consider himself as valuable as his king and when all citizens took themselves together, they would consider themselves even more valuable than any monarch.

The Caesar's Withered Laurels

All the clues that make up the reign of James I confirm the suspicion that we laid out at the beginning of this chapter: The Templar order, holder of great power in the shadow of the crown of Aragon, believed the moment had come to rehearse its synarchic plan when it fell upon the possibility of conforming to its image the destiny of the boy-king who had been entrusted to it. They prepared him carefully so that in him the first stage of their universal theocratic ideal could come about.

If we add up criteria and events that may seem episodic and lacking in deeper significance, we could establish a series of principles that King James I retained throughout his reign and which, although generally interpreted as common to any of the other monarchs of medieval centuries, reveal that James the Conqueror acted with an assumption of his own messianism inculcated in him by Templar education. Further, it seems his actions were always accompanied by the clear conscience of a destiny reserved for him, which ultimately surpassed the condition of his obedience, as a Christian monarch, to the consignments of the Holy See.

In the history of James I we must find the balance between his actions that were diametrically opposed to the norms for rulers of the time and those that clearly followed established customs and orthodoxy. He was a Christian open to listening objectively and respectfully to the principles that the official Church anathematized. He knew how to listen to Nahmánides and allowed Occitan Catharism to find refuge from inquisitorial persecution in his territory. He forged a humanistic idea of the holy war, and not only did he fulfill it to the letter in his conquering campaigns, but he also attempted to export it to the Holy Land, even at the risk of the Holy See vetoing his venture. He promoted the cult of the Great Mother through popularized images known as the Merced of Lluch or of Puig, and silenced his role for the sake of the more universal idea from which those cults emerged by the demands of a majority in the populace that claimed them. He surrounded his life with supernatural elements and promulgated them as everything innate to the monarch is promulgated, so that he himself could be judged above good and evil. He viscerally took on the Templar ideology, though he barely mentioned it when accounting for himself through his own story, as if his connection to the Templars should remain discreet, as if the future should be structured in part with his silence. He gathered knowledge forbidden by the triumphant Church, yet revealed himself to history as an uncultured prince who was incapable of thinking for himself. He conquered whole kingdoms and, with a synarchic sense that went against all ruling ideals of the day, chose not to assimilate them into an expanding kingdom, but instead to fight for the preservation of their characteristics. This worked toward his attempt to establish a community of states united by an exclusive synarchic messianism, the potential tranquillity of which was broken by his will and testament; for in it he ignored the precariousness of this unity and divided these states among his sons, perhaps aware that the unity he had forged was the exclusive fulfillment of his own plan, one not to be maintained by any other.

Curiously, all these clues coincide with a vague Templar ideology obsessed by the political and religious unification of a meta-Christianity that not even the Church or the other great Mediterranean belief systems seemed disposed to take on. From this time forward, the Templars did not have the cards that would carry their plan to success, that would make for the triumph of their ideology. From here their task would be discreetly to find someone capable of realizing their great enterprise. To this end, the Order saw to it that documentation would not go beyond titles, donations, loans, transactions, disputes, and the like. The fulfillment of its ideology would be seen only when the work was near to being accomplished.

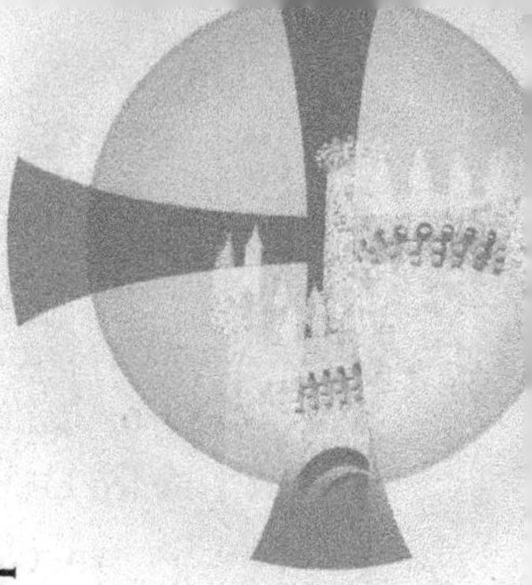

7
Twilight of the Idols

If we look at only known historical data, ignoring suppositions that advance or push back foundational Templar dates, the Order was born in 1118 and it was made official in 1128. On October 13, 1307, the French Templars were captured, in 1312 the Order was suspended, and in 1314 its grand master Jacques de Molay was burned alive on the Island of the Jews. The Templar order lived between 176 and 197 years, which means that midpoint between its rise and decadence can be fixed on the year 1216. This is the year in which Pope Innocent III died and Domingo Guzmán saw the confirmation of the Rule that signified the birth of the Dominican order. It was also the year in which the Templars agreed to present to the world their disciple, the king they educated to fulfill their plan—James I, the Conqueror—and the year in which Genghis Khan crossed the Hoang-Ho River on his way south.

Special interest groups, just like empires and peoples, are born; grow; and reach their vital, ideological maturity, where they remain for a relatively short time; then enter an unavoidable twilight until they disappear and fall into oblivion, fulfilling the inexorable cyclical laws of history. History is, of course, made and lived by humanity, and its laws are the immediate consequence of the behavior of those who establish themselves among individuals and groups as the interests defended by groups concur or collide.

The Twenty-Five Decisive Years

We need simply to review what occurred between 1214 and 1240 to realize the accumulation of factors that contributed, on the one hand, to marking the zenith of the Templar order, and on the other hand, to forming the clues to its decline and disappearance. Let us travel through these years together.

1214: James I is taken to Monzón in the middle of the crusades against the Occitan Cathars. Barely six years old, his Templar initiation begins. This is the year of the death of Alfonso VIII of Castile and Fernando III's rise to the throne when he too was a boy. The Templar order holds firm reins over the crown of Aragon when it is confronted with the power struggle between Prince Sancho, who is inclined toward Catharism, and Prince Ferrán, who is committed to strict orthodoxy. This very year, for defending those who killed Pedro II in Muret, Raymond IV of Toulouse bows to the will of the pope and accepts the penitence imposed on him. Innocent III hands over Toulouse to Simon de Montfort.

1215: The Fourth Council of Lateran announces new repressions against heresy, while Frederick II Staufen, still a friend of the Templars, triumphs in Germany and confronts pontifical authority. Innocent III considers him the Antichrist. This same year, Genghis Khan commences his unstoppable ascent by taking over Peking.

1216: Pope Innocent III dies and is succeeded by Honorius III. The first acts of the new pope are the confirmation of the Dominican order and the preaching of the Fifth Crusade, in which he intends to involve Frederick II in order to check the emperor's desire for power in the territories the Holy See considers its own. The Dominicans embark on an extensive campaign of forced conversions in Occitania, backed by the Church's Cathar repression.

Numerous Cathars take refuge in Templar houses and in the Hospital at Langedoc. Genghis Khan starts on the road to the West.

1217: Raymond VI of Toulouse wins back his estates from the Crusaders, though the Fifth Crusade fails emphatically in Damietta and in Mount Tabor. In the assembly in Monzón, the exit of James I and his precocious ascension to royal duties is decided. The monarch is eight years old and the Templars are collectively on his side. The Portuguese Templars continue their campaign of territorial conquest and take over Alcácer do Sal. Fernando III of Castile begins his rule.

1218: For the first time, the Leonese Templars of Ponferrada engage in disputes over lands with the monks of San Pedro de Montes. Simon de Montfort dies in Toulouse. In this year, pious tradition says Our Lady appeared to both Pedro Nolasco and the boy-king James I. It marks the founding of the Order of Mercy and is the second Marian apparition in the life of James I (the first being the Virgen de la Alegría at Monzón).

1219: The Grand Master of the Templar order, Guillaume de Chartres, dies from the plague in front of Damietta. He is succeeded by the master of Aragon and Catalonia, Pere de Montagut, who keeps the Order exempt from the jurisdiction of the king of Jerusalem. The king of France, Louis VIII, organizes a new campaign against the Cathars with Crusaders from the north. St. Francis travels to Egypt and neighboring Islamic realms, where he learns the mystical techniques of the Egyptian Sufis, spiritual heirs of the Christian hermits of the first centuries. The Mongols continue their advance through the Valley of Tarim, forcing great migration toward the West.

1220: Frederick II crowns himself emperor and temporarily allies himself with Rome against the Cathar heresy. The Leonese Templars continue their disputing, this time in Zamora against the Order of Santiago (the Order of St. James, or the santiaguistas). The dispute becomes so tense that the intervention of Pope Honorius is necessary. He declares himself in favor of the santiaguistas. At the same time there occurs the supposed apparition of the Templar Virgen de la Encina in Ponferrada, which awakens Marian devotion in Bierzo. Retreating from the Mongol advance, the Ottoman Turks appear in the lands of the high Euphrates.

1221: The provincial Templar master in Aragon, Guillén d'Azylac, travels to Agreda with James I (who is now seventeen years old) to retrieve the monarch's fiancée, Leonor of Castile. Fernando III begins construction of the Burgos Cathedral. St. Domingo de Guzmán dies. Damietta is once again lost and Robert de Courtenay becomes the first Latin emperor of Constantinople. The last knights of Extremadura's Order of Montsfragüe ally themselves not to the Templars, as the Aragonese branch of the order did, but to the Order of Calatrava instead.

1222: King Andrew of Hungary, the future father-in-law of James I, who is as deserving of sanctity as his holy daughter Isabel, shores up his kingdom with the Gold Bull, which allows him personally to adjudicate the kingdoms of Bohemia and Moravia. Raymond VI dies in Toulouse and as a result, Catharism suffers a setback, despite the fact that the torch is passed to Raymond VI's son, Raymond VII. Frederick II establishes the University of Padua.

1223: Louis IX is in his boyhood and Frederick II launches an anti-Islamic crusade by conquering all of Sicily and jumping to the Maghreb. The Mongol advance continues through Russia with the conquering of the Crimean peninsula.

1224: The Franciscan expansion begins in England and on the Iberian Peninsula. The Templars of Segovia receive from the pope the reliquary with remnants of La Vera Cruz (the True Cross), accompanied by a donation title. Frederick II founds the University of Naples.

1225: Fernando III conquers Andújar with Templar assistance. Prince Louis takes charge of the Cathar crusade, which he then hands over to Amaury de Montfort, son of Simon, the first Crusader. St. Thomas Aquinas is born. Construction on the Cathedral of Toledo begins.

1226: Louis IX, the future saint, ascends the throne of France. The latest Cathar crusade comes to an end, but the Cathar repression continues. Raymond VII of Toulouse is excommunicated. St. Francis of Assisi dies. The Teutonic knights have their day in Prussia, called to the assistance of Conrad of Moravia. Honorius III does not recognize as a Crusade the efforts of Frederick II against the Mahgreb; instead, the pope urges Frederick to take on the confrontation as penance. The followers of St. Francis who have not been ordained explode onto the roads of Europe.

1227: Genghis Khan dies. Frederick II leaves for the promised Sixth Crusade (1228–29). Honorius III dies and Gregory IX is designated his successor. The Holy See proclaims itself the protector of the Franciscans—distinguishing them from the *fratichelli*—and urges them to study, which provides good results among the Dominicans at the European universities. Supported by the Templars, Guillén de Montcada and the viscount of Béarn bring a dispute before James I. Alfonso IX of León conquers Cáceres with Templar support. James I, receiving the first news of the Balearics and their potential for conquest, organizes a campaign there with the help of the Templars.

1228: James I undertakes his expedition to conquer Mallorca. Numerous Cathars join it, while in the Languedoc the peace of Toulouse is signed, which puts an end to the Cathar crusade, but not to the hunting of Cathars. Frederick II arrives in Syria and the military orders of the Holy Land gather to negotiate the *pactio secreta*, through which they declare that Emperor Frederick II will be king of the world if he manages to conquer Jerusalem.

1229: James I conquers the city of Mallorca. The 1228 Treaty of Toulouse is finalized with a treaty from Paris, which makes Raymond VII a vassal of France, and obtains his guarantees against the heresy. In the Holy Land, Frederick II and the Egyptian Muslims sign the Treaty of Jaffa, by which the emperor is to be called king of Jerusalem, though the city will never belong to him. Instead, the city, including the houses of military orders and convents, is the property of the Islamic authorities, although Christians will be allowed to visit freely the holy sites there. The Templar order loses its principal feudal domain as it continues its disputes with the Order of St. John. The Templars are outraged when it is confirmed that the emperor Frederick II not only engaged in a Crusade, but also established agreements that, for legitimacy, should have been signed with Baghdad instead of Egypt. Without the acquiescence of the Templars, Frederick crowns himself king of Jerusalem. The Templar order manufactures a legend regarding this coronation: Angels appeared from the sky and took from the patriarch of the Holy City the relic of the Lignum Crucis that he carried around his neck as a sign of his rank. The University of Salamanca is founded.

1230: The Hanseatic League is founded, promoted by the Teutonic Knights, with the intention of slowing down the growing importance of the Genoese, Pisan, and Templar fleets. At this time the Templars keep important ports in the Atlantic and on the Iberian Peninsula (La Rochelle, El Burgo in La Coruña, and important bases in Portugal). James I begins the division of Mallorcan territories; the Templar order receives enormous portions around Pollença and its port, as well as Alcudía's, plus an important house in the capital's Jewish quarter. The union of Castile and León is realized under the crown of Fernando III. The site of Montségur becomes a refuge to a great number of Cathars. (Its capture took place in 1244.)

1231: James I and Sancho the Strong become friendly and, out of mutual admiration, establish a treaty by which one is to become the heir of the other, depending on who lives longer. The master of the Templar order, Ramón Serra, captures Menorca for the crown of Aragón. The Teutonic master Hermann of Salza establishes a state for his order on the Slavic frontiers of Prussia.

1232: Pope Gregory IX officially establishes the Inquisition in Occitania, under the auspices of the Dominicans and apart from the bishops. James I legitimizes his firstborn, Alfonso, and names the Templars and the Hospitallers as his tutors. The organization of the Mallorcan Templars begins, as a state within a state. The construction of the Nazarite Alhambra begins. The Catalan grand master Pere de Montagut dies and his successor, Armand de Périgord, commences negotiations with the sultans of Damascus, with a view to breaking the treaties signed by Frederick II. In Extremadura, the Templars capture Trujillo, and in Portugal the conquests of the Bajo Guadiana and the Algarve continue. In Aragon, the Templars contribute to the conquest of Morella. Ramón Lull is born in Mallorca.

1233: The conquest of Peñíscola, Burriana, and Xivert is realized in the kingdom of Valencia, whose castle passes on to the Templars temporarily. At the home of the Templar order, the total conquest of the kingdom is projected. Sancho the Strong of Navarre dies and is succeeded by the crusader Teobald I. Fernando III takes over Úbeda with the help of the Templars and other military orders. Medellín is captured.

1234: James I and Violante of Hungary are wed. In Portugal, Aljustel is conquered.

1235: Córdoba is conquered by Fernando III. Donation of a house in Córdoba is made to the Templars. With the conquest of Faro by the Templars in Portugal, the Order reaches the southernmost point of the kingdom; it becomes its second most important seat. Ibiza is conquered.

1236: The Almohavids retire from the Peninsula. The domains of the Teutonic Knights advance to the Vistula River.

1237: Fernando III grants high privileges to the Templar order. In the campaign to conquer Valencia, the Templars form the garrison of Puig de Seba, the future Puig de Santa María, where an apparition of Our Lady is seen. Frederick II sees to the election of Conrad as king of Germany.

1238: The city of Valencia is conquered. The Templars receive the poor outskirts of Ruzafa and the tower of Barbazacher, where the Order installs its house. Pope Gregory IX sends a letter to the Templars in which he reproaches them for their doctrinal carelessness.

1239: There is much preaching on the Sixth Crusade. Teobald of Navarre joins it and drives the Templars from his kingdom. Afterward, he still has disputes with the Templars for not following his strategic counsels. Frederick II is excommunicated for attacking the papal states.

1240: Teobald I returns from the Sixth Crusade. Murcia is conquered by Aragon. Castile begins an active collaboration of the Aragonese and Castilian Templars.

Those of Lime and Those of Sand

Let us carefully examine the data we have just outlined. Some information directly concerns the Order of the Temple, while other facts, at least in appearance, do not. Yet they all constitute a European historical panorama that could potentially account for a long-term influence on the Templars as well as the development and outcome of their enterprise. The Templars' own efforts toward the fulfillment of their plan are altogether separate from the circumstances that came together to prevent it. Some historical circumstances were the result of the Templars' own attitude; others were completely foreign to them but promoted events that would spoil their hopes and eventually threaten the very survival of the Order.

With regard to what directly concerns the Templar order, let us say that these years were probably the ones that witnessed their peak as an influential political and economic collective. They had in their hands, at least unofficially, a very important part of Europe's destiny. They had reached an economic power that made them superior as a group to any of the states in which they had settled, and some of these entities for a time entrusted the care of their finances to the Templars. They had educated at least one monarch—James I, the Conqueror—according to their values and the image of the political plan they had conceived. With an eye to total control, they partially controlled the strategy that, in theory, would lead to the conquest of the Jerusalemite Axis Mundi, the nucleus of their great synarchic enterprise. They maintained officious but very solid relations with qualified representatives of the great Mediterranean religions, who came to consider the Templars the firmest speakers to a mutual understanding that constituted the basis for that union on which would be built the dream of a universal theocratic government. As if that was not enough, the Templars promoted, however silently, the development or at least the survival of condemned forms of Christianity, which theoretically could presume the birth of a Church with different political as well as theological attitudes, a Church capable of embarking on the syncretic path for which the Knights yearned. In this manner they hid as well as they could many of the Cathar Perfects from the persecution to which the newborn Dominican order subjected them, helping them to cross the border of the Pyrenees and allowing them to hide in territories such as the Maestrazgo, which was practically dominated by the Templar order. In addition, the Knights opened new routes to new lands, such as Mallorca and the Balearics, in which the Cathars could live discreetly in relative peace, sheltered from the claws of an Inquisition that had been created precisely to finish off them and their beliefs and which was already starting to carefully snoop into the complexities of the Templar order.

As the obsessed owners and confirmed seekers of places long marked by sacred tradition, the Templars knew they were to be the ideal arbiters to channel certain religious tendencies that throughout history had been the triggers of the impulses to inspire essential changes in human events. For these places they created very special cults, such as the Christian representations of the Great Mother, or fomented others that the official Church had systematically hidden since it had become owner and mistress of beliefs in the West. And although they always proved themselves to be the best defenders of the Christian faith recognized by Rome, they took that Christianity upon roads of syncretism that could bring about unity and understanding with other creeds when the occasion became favorable.

Naturally, it is logical to think that such an attitude could stir up jealousies, even if caused not by hard evidence, but by its exact opposite: the lack of concrete elements that would cause its authentic dimension to be guessed at and foreseen. It is certain that the Templar order always maintained such a discreet attitude about its own organization that it often aroused curiosity regarding what it could be hiding.

If unsatisfied, curiosity immediately provokes distrust and even fear of what might lie beyond the obvious. If this fear is personified—as occurred centuries later with Freemasonry and other secret societies—it could lead to the desire to destroy what is unknown or, at least, to the conviction that what is ignored is essentially malignant and dangerous to the survival or stability of the society as a whole. The purpose of this book is not to judge whether the Templars' attitude and their long-range plan were good or bad with regard to the well-being of the world in which they emerged. But if that project had come to fruition, much of the medieval spirit would have had to violently transform itself, destroying institutions and attitudes that were far from the Templars' ideology and vision. And this, however wrapped in the fog of ignorance, is what the powers at the time began to suspect. Little by little, they started to see in the Templar order if not a clear and overwhelming threat, then a group attempting to impose criteria that did not always agree with the plans of that medieval world—a world that was structured on beliefs and principles that were hardly flexible to Templar ideology.

But in that precise instant of Templar ascendency, another factor was at work that both marked the zenith of the Order's power and announced the beginning of its twilight. To those wielding power, it imparts pride in authority and the conviction that nothing or no one can stand in the way on the path that leads inexorably to a proposed objective. Additionally, those in power are gripped by the conviction that they stand above good and evil and that the power they have acquired allows them attitudes and behaviors they would never consent to for others. I suppose we could call this wielding of power the sin of pride, which the Church has constantly used and abused as much when it condemns it as when it exerts it. But the Templar order also certainly fell into this trap of pride, and this could well be the reason why it was hurled into a premature decline, frequently failing in the very principles on which it had been created, both exoterically and esoterically.

The Nefarious Sin of Pride

Within this specific period of time marking the height of Templar power and influence, most telling are the years in which the balance begins to waver before moving to the side of the Order's decline.

In the conquest of Valencia in 1238, the Templars played a decisive role, complemented by the earlier success in the conquest of Faro, in Portugal, in 1236, which nearly completed the expansion of this peninsular kingdom and provided the Templars with one of their most significant enclaves: the southwestern point of the Peninsula, and the fortress of Sagres* at the far end of Cape San Vincente. In addition, two years before the conquest of Valencia, the Templars had actively collaborated with Fernando III of Castile in the conquest of Córdoba and in 1237 had obtained from the saintly king a general privilege that placed the Order over others with respect to rights and privileges from

*The Knights of Christ, successors to the Templars, established a nautical school in Sagres. Recruited for the institution were a number of well-known Jewish cartographers (many of them Mallorcan), who were experts in the design of nautical maps.

the Crown. The 1238 letter of reproachment from Pope Gregory IX, sent the same year in which Valencia was conquered, seemed to deny, or at least minimize, the Templars' efforts. According to the Holy See's criteria, the sights of the Templar should have been on their original enclaves in the Holy Land and not in the countries of the Occident, where occasionally their influence began to acquire an eminently political tone in which the papacy likely found itself marginalized, though never officially.

It is probable that this fact contributed to activating Templar intentions as well as being the instigation of the events that followed. The first of these events was the rushed organization of Teobald I's expedition to the Holy Land, which ended in colossal failure because of the difference in strategic philosophy between the Navarrese monarch and the Templars' military leadership, which undoubtedly wanted to demonstrate at all costs that the organizational spirit of the Crusade was its personal prerogative and that its own objectives should prevail over any attribution that some recently arrived upstart would want to take for himself. In good part, this must have been the first cause of the Templars' break with Emperor Frederick, and also, as we will see, the cause that distanced the Templars from France's Louis IX when he once more decided to take on the conquest of the holy sites.

On the Peninsula, the Templars actively collaborated in the conquest of the Moorish kingdom of Murcia, which was undertaken jointly by Aragon and Castile, although with the understanding that the conquered territory would form part of the Castilian crown, given that James I, through the treaty signed in Almizra, recognized that his campaigns of conquest ended with the kingdom of Valencia. It was in Murcia, specifically in the plaza of Caravaca, where the Templars would establish their last great military and ideological redoubt, given its position on the Muslim frontier. By immediately occupying it, the Order could make it a very powerful center of religious syncretism, through the cult established to its Lignum Crucis, which went on to become a paradigm of some popular devotions that were linked to the firmest beliefs of the region's pre-Christian ancestors, worshippers,

Fig. 7.1. Caravaca de la Cruz, where the Templars installed the most important of their Ligni Crucis

and invokers of the earth's fertility.[1] If we add to this the supposition that the cross was transported from Jerusalem, after having supposedly disappeared from the neck of the Holy City's patriarch while he proceeded with the crowning of Frederick II (contrary to Templar intentions and interests), we can see how the Order went on to ruin the subtle ideological weave that, according to their intentions, would make up their grand objective: to unify allegedly supernatural events that could contribute to the consolidation of their prestige and the view that the Order was in charge of designing some great synarchic future.

Naturally, Templar pride and the Order's decision to accelerate the solution before the implementation of its own synarchic project did not end there. They had at their disposal an important figure whom they created and in whom they had deposited their trust and hope of reaching their goal's first steps. James I, still at the top of his game as king and warrior, and having fulfilled his particular Reconquista, could be the engine of a new Crusade, which could fulfill the ideology forged by the Order and finally achieve the goals that had not been reached by those who preceded the Templars. Thus the first (though failed) attempt of James I's crusade took place as the martyrdom of Catharism and the end of the Occitan dream occurred with the tragic fall of Montségur in 1244. The Catalan-Aragonese monarch, the designated king of the world promoted by the Templars, cheerfully faced the warnings and threats of Pope Innocent IV and prepared a crusading expedition that would never take place—not out of respect for the pontiff's wishes, but because the elements were against the king and his forces, preventing the fleet from sailing out to sea. Interestingly, it was a fleet that, like the one that reconquered Mallorca, counted among its crew a number of Cathar fugitives.

The Templars were faced with a dilemma: Either support the Aragonese king in an enterprise vetoed by Rome—and thus be forever marked as disobedient—or acquiesce to the pressures from Rome and join the enterprises that had won the pontiff's blessing. Surely, this dilemma and their eventual choice were the impetus behind their active collaboration with the Seventh Crusade, spearheaded by Louis IX. Ultimately, the Order put all of its fleet at the disposal of the French monarch after a deposit of royal treasure in the Templar coffers. Once more, however, the strategic harmony between the Templars and the Crusaders was broken, provoked by the 1250 disaster at Mansurah, which resulted in the death of Grand Master Guillaume de Sonnac and the imprisonment of St. Louis, for whom the Templars reluctantly paid a high ransom (which they charged to the Templar-administered French royal coffers). Curiously, this operation was carried out at a moment when the Templars lacked a grand master; Sonnac had recently died in battle and the chapter in charge of looking for his successor had not yet been convoked. The ransom payment was made during this interregnum and against usual Templar practices, which forbade acceding to any type of rescue. Marshal Reynaud de Vichiers was immediately named grand master by the chapter gathered at San Juan de Acre, and he in turn named Hugues de Jouy as marshal of the Order.* Hugues had been the firmest opponent of the royal rescue, even though the one being saved was Louis IX and the ransom was charged to the monies deposited by the French crown into the coffers of the Templar order so that it might act as its custodians and administrators.

Louis IX had barely been freed when he heard of the vicissitudes suffered by the Templars in the negotiations for his freedom. This put him on his guard against the Order. He no longer depended on it for anything, and he initiated contacts with the Sunni Muslims of Egypt—just as Frederick II had done in his day—to obtain the return of the prisoners of Damietta and Mansurah. In the meantime, the new Templar grand master, Arnaud de Viciers, following the tradition of good relations maintained by the Templars and the Shiites, began negotiations with the Muslims of Damascus in an attempt to create a peace that would be favorable to their future projects. These formalities were carried out through Marshal Hugues de Jouy, to whom the Shiites felt more disposed than did the orthodox Egyptian Sunnis.

St. Louis, however, considered these maneuvers a betrayal of the spirit of his crusade and to his unwavering orthodox Christian perspective. Thus he forced the Templars to break off the talks, with the excuse that he had not been informed that they were being held. The Templars had no choice but to side with the will of the French king. Marshal Hugues de Jouy was immediately removed from the Holy Land—and was named master of the Catalan-Aragonese province, where he was warmly received by James I, who, two years earlier, at the height of his fidelity to the Order, had made the formal promise to place his next male child in the Templar militia.

Fissures and Cracks

Having concluded the campaigns of conquest under the crown of Aragon, the Templars possessed so many houses, bailiwicks, encomiendas,

*The rank of marshal included the custody and administration of the goods of the house or of the Temple.

and donations in that territory that a member of the Order could cross the entire kingdom and sleep in his own house each night.[2] With the Castilian expansion having been completed under Alfonso X, the Wise, with only the kingdom of Granada remaining as a vassal state of the Christians, the Templar order was thus established in the territory of Castile-León. Although it had to share its privileges as a military order with the native orders created in its likeness—Santiago, Calatrava, and Alcántara—the Templar order maintained an ample range of influence that made it owner of important possessions extending to the north of the Tajo and the Central System, in Extremadura and Andalucía. The region of La Mancha was left largely in the hands of the native orders and the Sanjuanistas, who would accumulate their most important *latifundios* (large estates or landholdings) there. Concerning the Portuguese kingdom, the Templars were in fact the arbiters of its politics and exerted influence there as actively as in the Catalan-Aragonese kingdom, although in Portugal their fundamental goal was to keep control over the Atlantic ports, with an eye to a future that documents have always preferred to ignore, but that evidence clearly proclaims: a trans-oceanic synarchic expansion, once the theocratic project of the Great Mediterranean States had been concluded.

There is no doubt that the Templar order had reached a certain height of power, although it harbored aspirations to other, more ambitious goals. In fact, of the four peninsular kingdoms, it held firm influence over two, and in the other two it controlled enough possessions to be able to raise its representation quotas when it was to their advantage to do so. For this reason, it maintained good relations with the rulers of these kingdoms, although the two that were not clearly under Templar influence tried to keep from falling into a situation that would force them to depend on the Order's criteria much more than seemed prudent.

At this point we can recall an episode that has been widely known since the discovery of the document in which it was originally recounted as part of the trial of the Templars in Castile:[3] Alfonso X was curious about what was happening behind the closed doors of the Templar houses. To find out, he had one of his most faithful servants enter the Order. After a year the king summoned this man to appear before him, but the infiltrator, being afraid, told the monarch he preferred death to speaking of what he had seen in the houses of the Templars. All wild imaginings aside, there is no doubt that the Templar order raised suspicions because of the secretiveness and unmanifested intentions it may well have displayed. This awoke jealousies and, at least in Castille, led to a tolerance of the Templars that was marked by hidden reservations. This ensured that native orders enjoyed private royal favor at the same time as the Crown was publicly hailing the merits of the Templars.

Although there are not many accounts such as this in the fairly thin Castilian documentation referring to the Templars, it constitutes an example because of the worries it aroused and because it points to a kind of behavior that is a common distinguishing feature of any group assigning itself high political aims. The members of these groups meddle in public life as a single-minded entity and allow themselves to be known as an active and even indispensable presence. Yet although they are involved in important public and governmental affairs, they try at the same time to preserve their privacy. They never reveal what transpires behind the walls of their sees, and thus never reveal the true intentions of their behavior.

Another important factor was at play at the moment when Templar power began to show fissures that ominously foretold the Order's twilight. The Templar order, an organization born in the Holy Land as a fruit of the originating spirit of the Crusades, justified its power and its insatiable economic ambitions by the necessity of gathering the most means for supporting a struggle in the Middle East that circumstances were proving was unsustainable. Early on, the Roman papacy had distorted the intention of the Crusades and had begun to make use of the thaumaturgic word for some ends that had nothing to do with its original meaning. From 1202 to 1204, the Fourth Crusade gorged itself violently on the Byzantine Christians. In 1208 a crusade was launched against the Languedoc that did not make even subtle distinctions between the heretical Cathars and the Catholic faithful in those territories. For his part, Pope Innocent III, promoter of the imitation crusade against the Cathars, threatened Frederick II and any other sovereign who dared to think outside the margins of the Vatican's desires. In 1252, a crusade against the kingdom of Sicily was once again being preached.[4]

The word *crusade* had lost its original meaning and had become simply a weapon in the hands of the pontiff on duty. The pope could brandish it as a formal threat against those who did not fall in line with the orders emanating from Rome and who showed themselves unruly toward the papacy's designs. Overall, Europe began to grasp how ridiculous this was, and the Templar order, as a qualified representative of the spirit that it bore more than a hundred years before the first expedition to the East, suffered the consequences of this shift in the popular mood. The Templars became victims of the doubts that were being generated about the authenticity of the word *crusade,* a term the Order had used as a battle cry to justify its power, its influence, and, above all, its accumulation of holdings that, at least officially, were intended for the maintenance of a situation some considered lost.

During their unstoppable ascent, the Templars had been able to maintain themselves at the margin of semantics by living together as a monastic entity. The Order's Rule forbade them to fight against Christians, and to the displeasure of the pope, who could not twist such a consistent code, they managed to face undaunted the violence of the Cathar crusade without participating in it.[5] Similarly, without active involvement, they passively collaborated to ensure that the Portuguese state was able to maintain its integrity against the kingdom of León. This freed Alfonso Enriquez from the necessity of intervening in the civil conflict, which would have been a distraction for his forces and prevented him from taking the leading role in the fight against Islam. The Templars' stand gave him the support he needed until the Portuguese kingdom obtained its independence.*

---

*Campomanes, *Dissertaciones:* ". . . due to their possessions being a type of fief, they lent their military services, which is what the rest of the orders in the land did in case of invasions, even if they were from Christian princes."

As the Western Templars reached the summit of their influence, the synarchic dream, although it had not disappeared from Templar ideology, was merely fueling an ambition for more power and prestige. With the failure of the plan they had constructed around Frederick II and the enterprise they forged for James I, with the obvious ill will of St. Louis of France and the pope's loud protestations regarding the Order's lack of commitment to the whims of the Holy See, the Templars largely succumbed to a more immediate ambition for power and began to exert the influence they had amassed to their personal benefit rather than toward the goal of their universal synarchic vision.[6]

Ramón and the Real World of *The Blanquerna*

Ramón Lull was probably one of the most distinguished intellectual personalities of the European Middle Ages. Though he was popularly considered to be a saint in his Mallorcan homeland, the Church always found sufficient motives not to accept his official canonization. He was regarded as a sage by the open-minded of Europe, but official science has always found reasons to cast doubt on his knowledge and place him in the obscure heap of pseudoscientists who have always been looked upon with suspicion by academics. In any case, Lull was a curious and original sample of what knowledge can manage to obtain in the field of belief. He was a mystic scientist and, as much as possible, a thinker capable of transcending his time and the desires of his contemporaries and of glimpsing truth at each moment, beyond circumstances that impose partial truths, which merely serve to mend errors rather than work toward building new structures and visions of reality.

Lull had thrown together in *The Blanquerna** the archetype of a new human being: a seeker of a truth without conveniences, an aspirant to integrity, and an example of a new conscience based on the chivalrous idea—inspired by the Grail—of constructing a more lucid mental-

*This refers to *The Book of Blanquerna,* by the Mallorcan laic theologian and philosopher Ramón Lull, which speaks, among other things, of the practices of elementary and secondary education in medieval Spain.

ity that could be assumed by the human genus in its totality. Examining the Lullian *Blanquerna* today shows what Templar ideology might have been originally. It is more than probable that Lull himself would see it this way, after the discussions he had with the Templars in Cyprus, where the Templars had been transferred after having been thrown out of the Holy Land. Lull was forced to stay there under the care of the brothers because of a disease that kept him from embarking on his planned expedition to the interior of Asia. In Cyprus, as he tells us, he had the opportunity to converse openly with the last of the Templars' grand masters, Jacques de Molay. It is likely that what emerged from these talks was the complete vision that Lull would never abandon. Interestingly, this plan has convinced many scholars to declare him a sworn enemy of the Templar order—of its goals and its very structure.

Lull's stay in Cyprus dates from 1302 and his project was published in 1309, several years after the French Templars had been imprisoned and subjected to trial by the Inquisitorial powers. Curiously, however, Lull expounded his idea as if the Templar persecution had not occurred. He ignored the trial, asked for the convocation of a council that was already convoked, and pointed to the advisability of having the Order suspended when in fact the suppression had been decreed and the Council of Vienne's verdict was an open secret. It is not, however, the circumstances that we are interested in uncovering, but, instead, where possible, the idea that Lull proposed: a unique military Order, which he called "of the Holy Spirit" when he did not simply call it the Order.

Lull's *Libro sobre la recuperation de Tierra Santa* (Book on the Recuperation of the Holy Land)[7] is, in reality, a systematization of a suggestion made to the Franciscan pope Nicolas IV in 1292, in which Lull proposed something that had already been laid out: the unification of all the existing military orders (he cited only five, although there were others) into one group that might be called the Order of the Holy Spirit.[8] Later, for a period of some years, until the convocation of the Council of Vienne, this idea flourished in his mind and and even suggested to him the advisability of the Templar order's suppression.

One distinguishing feature of Lull's thought, expressed in the pages of his *Blanquerna,* is his formal rejection of an atomization of ideals that could only lead to petty quarrels and rivalries and struggles for influence, while the pure idea of *milicia* (militia), with the transcendent meaning he gave the word, presupposed a solidarity marked by shared goals and a unique ideological approach capable of unifying all the different tendencies that might arise in the search for an ideal. Lull knew that the losses of the holy sites in Jerusalem and with them, the possibility of accessing the Jerusalem's Axis Mundi, was due not only to the unstoppable push of the Islamic hordes (of which he was fully aware), but also to the lack of a unified set of criteria that could have coordinated all the efforts in the East and directed them, with a unique ideology, to a proposed end.

But Lull knew—or intuited—something else: The traditional synarchic state the Templars were trying to promote could not be born from the armed and vigilant class represented by the Templar order. Instead it had to originate from a superior spiritual authority that gathered the unifying requirements necessary to be universally recognized. It was this authority that would be in charge of creating high-minded militias intended to safeguard the fundamental essence of the ideology governing the community. This synarchy would develop exactly opposite from the plan the Templars proposed: According to the Templar scheme, the militia would have to conquer and preserve the Axis Mundi over which the supreme unifying hierarchy of the theocratic ideology would sit; then, an authority would have to be found or fabricated to be universally recognized. The military element would always necessarily find itself on a higher level than that of the supposedly supreme authority that had created and would hold decisive power. In this way, the fundamental essence of the synarchic idea would be lost. In actuality, the class in charge of vigilance should be a mere instrument of the superior authority that ruled the whole system.

The unification of military orders assumed the dispersion of the synarchic concept, for it was in fact present in all of these Orders, but only the Templars had seriously appropriated and proposed this idea. But at

Fig. 7.2. For many, the Cathedral of Palma de Mallorca was a Templar inspiration. In the foreground is the monument to the great Ramón Lull, who advocated for the Order's dissolution.

the same time, such unification represented another danger: an excess of immediate power that might turn the resulting single order into the arbiter of the destinies of the kingdoms in which it would be installed. In practice, it would be placed throughout Europe and the remote Christian enclaves remaining in the Holy Land. Curiously, James I of Aragon, a sovereign decidedly committed to the Templars and their ideology, declared himself against this unifying plan when it was proposed at the Council of Lyon in 1274. He alleged that such a union—which was by then reduced to the Templar and the Hospitaller orders—represented a problematic accumulation of power for the states in which both orders were already established.

The Awareness of Failure

An institution—political party, church, brotherhood, or sect—will always rise to certain quotas of power and prestige that place it on top:

then, once in such a postion, the group's foundational ideology becomes contaminated with the virus of that power. Original hopes fester, corroding the basic principles that constituted the structure in which the group had grown (and that permitted its growth). There is no longer a place for those claiming to preserve the sacred flame of that first founding impulse. If the Templar order, as a majority of historians claim, emphasized its origins as defending the holy sites, the loss of these sites made its existence obsolete. If, as we dare to believe, the Order originated with a wider and more complex ideal—the radical transformation of the political and religious structures of the medieval world—that ideal became contaminated by the Order's tremendous economic power, which was at that time, just as economic power is now, the only means capable of preying on any ideal in the interest of the immediate benefits that the forces of monies confer.

The Templar order had within its Rule, as it did later in its constitutions, a principle of personal poverty, which—as has been the case for all religious institutions throughout history—did not require that such poverty extend to the Order itself. Most, however, will admit and recognize that a wealthy society cannot exist with solemnly poor members and that it is very difficult, if not impossible, that a group's wealth will not benefit or somehow reach each and every one of those who make up that collective entity.

This saturation and dissemination of wealth must lead to the group's unrelenting defense of its acquired properties, and this defense leads, consequently, to the loss or forgetting of the ideology that originally compelled the formation of the group. Of course, the voices of those not yet contaminated might emerge, although it is difficult for such voices, even if they scream, to be heard beyond the walls guarding the collective's privacy. If they are heard, or if in the passing of years or centuries, we manage to recognize one of those screams, it may be possible for us to glimpse the radical abysses that separated the origins of an ideology from the nefarious consequences that resulted from its unstoppable ascent to the highest power.

In the aftermath of the Templars' road to degradation, we have been left the task of clarifying facts about the loss of their purpose as well as of making sense of the documented proof of what the Order planned to be and what it ended up becoming.

Much clarification can be found in documents that are most numerous in the Catalan-Aragonese archives. These tell us how the Templar order, in flagrant violation of its principles, fought with and showed no mercy to those who dared cast doubt on their land rights and their authority over peoples that had been donated to them both by the fervent devotees of the Order and by royal favor.[9] One such dispute took place in the lands of the valley of the Ebro River with the powerful Entenza family, resulting in the obliteration of whole villages, the killing of people, the taking of hostages, the destruction of crops, and the fierce fighting for the right of way to the river, which produced great benefits for whoever held it.

To balance this we find, not on the Peninsula but in the Holy Land, the almost desperate nostalgia for a failed and unrecoverable ideal in the 1265 poem "Ira et Dolor" (Anger and Pain), by the Templar poet Rigaud Bonomel, called Olivier the Templar:[10]

Ya ni la cruz ni la fe me socorren ni protegen
contra los infieles; a quienes Dios maldiga.
Mas parece que Dios mismo desee
ayudarles a ellos, para nuestra perdicion

(Already neither the cross nor faith helps or protects me
against the infidels; God curse them.
It seems more like God himself desires
to help them, to our perdition.)

This protest, directed at God himself, extends as a complaint against the maximum authority of the Church. By blaming it for the world's ills—which for the poet are the ills of the Templar order—the Church becomes the object of censure parallel to the one the Protestants advanced centuries later, at the hour when they parted ways with papal power and the institution of the papacy to form a new branch of militant Christianity:

> *. . . los clérigos venden a Dios y las indulgencias*
> *por dinero contante . . .* [11]
>
> (. . . the clerics sell God and the indulgences
> for hard cash . . .)

"Ira et Dolor" not only complains; it goes on the attack as well. And as it searches for those who are responsible, it discloses at least partially the ideology that the Templar order tried to keep hidden by always proclaiming itself a faithful child of the Church. In reality, it was trying to transform its structures of obedience into a plan that the Inquisition's Cerberuses already had in the crosshairs of divine justice. For the authorities of the Inquisition, neither the Church nor its authorities could be mistaken regarding the established paths to be followed by the faithful. Those Dominicans knew very well and remembered at all times that the Templars had protected the Jews of the *aljamas,* had respected the beliefs of the Moors who labored in their lands, and had taken in and continued to take into their houses the Albigensians who were about to be trapped by the long arm of the law that represented the Holy See.

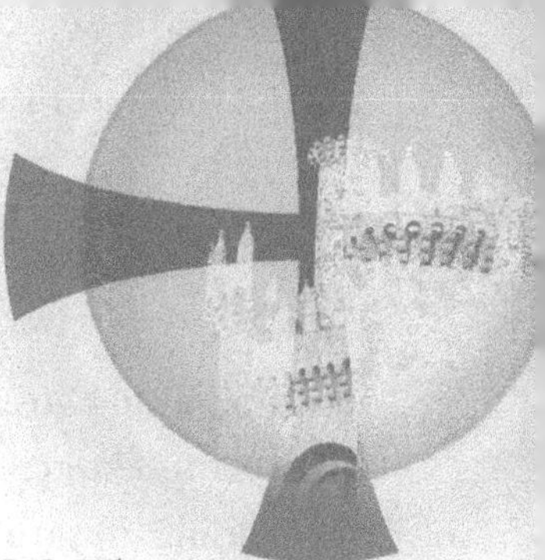

8

The Fall of the Clay Colossus

Few events in the Middle Ages are as documented as the annihilation of the Templar order, and few events have inspired such speculation, despite—or maybe because of—so much existing documentation. In contradiction to those who unquestioningly accept the evidence of the sources, this great speculation and questioning have shown that these documents were subjective from the very moment they were created. We can see that these accounts display the intentions of those who committed them to justify a specific attitude or to defend reasoning.

If a donation title exists, it is because the person who created it—donor or recipient—desperately wanted this act to remain marked by the benefit that it produced, while the authentic reasons for its realization are left on the sidelines. If the testimony of a trial has remained, it is because those who initiated it wanted at all costs to leave behind proof of their particular sense of justice, with their supporting rationales left on the sidelines. If we find the litigation of a dispute, we will see nothing but the unwavering defense of the interests of the participants. A simple receipt is proof that a service or product had been properly paid for to the benefit of the person who made the payment. A will, whatever its character may be, will always contain the secret motives that led the testator to have it redacted in precisely those terms.

Europe and Spain Confront the Templar Order

In attempting to establish more or less valid conclusions about the Templars' extinction, the different causes that promoted the Order's demise are all thrown into one bag, which, although there was but one outcome, does not take into consideration that the kingdoms and territories constituting medieval Europe had nothing in common but their assumed radical Catholicism and that even this commonality manifested itself very differently in each one of the communities that played a part in Continental history. Even on the Iberian Peninsula, which seemed to offer a certain unity in the face of other European countries, the political situation was very different in each of its five kingdoms, four Christian and one Muslim. This Muslim kingdom of Andalusia had ceded all of its prerogatives in acknowledging its vassalage to Castile. Yet even here, everyone from the monarch to the least of his servants felt that the complete realization of its territorial apex was still pending. With its cycle of peninsular expansion complete, the crown of Aragon concentrated its sights on the Mediterranean lands, and Portugal, in the same situation, had begun dreaming, however vaguely, about what might lie beyond the waters of the Atlantic. For its part, Navarre, barely a political appendage of France, vacillated between a subjection from which it could not escape and its essential Iberian Basque identity, which culturally linked it more to the kingdoms west of the Pyrenees, though its monarchs barely considered it more than a rest resort of the French crown.

The peninsular Templar order had adopted certain duties based on the circumstances of the various kingdoms in which it was established. In the kingdom of Aragon, where it still clung to the enormous influence it had enjoyed during James I's reign and campaigns of conquest, the Order was determined to maintain its grip on its power and prerogatives, even though the immediate successors of the Conqueror—Pedro III, Alfonso III, and James II—considered it to be scarcely better than a freeloading, unemployed guest living off past glories. Moreover, because of the Order's position as a religious institution, it could only poorly serve Spain's kingdom's when the hour came to mount military ventures against other Christians. Despite this, there is testimony that the Templars—like the Hospitallers—acted more than once as a militia in service to the Crown's political interest.

In Portugal, the Templars had figured out how to recycle themselves as efficient administrators, and, in communion with the views of their sovereigns, they began to project their future expansion in the Atlantic through the promotion of their fleet and the use of the kingdom's ports, not to mention the study of overseas perspectives—especially African—which would start to bear fruit only after the official extinction of the Order and the creation of its (largely semantic) substitute, the Order of Christ, which would presume the permanence of the Templar spirit without directly continuing it.

In Castile, the Templar order continued its existence as a militia facing a potential but unlikely Islamic threat. Although committed to its duty of vigilant watch, it was short of reasons to justify its military role. Operations in the Holy Land had ceased and the Order's accumulation of properties and donations had been in serious decline for some time. The Templars also had serious rivals in the native regional military orders, which had always tried to obtain the lion's share when the time came to divide the spoils and were always seeking to increase their political influence over the region's sovereigns.

Concerning Navarre, its monarchs did little else in this land but use it as a training ground in order to rule more effectively on the other side of the Pyrenees. The Navarrese Templars, however, preserved up to the very end a special kind of freedom of action and a unique independence with regard to royal authority, which surely played a primary role in the Order's development of its particular ideological proposals. It did not propose restarting its venture from Navarre, but, keeping the profundity of its original esoteric values intact, instead taking advantage of the Templars' proximity to the route taken by the St. James pilgrims.

None of the peninsular kingdoms had real motives to rid itself of the Templar presence, whose function during the high points of the wars against Islam had been frequently decisive. But nor did any of them, except perhaps Portugal, have special reasons for defending the Templar presence. In contrast to the strictly monastic orders, to which could be conceded the benefit of an evangelizing role, without open war against peninsular Islam and sacred sites to guard in the Holy Land, the Templar order had few reasons for its continued existence, save for its hypothetical role as the consecrated militia in service to Rome, which did not satisfy anyone, no matter how much all proclaimed themselves faithful servants of pontifical authority.

The Conscience of the Templars

All of these political situations were, to varying degrees, posed in each one of the Christian kingdoms of the West in which the Templars had settled. The only entity that could see things from a different perspective was the papal state. The popes considered the extent to which their authority could be reinforced by relying—at least in theory—on a monastic militia subject to rules and vows that would allow it to defend its interests against any threat that might transpire in the bosom of Christendom. After having experienced more than a century and a half of Templarism, during which the brothers had exerted their force in the Orient and the Occident, the Church was conscious that the Order had maintained its obedience to the mandates of Rome by conditioning these orders to the interest and convictions of its own criteria, as could be verified by the Cathar crusade, which the Templars never considered as such and from which they abstained, despite the pressures Pope Innocent III and the whole clergy attempted to exert over them.

It remains to be seen—and this continues to be a mystery that the exhaustive research of documents has not been able to clear up—how aware the Templar Order was of its own role at the moment its persecution and destruction took place. To give ourselves an approximate idea, one that may never conform to reality, we must clearly distinguish between the goals of the external, public, historical Order and those it attempted to gain at levels higher than immediate reality, those it sought to attain but never managed to touch.

From a purely historical perspective, which sets aside their greatest hopes and visions, the Templars, spread throughout different lands, formed a coherent and unified group, a supranational entity centered on the Palestinian nucleus, to which were allocated all the benefits accumulated through financial operations and donations, war loot, and alms. The documents that make reference to this perception of the Order, written no doubt by Templar scribes, almost always also make reference to the Holy Land, for whose defense and maintenance all deliveries were officially made. This is significant in that it represents a constant subliminal call to that Axis Mundi from which would emanate, at the margin of exclusively orthodox Christian tradition, that beam of light that would illuminate a more wholesome humanity, including—according to the great and inconclusive enterprise of the Templars—Muslims and Jews as well as those Christians who had chosen rites, dogmas, and devotional forms different from those accepted by the "official" and "authentic" Roman Church.

The Holy Land, or the reduced zone it was increasingly becoming, constituted not only the great bank where the majority of the resources of the Order were deposited (in fact, there were serious complaints during the Reconquista that the Templars lacked the appropriate means for combat because so much had been exported to the Middle east), but also the place of Templar initiation where, as in other religious orders, those chosen for the highest positions in the organization would find themselves to, receive their "doctorate," as it were. In crucial moments of the Palestinian wars, and especially during those hopeless battles that ended the Christian domination of the land, we can detect the presence of the Catalan Templars, In the siege of Tripoli, for instance, we find Pere de Montcada,[1] a member of a family closely linked to the Catalan-Aragonese Templars,[2] who was provincial master between 1244 and 1255, and a son of the count of Ampurias, Friar Hugo. Both died during that siege.

With the loss of the Middle East holy sites as well as their strategic surroundings, the Templar order took refuge in Cyprus, where it ineffectively tried to form a Templar state much like the one the Teutonic Knights actually achieved in eastern Prussia and like that of the Hospitallers on the island of Rhodes. There it had to realize that its purpose had touched bottom. The petitions for more help to launch a new attempt at conquest of the Holy Land stumbled on the indifference and even the mistrust of the kings and others in power, who were the only ones with the means to support this impossible task. Although they still had access to their own powerful resources, the Templars knew it would be impossible to bring about success in the Middle East by relying solely on their own determination, not only because of the daunting nature of the task of recapturing the Holy Lands, but also because of the potential danger of destroying themselves in a vain effort; an attempted Middle East reconquest would bring about the death of the order through complete depletion of its liquid assets that no one would replace. Joining with other military orders was unthinkable; putting aside the Templars' traditional rivalry with the Hospitallers, any such union, even if achieved with the best guarantees, would automatically presuppose the loss of the Templar personality and the abandonment of their synarchic plan, which, although now impossible to achieve, formed part of the Templars' raison d'être.

This, then, is the intimate tragedy of the Templars: By desperately clinging to an ideology that theoretically overcame the conditioning imposed by their era, their survival was not viable, although, ironically, their ideology formed their sole purpose for existence. To abandon their vision, no matter how impossible its achievment had become, meant becoming a religious order *contra naturam;* because of its military character, despite the declarations of its last grand master, Jacques de Molay, in his 1303 letter to Clement V, the Order had no other purpose than to make war. This was in contrast to the Hospitallers of St. John, who could and did fulfill other commitments, which enabled this order to survive into the present, albeit under a new name.*

*In reality, the Hospitallers constituted the Order of Malta, dedicated at least officially to mercy acts, which didn't prevent it from maintaining an economic structure whose connections and complexities have not been studied in depth.

The Incredible Dawn of October 13

Another subject of endless debate, one that an abundance of existing documentation has not managed to clarify, is the synchronized arrest of the French Templars on the night of October 12 and 13, 1307. The strategy of King Philip IV required a long time to prepare, which casts serious doubt on the possibility that the Templars where caught off-guard and were unaware that their capture was imminent. But if this is how it actually played out, how could the Templars have waited passively to be arrested, without taking any steps to avoid capture by fleeing in search of refuge and safer locations? Only two answers are possible, but whenever more than one answer is possible, doubt prevents us from taking a stand that we prefer to be true.

The first answer is most likely to figure in a Templar internal history. The brothers had advance knowledge of the arrest, though did nothing to avoid it, being aware that their end was nothing but a consequence of the Order's own failed attempt to change the structures of a world that had turned hostile to them. They preferred to become martyrs to their own lost cause rather than to become obscure unknowns condemned to oblivion. There is no doubt that this idea of self-immolation is beautiful, something like the ending of a Greek tragedy or like an end that the Romantics of the nineteenth century envisioned and exalted. It has only one drawback as an explanation: The Order was a perfectly organized institution with clear communication throughout its ranks. This submissive posture was assumed by only the French Templars, while members of the Order in the rest of the kingdoms of Christendom—including Cypress, which took its last stand—had a very different reaction.

The second possible explanation: Despite the fact that for some time he had made no secret of his hostility toward the Templars and made a public display of his dislike of the Order when it suited his purposes, Philip IV, the Fair, prepared his action in absolute secrecy. To his delegates throughout the kingdom he sent sealed letters that most likely included instructions specifying that the seals not be broken and the

Fig. 8.1. The burning of the Knights Templar by the Inquisition

letters not opened until the time appointed for organizing and putting into action an uninterrupted operation. The Templars were thus caught by surprise and very few managed to escape. These may have received news of the arrests after they were in progress. The result was that almost all the Templar friars in France were the first of the Order to fall, without the pope knowing about it until sufficient time had passed, which meant he could not even claim jurisdiction over the prisoners, who had already confessed the sins of which they were accused, among them the most horrendous and abominable of the medieval repertoire.

There are those who assert that the abolition of the Order was one of the conditions that Philip IV imposed for his support of the papal candidacy of Clement V, with whom he spoke at least twice before that forceful strike. King James II of Aragon received letters from the French king that, without providing any indication of what actions to take, gave him notice of the nefarious and sacrilegious sins clouding the Order's reputation. To these comments, James II, who did not feel any great sympathy for the Templars because of their commitment to the permanently weak kingdom of Mallorca, nevertheless replied that he did not believe the Templars in his kingdoms could be party to the aberrations of which they were accused. It seems he reasserted this when he was visited by Esquieu Floriano, who was responsible for officiously planting suspicions and slander about the Templars. Not only did James II pay Floriano little heed, but also he let his visitor know how evil he found these calumnies. The reactions of the rest of the peninsular monarchs were in this sense very similar.

Given these facts, the real explanation is found somewhere between the two possibilities: The Templars saw and suspected the growing hostility that weighed over them in Europe, above all in France. They were very probably aware that the time was coming when it would be difficult or almost impossible for them to overcome this hatred. The end, in any event, was drawing near. Those they could see now actively working against them or those absorbed by passive indifference were many of the same parties in power that had earlier given them their unconditional support and had shared in their high-flown theocracy and work in the Holy Land. First and foremost among these was the pope in Rome, who would not lift his little finger for them now. Lacking any immediate objective but their own survival, condemned to an existence without any goals other than the overseas Portuguese enterprise, which had not matured sufficiently to become an alternative task, many members of the Templars had fallen asleep, lulled by their own inertia, or had reckoned with a present that had lost all perspective. They were merely attempting to save the position they had acquired, although they were at a loss as to what purpose this position now served.

In this situation, even in those places where the prestige of their heroic past still survived, the Templars had become increasingly ignorant as to what role they could play. We have already seen that they did not hesitate to take part in territorial squabbles and wars between Christian princes in the absence of any higher purpose. The last milestones, in Tyre, in Sidion, and in Acre, were those of martyrdom and not of victory. They did not even receive laurels for transcending defeat, for practically all of Christendom held them to blame for these losses, although no one had mobilized to intervene and stop them.

They now existed in a world that, in addition to no longer recognizing their merits, had begun to view them with anger or suspicion due to their reputation as sorcerers and occultists, which their enemies advanced with adverse propaganda. They were also accused of practices that most suspected were taking place in many monasteries and convents. In this milieu, the Templars, who depicted themselves as the purest of the pure, convinced of their own essential difference, prepared themselves—with varying degrees of enthusiasm—for the sacrifice in store for them. As time would bear out, this sacrifice made them martyrs to an ideal, and though the populace could not grasp this ideal, the Templars' demise would transform their destruction into a heroic sacrifice. In time, other groups, believing they had grasped the Order's true purpose, attempted to re-create this ideal, which emerged from the shadows of other secret societies.

Waiting for Decisions from Heaven

We should recall that, much like the great monastic orders did previously and like the minor orders did later, the Templar order enjoyed privileges that it may well have turned to its advantage throughout the course of its history. Among these was an absolute independence from lay clergy and bishops, although they did have to account to these groups for the holdings they possessed in different dioceses. Yet the Order frequently assumed the right to the tithes from these holdings, which had previously gone to the ecclesiastical establishment. Regarding their obligations to monarchs, the Templars never had to account for the riches of their generally prosperous properties because all benefits were theoretically intended to subsidize the Order's needs and expenditures in the Holy Land. For this reason, not only were all donations received by the Order exempt from taxation, but the benefits of this untaxed wealth did not even revert indirectly to the kingdoms in which the Order was established. Instead, the lion's share easily left the country to fatten Templar coffers across the sea, beyond the reach of anyone—including the pope—but the Knights themselves.

The less people knew of the reality of the riches of the Templars, the more this wealth was coveted. Undoubtedly, Templar wealth was suspected of being more substantial than it actually was. Because of this supposed great wealth, along with its independence and freedom from accountability, the Templar order largely existed as a state within a state in the kingdoms in which it settled. Even more, it was an untouchable state, thanks to the papal bulls that, since the Order's founding, gave the Templars such freedom, for the Order's ends were supposedly religious in nature, although they were actually political, especially regarding the degree of influence it had over the monarchs of Europe. In fact, the Order's possessions gave it the right to be part of any of the councils of state that decided the destinies of the countries of which they were a part, including matters of peace and war and even the amount of taxes to be raised.

The operation to capture the Templars was barely concluded when Philip the Fair hastily sent urgent missives to all the European monarchs, urging them to follow his expeditious methods and imprison the Templars of their lands. The letters, arriving one to two weeks after the French raid, amazed their recipients, for they had not anticipated such a violent, forceful reaction, despite the fact that they had heard the rumors and suspicions concerning the supposedly sinful life attributed to the members of the Order.

The monarchs of the Iberian Peninsula rushed to reply to the French king and exchanged letters among themselves in which they expressed their opinions, which were unanimously in favor of the Templars. They gave no credence at all to the calumnies that had been ascribed to the Order. James II of Aragon noted that the Templars "had lived in a praiseworthy manner as men of religion" and that they had always been faithful in their service to the Crown while repressing infidels. In short, Iberian rulers did not believe in the prerogative assumed by the king of France in judging the Templars for crimes that, for the moment, only his interrogators corroborated. Above all, they believed that because the allegations concerned members of a religious community, only Rome and the pope had the authority to make such declarations. Their decision was to wait for such a declaration from the pontiff, and then take appropriate action.

For his part, Pope Clement V also seemed to have been ignorant of the Templars' capture until after it had occurred. But he was forced to immediately silence his protest because Philip IV, with a diligence worthy of the best politician, enclosed with his notification to the pope the written and endorsed results of the first Templar interrogations: The methods of the king's tribunals had wrested the desired confessions from the accused. We must take into account that in the Middle Ages, a suspect's confession was the primary proof of guilt and that this confession could be obtained by any means, including torture. The pope, who was the first to approve and hold them irrefutable, agreed to ask that official inquisitors confirm these first presumed confessions. Further, his main request was that he have a say in what was essentially the underlying motive of the entire sham: the divvying up of the Order's goods and their temporary safe storage while the Church decided what was to be done with them permanently. Some believed there was a chance the Order would emerge from this process unscathed and reinforced, and would return to its realms with even more strength and influence, though few, not least the Templars themselves, thought this was realistic. This papal disposition informing monarchs of the charges against the Templars was transmitted to all Christian kingdoms where the Templar order was established. The bull, *Pastoralis Preemientiae,* arrived in Spain in early January 1308, accompanied by a personal brief addressed to the monarchs, which granted them permission to act against the Templars in their respective jurisdictions, including interrogating them to clarify responsibility and assess blame. The letter also made recommendations that Templar property be confiscated for eventual disposition in accordance with the outcome of the trials.

Three months after the arrests that had taken place in France, the Templars in all the kingdoms of the Peninsula knew very well that, sooner or later, action would be taken against them. They did hold several favorable cards, however: First, they had been allowed time to prepare for what might befall them. Second, during those three months, nothing had happened to them and no monarch seemed in a hurry to follow the French king's example (with the exception of the king of Navarre, Luis Huttin, who happened to be the son of Philip the Fair). It was hard to believe that the arrest and censure of the Templars would take place on the peninsula—and even if it did, it would surely not be characterized by the violence and viciousness of what had taken place north of the Pyrenees.

Yet the Spanish Christian kings, with Pope Clement V's bull in hand, were reckoning with something that could immediately benefit them: permission to pillage Templar properties and take control and possession of any goods they held. After this, they could sit tight and wait for whatever events or skillful manipulation would give them full ownership of these properties without incurring the wrath of Rome. In this way, the Templars played the game that would best serve them or that at least would not be detrimental to them.

License to Plunder

As we have learned, the contemporary chronicles of the peninsular kingdoms tend systematically to hide the role the Templars played in the political and military events that took place during the Order's existence. Between this and the obvious interest of the heirs of the Templar properties to disguise the provenance of their holdings, there exists a considerable gap between the scarcity of Castilian Templar documentation and the relative abundance of documentation in the Catalan-Aragonese archives. Thus we must use other sources of information, such as folk traditions—so unjustly denigrated by academic research—to reconstruct, at least partially, what transpired during the time of the persecution and fall of the Templar order.

The official chronicle recounting the reign of Ferdinand IV of Castile, the *Emplazado* (Supoenaed), was written by Fernán Sánchez of Valladolid many years after Ferdinand's death. As is the case with the majority of commissioned chronicles, because the author takes great care to exalt certain virtues that this king barely possessed, it is possible to catch a glimpse of his immature and sick personality only if we read between the lines. He was a capricious figure who was pathologically submissive to the strong-willed nature of his mother, María de Molina, who determined the destiny of Castile from the shadows of the reigns of three monarchs.[3]

In the *Emplazado,* among a jumble of information unrelated to our subject, there are a mere two paragraphs that reference the Templars. Yet these are significant enough to invite reflection. The first one, given that the papal orders were established, recounts that "the king had sent word by which he ordered that the Order's castle be handed over to him."[4] But the provincial grand master, Rodrigo Yañez, appeared in Valladolid, where he found doña Maria Molina (whom the chronicle always calls the Queen, in acknowledgment of her power and influence in matters of state), and implored her "that she would willingly take up this dispute"—that is, assume the responsibility of accepting the custody of those fortresses "until the Pope made his ruling on the landed estates of the Order as he pleased." The queen refused to accept this proposal "without at least knowing the will of the king and if he wanted it, and about this matter she sent her message to the king," who, it seems, gladly accepted the proposal of the provincial grand master. Yet Rodrigo, who for good reason was suspicious of the monarch's true feelings, delayed for as long as possible the fulfillment of the conditions of his proposal. Because of his apparent mistrust of Ferdinand IV's quick acquiescence, he sought an audience with the king's brother, Prince Philip, in Galicia and delivered to him the most important Templar sites in the northeast of the Peninsula—Ponferrada, Alcañices, San Pedro de Latarce, and Faro—in exchange for the prince's promise to defend the Order and speak on its behalf to the king and bishops to facilitate establishing the date and conditions for the Templars to account for the accusations lodged against them. If this diplomacy had any success, the Order would gladly hand over to the prince the rest of their fortresses; if it did not, the prince was to commit himself to defending the Templars and ensure that their desire for justice prevailed over any royal's whims.

The second mention of the Templars appears in the following chapter of the *Emplazado*[5] and tells how the king, looking for a way to finance his campaign against Gibraltar, looked to his uncle, Prince John, who suggested the king request from his brother the profits made from the use of the Templar fortresses. Once again, Maria Molina, the queen, intervened, arranging a meeting, and told the prince he was acting wrongly by making this kind of deal with excommunicated men who were accused of heresy before the pope. She advised him and ordered him to pull out of this deed, and showed him letters the pope had sent to the king and to her asking them to hold all the Templar fortresses and to keep them and all their goods under guard until the pope ruled on what to do with them. The prince acceded to the queen's wishes and the Templars ceded to the king their hopes and, along with the fortresses they previously placed in the custody of Prince Philip, turned over those at Montalbán, Jerez de los Caballeros, Badajoz, Burguillos del Cerro, Alconchel, and Frenegal de la Sierra. As if the Templar situation ended with these deliveries, the rest of the chronicle makes further mention of the Order.

We must keep in mind the scarcity of preserved documentation when considering what happened next to the Order's goods and properties. The king quickly took charge of them, but though he did ask for the cataloging of all Templar possessions that had not been voluntarily handed over to him—an inventory demonstrating in fact that the Templars had few remaining goods that could be pawned*—he did not seem interested in keeping in his custody any Templar goods, as ordered by the papal bulls. In July 1309, before the judicial procedures against the Order had begun and, of course, long before the pope made any decision concerning the Order's legacy, the king ceded to the Order of Alcántara the villas and castles in Extremadura—Capilla, Garlitos, and Almorchón—for 130,000 *maravedíes,* specifying in the corresponding transfer document that if the Templar order was once again recognized, it would have to provide the Order of Alcántara that same amount to recover these holdings. This operation was merely one among many the Castilian monarch schemed at the expense of the Templar estate, but the majority of the proof that could confirm this has been lost.

Yet there is an episode appearing in the *Emplazado* that raises suspicions concerning the behavior of the Castilian king toward the Templars. It tells us that in Martos he ordered two brothers, whose names are not mentioned, to be caught and summarily executed on the charge of having slain the king's favorite in Palencia, don Alfonso Benavides. The chronicle says that both brothers vainly proclaimed their innocence, and as they were taken to be executed—tradition says they were thrown from the rock on which the castle of Martos sits like a crown—they subpoenaed the king to appear before God's tribunal in thirty days to answer for their murder, which he did in Jaén with perfect punctuality.

Historical research and study of the existing documentation have shown this episode to be nothing more than a legend. In addition, the figures in the story lived many years after the events in which the chronicle involved them. Yet there are clarifying details in the story that prevent us from declaring it simply false.

First, the sacrifice of two brothers who never existed is a curious parallel to Templar symbolism. One of the Templar seals—possibly the one

*We are told there, for example, that the bishop of Jaén communicated to the bishop of Toledo that the Templars did not own anything in his diocese and that a place like Birhuega possessed nothing belonging to the Templars but a horse and an old wool hat.[6]

used most by the Order—depicts two knights galloping on one horse, an image that seemed to point to one of the mysteries surrounding the Knights of the Temple of Solomon: the pairing or twinning of initiates in the study of the arcane mysteries.

Second, the act of subpoenaing a king to appear in an expected period before God's tribunal is also said to have occurred when Grand Master Jacques de Molay climbed the pyre on the Île-de-Javiaux (Isle of Jews) near Notre-Dame in Paris and subpoenaed Pope Clement V and King Philip IV to present themselves that very year before God's tribunal to account for their acts and the crimes committed against the Order.

Third, those two brothers, which the chronicle cites without even mentioning their names, were baptized by later tradition as the Carvajal brothers, knights of the Order of Calatrava—the same Order that assumed ultimate possession of the holdings of the Templars of Castile, where, it is said, all the lost documentation referring to the Order was kept.

What we may deduce from this legend embedded in the chronicle is that its author, Fernán Sánchez of Valladolid, who wrote it by royal command surely during Enrique II's time, felt obligated to tell the truth about the facts that he knew and, at the same time, not to denigrate any member of the Castilian monarchy, who were the ancestors of the monarch who had commissioned him to write the history. The solution lay in telling another encoded history, which could eventually be fully understood by those who were adept at decoding certain ciphered languages commonly used throughout the Middle Ages.

Fourteen Accusations

The avarice of the rulers of the European kingdoms—including those on the Peninsula, with the honorable exception of Portugal—was made glaringly obvious by their attempts to recover the holdings that had belonged to the Templar order. These rulers ignored for as long as possible the papal orders to transfer these holdings into the hands of the Hospitallers. The Templar demise did not cease with the simple suspension of the Order, which did not take effect officially until the accords of the Councils of Vienne in 1312. The Templars had to be tried to discover to what degree they could be found guilty of the accusations lodged against them in France (to which almost all of them had confessed in principle). Rome was very careful to follow secular custom of the Church and gave to bishops and inquisitors a precise series of questions to be answered at the trials. These varied according to the tribunals that ultimately formulated them, but fell in number between the 127 that the papal curia developed and the eighty eight that were finally used by the Catalan-Aragonese tribunals.[7] Campomanes summarized them in fourteen points:[8]

- When admitted to the Order, were the new brothers forced to renounce Christianity?
- Did they deny Christ's divinity?
- Did they consider Christ a mere prophet?
- Did they believe the grand master could impart sacraments?
- Did the writings of the Order include dogmatic errors?
- Upon entering the Order, were brothers urged into homosexuality?
- Did brothers swear to promote the expansion and progress of the Order?
- In joining the Order, were brothers encouraged to hold any hope of salvation in Christ?
- Did they spit on the Cross during the Order's initiation ceremony or during other ceremonies?
- Did they worship a cat idol or simulaca (baphomet)?*

*[The worship of the baphomet was central to the charges against the Templars. This idol was said to take the form of a head or the shape of a black cat. Some believe the name to be an anagram of Temp ohp Ab, which comes from the Latin *templi omnium hominum pacis abhas*, meaning "father of universal peace among men." Others suggest it is a garbled spelling of the name Mohammed. —*Trans.*]

- Did they wear belts that previously had been wrapped around such idols?
- Did brothers behave lasciviously with young novices?
- When celebrating religious services, did they omit the words of consecration?
- Did they understand the commission of such crimes as evil?

As we might expect, the authentic intentions of the Templars had no place in their interrogation, for they could pose a real threat to the structures of the medieval world. Although the inquisitors' questions seemed designed to judge the entire Order, in practice the interrogations were conducted individually and subsequent indictments or absolutions were individual, although the final result affected the destiny of the Order as a whole. Without a doubt, this situation was one of the many absurdities that emerged during the process of the trials, but if we take into account the political interests at play throughout the scheme, we can see that the immediate motive, prevailing over all others, was to disempower the Templar order without turning it into a target for persecution. Its members could still be useful, if they were incorporated into other organizations that posed less of a danger to the Church and offered fewer grounds for worry for the European monarchies, which undoubtedly suspected the Templars' true goals.

Obedient, Disciplined, and Innocent

Every time they were required to give a statement or were interrogated by bishops and inquisitors in the kingdom of Castile-León, the Templars exhibited the same obedience they had shown in the surrender of their fortresses in Castile. Pope Clement V had especially commissioned the bishops of Toledo and Santiago de Compostela and the bishop of Sigüenza, together with the apostolic inquisitor Friar Aimerico de Plasencia of the Order of Preachers (the Dominican order), to arrange the sites and most appropriate times to carry out the interrogations. These took place in Medina del Campo, Alcalá (1309), Toledo (1310), and Santiago, and each time the Knights Templar faithfully attended and responded in a disciplined manner to the accusations reflected in the pontiff's questionnaire.

As might be expected, the results served to swell the documentation to be presented at the Council of Vienne, which the pope announced in 1309 and that actually took place in 1312.[9] The results of all the interrogations should have uniformly matched those presented at a provincial council that took place in Salamanca on July 15, 1310. This earlier council confirmed the findings of the local tribunals, which declared all Templars of the kingdom, without exception, innocent of the charges for which they had been accused. Some of the questionnaires reflected only some sins that were considered to be minor, those related to ancestral superstitions that the Templars continued to practice, such as painting crosses on the stirrups of their mounts to protect riders from the dangers that could threaten during battle.

When considering these questionnaires and councils, we must bear in mind that according to Templar organization, Castile and Portugal constituted one Templar province. Portuguese Templars, however, were rarely interrogated by the Castilian commissions. On the contrary, King Dinís of Portugal confined his actions to claiming the Order's relinquished goods, as ordered by the papal bulls, and waited patiently for a new pope to replace Clement V. Following Clement's death, he solicited his successor, Pope John XXII, through João Lourenço, an envoy who was, not by chance, a Templar, for the pontiff's permission to create a monastic order bearing the name of Christ. This order was not only to take the Portuguese Templars as members, but would also have at its disposal all the goods and properties the pope had officially removed from the Templars' possession.

The Portuguese case was atypical in the whole Templar adventure; this was the only kingdom in all of Christendom that did not interrogate its Templars, looking for possible guilt and hypothetical heresies. In fact, it extended indefinitely the survival of the Templars merely by

Fig. 8.2. A knight of the Order of Christ, which replaced the Templars in Portugal after the Order's demise

changing the Order's name and suggesting it would follow another Rule—the Rule of Calatrava, which, since its founding in Navarre by Raimundo de Fitero, had been guided by parallel Cistercian ordinances that the Order of the Templars has also incorporated in its official Rule.

In what eventually became the Portuguese national archives of Torre de Tumbo, an essential part of the Portuguese Templar documentation has been preserved and was jealously guarded by the successors to the Order of Christ. That documentation, however, contains some inexplicable gaps that have caused some scholars to suspect that the Order was more powerful and influential in Portugal than the actual documents reflect. Particularly suspicious is the absence of any record of the considerable number of Templars with French surnames (some hardly altered) who appeared as members the Order of Christ from the very moment of its establishment. This absence might suggest that Portugal, possibly through the port of La Rochelle, took in the majority of the few Templars who managed to escape the trap set by Philip the Fair. Once in their new home and unmolested by any tribunal, these men actively collaborated in the formal transformation of the Templars into the Order of Christ, which, in contradiction to the many spurious attempts to claim otherwise (a claim having behind it a paucity of documents), was the true heir of an essential part of Templar ideology.

The Adventure of the Catalan-Aragonese Templars

The Catalan-Aragonese crown can boast ownership of a wealth of medieval documentation which, at least in regard to the Templar Order, surpasses that in Castile's archives. This abundance has allowed researchers to follow much more accurately the steps taken by members of the Order. They provide a more truthful account of its encomiendas (possessions)—what they were given and what they bought—along with many of their ambitions and some of their great plans. This plethora of documentation has resulted in one of the most definitive studies to date on the fall and the trial of the Catalan-Aragonese Templars, which was recently undertaken by Professor Sans i Travé.[10] This study allows for few remaining doubts concerning what happened in the lands of the Crown on a day-to-day basis during those crucial years.

Summarizing Professor Sans i Travé's research—which leads to ideas that have already been presented, although with less rigor—we find that James II, called the Just, thanks to the trust he invested in Esquieu Floriàni (or Floyrán), knew of the accusations against the Templars years before they came to the knowledge of Philip IV, but he refrained from giving them credence or making use of them until the French king made his drastic decision to finish off the Order. It was as though James II had quietly waited for someone to go ahead of him in this regard to avoid having to accept responsibility for the disappearance of the Templars from his lands. Such an elimination, however, would be to his advantage; it would spell the end of an overly powerful organization that, since the time of his grandfather the Conqueror, had regarded his crown as belonging to them. The kingdom's history had been marked by the Order's attempts to determine the land's policies and destiny, when the opinion of the Templars was solicited and when it was not.

It's more than probable—although it could never be documented—that the Catalan-Aragonese Templars were aware of the impasse they faced the moment they received news about what had happened on the other side of the Pyrenees and realized that a similar fate threatened them. When it became known that James II had received his neighbor's first letter, and when the briefs arrived with a copy of Jacques de Molay's first incriminating confessions and the letters of the Dominican Bruguera, a personal friend of the king who taught in Paris and gave him unofficial news about the case, the Templars began to be seriously alarmed, despite the monarch's insistence and the hope, however naïve, of some of the Templars that no one would act before Pope Clement V explained his point of view and will on the matter.[11] At the request of his Templars, the king limited himself for the time being to asking for the return of three Catalan Templar brothers who had been caught in Navarre in a trap prepared by King Louis. In Aragon the Templars did not quite have their act together, as can be seen in the chapter meeting of commanders that took place in Miravet. Here the provincial grand master, Ximén de Lenda, decided with those in assembly to prepare a resistance in the Order's primary castles and to name a commission to pressure the king to their favor, before anything was decided against them.

The commission found itself confronting a king whose evasions did not exactly portend decisions favorable to their cause. As a result, the grand master took action, sending urgent missives to the main fortresses and ordering them to be on their guard against events that were growing ever more imminent. In this way, first Peñíscola and then Castellote, Villel, Miravet, Cantavieja, Monzón, Libros, Chalamera, Alfambra, and others—curiously, those fortresses that had previously belonged to the extinct Order of Monsfragüe and the ones that were guarding the Maestrazgo—became strongholds in which a good many Templars from the province prepared to resist attack and, if neces-

Fig. 8.3. The remains of the interior of the Templar castle of Miravet (Tarragona)

Fig. 8.4. Ruins of the chapel dedicated to the archangel St. Michael, in the Templar castle of Miravet

sary, to resist unto death the imprisonment and destruction that had befallen their brethren in France and which they believed awaited them in Iberia.

The Templars' actions served as an excuse for the king, who, without waiting any longer for the pope's decision, ordered the fortresses besieged. He seized the holdings outside of these strongholds and preemptively imprisoned those soldier-monks who had not been able to enter the castles. With this course of action, James II fulfilled one of his desires: to take control of Templar wealth, even if only partially. The rest of the case against the Order, including its supposed nefarious sins, was of much less concern to him; in fact, he found these accusations as unbelievable as when he first heard them and was convinced the Church would be perfectly equitable when the time came to judge his prisoners. Therefore, when the papal bulls and briefs arrived, he left the bishops and lower friars to fend for themselves as God pleased and, as the castles gave up their resistance—the siege for some lasted a whole year—he limited himself to claiming whatever they might hold of value or importance. Thus, from the fortress in Miravet, according to the letter he wrote to his representative, Mascarós Garidell, he claimed the books, including two samples of the Bible that, along with a spear, had been donated to the Templars by his ancestor Ramón Berenger IV when the castle was captured in 1155.[12]

The Council of Tarragona

It seems beyond doubt that after having plundered Templars' possessions, James II would have wanted the provincial council in charge of acting on the pope's behalf to condemn the friars, just as they had been condemned in France. In 1310 Pope Clement V had not yet decided to convene the grand council that he had been announcing for almost two years, and therefore no one really knew what outcome awaited the Order. The inquisitions that had taken place throughout 1308 and 1309 by the different diocesan commissions of the crown of Aragon had resulted in the presumed innocence of the Templars called before them, and all the compiled material was gathered in Tarragona, awaiting a global decision while the imprisoned Templars benefited from a notable mitigation of their confinement.

In mid-March 1311, for the third time, the archbishop of Tarragona, Guillén de Rocaberti, gathered the council fathers and asked that all Templar prisoners except the sick and handicapped be brought before him. In this, it seemed, he was playing out a hidden desire to buy time while waiting for the Church to make its ruling and save him and his colleagues from the responsibility of coming up with a solution that might later be rejected. In one respect, though, this conclave demonstrated its relative independence, for it systematically rebuffed the feigned pressures from the king in favor of conviction. Instead of acceding—and without overtly taking the side of the Templars—the council agreed that while they waited, the Templar friars would receive a subsidy to make their confinement more bearable, the amount to vary according to each brother's standing. The grand master, for example, would receive two *sueldos* and six *dineros* a day; the sergeants would receive fourteen dineros. All these monies were to come from the Templars' confiscated goods, which indirectly harmed the king, who wanted to personally profit from the Templars' money.

Finally, in October 1311, the long-awaited council was convoked in Vienne and James II was invited to it, as were the rest of Europe's monarchs, but the king of Aragon sent in his place three representatives, who, together with the archbishop of Tarragona and the bishops of Mallorca and Valencia, formed the close-knit Catalan-Aragonese delegation. The king also gave strict instructions to his assistants to accept the conclusions and wishes of the pontiff concerning the culpability or innocence of the Templars, but to press and defend at all costs his determination that the Order's dissolution, which was already taken for granted, did not presume that Templar goods had to be distributed to another existing military order such as the Hospitallers.

On April 3, 1312, after a feverish burst of diplomatic activity, Pope Clement V made public his bull *Vox in Excelso,* by which the Order of the Temple was suspended not by a sentence of condemnation—which was impossible to decree, given that the greater part of the delegations had declared their respective Templars innocent—but by sanction. The subsequent bulls, *Ad Providam* and *Nuper in Generali,* stipulated the transfer of the Templar possessions to the Hospitallers. In the final bull on the subject, *Considerantes Dudum,* a milestone in twisted diplomacy, the Order of the Temple as a whole was for all intents and purposes suppressed, but the provincial councils were free to judge their Templars individually, condemning each man or declaring him innocent according to the evidence and testimony collected on each.

The Tarragonese Council thus met again in October 1312, after having brought together all the imprisoned Templars for the determination of the council fathers. On November 4, the council decreed the innocence of all the Templars of the Catalan-Aragonese province, the kingdom of Mallorca, and the kingdom of Valencia. Each brother could reside for life at his old monastery. Each was to receive a pension for life according to the position he held in the Order, which was to come out of the rents that diverse encomiendas provided.[13] As we might suppose, these solutions, although they were not discussed, were not much to the liking of King James II, whose greed led him to strip the most significant sacred ornaments from a number of Templar churches, leaving them lacking in what was most necessary for worship to proceed as usual. Archbishop Rocaberti, however, "demanded James II to put at their disposal the reliquaries and other objects taken from the friars, to allow them the fate approved by the Council."[14]

The Templars' Heirs

While there is never any shortage of questions concerning every stage of Templar history, questions about one event stemming from the case of the Templars of the crown of Aragon managed to linger long after the Order's suppression. The Order of Santa María de Montesa was proposed by James II to Pope Clement V through the king's ambassador, Vidal of Villanova, though it was not actually instituted until 1317, three years after the pope's death, by Clement's successor, John XXII. The Catalan-Aragonese king seems to have focused all of his efforts on obstructing the Order of St. John of the Hospital in his domains to prevent them from accumulating the excessive power that would come with the addition of the Templars' goods to their coffers, in accordance with the pope's decision outlined in the bulls issued by the Council of Vienne. In the monarch's opinion, as his delegation insisted before the pontifical court at Avignon, the Crown could in no way allow this adjudication, for if it was carried out, the Hospitallers would become not only the most powerful force in the kingdom, but also a force more powerful than any the sovereign could have put together, thus making the Order the master and lord of the destiny of the Crown. To give this position more muscle, James II undoubtedly contacted the other peninsular monarchs—with the exception of Louis of Navarre, whose interests were absolutely tied to those of France—to gather their support.

During the years of this give-and-take, the Aragonese monarch made

Fig. 8.5. After the Templars were abolished, Ares del Maestre (Arches of the Master) became one of the principal plazas of the new Order of Montesa.

a series of offers concerning the power and territories of the proposed Order of Montesa. It was determined that the new friars would take possession of the Templar holdings in the kingdom of Valencia, with the exception of the capital's encomienda and the villa and castle of Torrent, which would remain the property of the Hospitallers. The new Order was to be a subsidiary of the Order of Calatrava, by whose Rule it was to be governed. Its members were to submit themselves to the control and norms of this Calatrava, and Calatravese representatives overseeing them were to make regular visits to and inspections of their monasteries and castles. The new Order was also to be responsible for the kingdom's border security against any possible attacks from Granada's Muslims, the only Islamic force left on the Peninsula.

One unanswered question remains, however, despite the understanding that it has been resolved: The Order of Montesa was created with holdings that had been in the possession of the Templars of the kingdom of Valencia. Up to the nineteenth century, then, the *montesinos,* as members of the Order of Montesa came to be known, considered themselves heirs of the Templars and occasionally even proclaimed themselves Templars. Unlike the Order of Christ instituted in Portugal, however, the Order of Montesa was not made up of a good number of dispossessed Templars, but rather of some isolated brothers; its membership comprised those chosen by the Order of Calatrava and friars who joined a brotherhood for the first time. Thus, while this cannot be proved (surprisingly, given that its history has been well documented despite the disastrous destruction of its main see in an earthquake in the eighteenth century), the Order of Montesa's Templar inheritance seems to have been exclusively material, consisting of goods and lands, houses and castles, but never an ideology or goal. What is more, as Sans i Travé's book demonstrates beyond doubt, the chief players in the Templar Order in the Catalan-Aragonese province preferred to stay on the sidelines and quietly ended their days on the pensions religiously paid by the Hospitallers out of rents accumulated from former Templar possessions.

The Order of Montesa was the physical successor to the Templars, but in no way was its spiritual or ideological successor, as some, myself included, have suspected. While the Templars—not only the Portuguese Templars, but also those who considered the Temple their own and worthy of remaining in play—threw themselves single-mindedly into the foundation and development of the Portuguese Order of Christ, the majority of those in the kingdom of Aragon, including its principal leaders, appear to have been willing to mute their Templarism (even their own status as friars, which they did not lose when the Order was supressed) for the sake of a life, if not more free, then at least exempt from worries and responsibilities. Yet a number of them dedicated themselves to what the public did not hesitate to recognize as a "holy life" by becoming hermits who ended their days as penitents in the vicinity of the former missions, or as helpers in their former churches, or, most frequently, as guests in the same castles where they lived their lives as friars or sergeants of the Temple, which was destined to remain a mythical remembrance in the minds of the people.

It is not possible for us to arrive at a definitive conclusion about why the Templar Order entered so passively into its own extinction. Surely those Templars who were aware of the greater mission of the Order suffered a certain ideological defeat. There are many, perhaps too many, pointing to a secret Templar continuity. Most of them fall under the weight of their own inconsistency. Yet history—or inner history—continues to be peppered with signs of the Templars even after the abolition of the Order. These references, however, are much more ethereal and much less concrete than the public history of the Templars during its birth, ascendancy, and decline.

PART 3

THE TEMPLARS' LEGACY

*Veritable chose est que vos es done especiaument, si come por dette, que vos devés metre vos armes por vos freres, ensi com fist Jhesu Crist, et defendre la terre des mescreants paiens que sont enemis au fill de la Verge Marie. Ceste deffense dessus dite n'est mie entendue dou lion, car il vait avironant et cherchant que il puisse devorer, et les mains de lui contre trestous et les mains de tous contre lui.**

ARTICLE 56 OF THE FRENCH TEMPLAR RULE, WHICH CORRESPONDS TO ARTICLE 47 OF THE CASTILIAN RULE, REDACTED BY CAMPOMANES

---

*The truth is that you owe, as if you were in debt, and are thus commissioned to lay down your souls for that of your brothers, and eradicate from the earth the incredulous who always threaten the Son of the Virgin, for from León we read the following: Because he walks in circles, looking for whom to devour. And in another part: His hands against all, and all others against him.

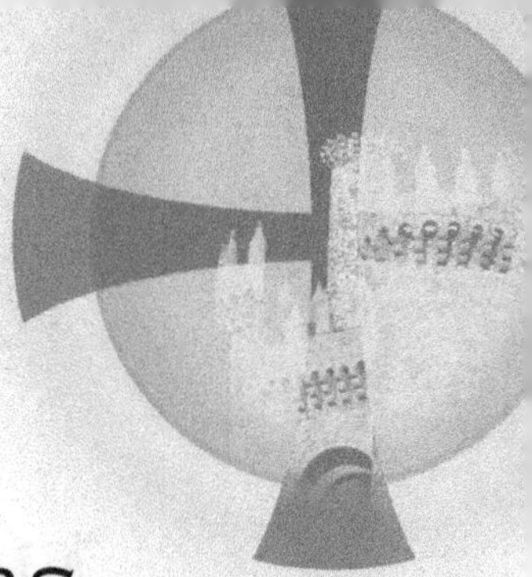

9
The Templars in History

The adventure of the Order of the Temple constitutes a decisive and significant episode in medieval European history. The Templar order was born, developed, reached its zenith, declined, and disappeared during a period of two hundred years (1118–1312), which marks, on the one hand, a crucial moment in Western culture, a milestone in the creation of this culture's identity and the incubation of the germ of a collective consciousness that, for good or evil, still defines us. On the other hand, this period of time—albeit a mere second in the life of humanity as a whole—summarized the entire legacy of a past that reached its ultimate goal and cast doubt on the values it had accepted up to that point. European society at the time then proposed substituting a new set of values more in accord with the stockpile of judgmental elements accumulated by that collective conscience that struggled to structure itself and take form despite the mortal obstacles placed in its way by the dominant organization of that society: the Church.

This radical change in mental scheme, essentially revolutionary and thus also destructive—as destructive as all such revolution is when it faces the monolithic structures entrenched in the powers that be—coincided with the Templar presence and was unleashed violently immediately after the Order's disappearance in the face of the Black Death, the

Western Schism, the Hundred Years' War. Anyone who seeks to penetrate the silence of history must ask if the Templar order merely coincided with such radical change or was one small factor among many that triggered it, or perhaps was the secret engine that put into motion such a great transition.

Some idealists who look at history somewhat simplistically and subjectively may attribute to the Templar order the role of exclusive engine of Europe's fundamental change, suggesting that it closed an era with its presence and opened another with its disappearance, but I am not among them. Idealists are always ready to look at history through a simplistic and subjective lens. Although the study of history is subjective and although historiography has not managed to free itself from the positive and negative aspects of those who have attempted to tell the adventure of humankind, too much subjectivity necessarily produces a striving for objectivity, forcing us to look at both sides of the coin, despite the fact that we may be attracted to one side more than the other.

The history of the Order of the Temple, like the history of Europe during the twelfth and thirteenth centuries, contains sufficient elements of mystery to cause suspicion—though no document could prove it—that a shadow reality pulled the strings behind the great conflict. We have been habituated, without asking any questions, to consigning to this reality responsibility for all changes. We are not accustomed to analyzing, without dangerous methodological impediments, what might hide behind conceited cultural appearances that interdict the framework of integrity upon which research and the behavior of individuals operate.

The Templar order responded to its era, an age in which the marvelous and irrational played leapfrog with droughts, the growth of universities, endless war, misery, absolutism, imposed devotion, the birth of the middle class, plagues, the conflict of priorities between the Church and the powerful secular authorities, and the rediscovery of commerce. The marvelous—the transcendent, perhaps—manifests itself in the everyday and the tangible, in the sudden emergence of the Gothic, divine war, the chivalrous science, the resurgence of the Kabbalah and alchemy, the unique adventure of the troubadours, the sudden appearance of

Catharism, the search for the Grail, the timid and heretical emergence of courtly love, the Masonic lodges, the recovery of the impossible hero. Significantly, if we take pains to carefully determine its essence, we find the Templar order integrated into it all those elements that constitute the reality of its time. Could the Order have been moving these elements, controlling the reality, perhaps? We must not be overly optimistic; in the Templar order we haven't found the philosopher's stone. But among the various threads woven into the cultural fabric that included the Templars, the dominant ones were those that formed the essence of the Order.

Is There a Templar Mystery?

Those who "know" and thus impose their criteria on others and disregard those who dare to disagree with them have suggested that the Templar order was a product of the Crusades. Further, they offer that it followed to the letter the ideological canons of its time and that it was nothing but an armed appendage of a Church that both used and abused its ecclesiastical military privileges and flourished thanks to its position. They maintain that it fulfilled its vital cycle and disappeared when at last a monarch was found who was more ambitious than the Order and there was in power a pope who had sold out completely those who confirmed him to his position and forced him to comply to their will and whims. The destruction of the Order allowed the pope to rid himself of an organization that had become both an irritant (due to its rivalry with Church power) and obsolete (due to the abandonment of the crusading spirit from which it was born). In its demise there is no mystery, no historical back room, no other wood but that which is burning.

Truth can be found in both academic investigation and scientific method, but not all existing truth can be found in these and I'm positive there is more to the picture than those who deal in "nothing but the truth" seem to suggest. Not only is the available documentation incomplete, but what does exist is an incomplete and partial expression of the truth or an expression of the truth that those who created or commissioned the documents wanted to assert. It is these compromised documents that are our only rational source of credibility.

Templar documentation, scarce or abundant according to the different national archives that preserved it, gives us an account of the Templars' immediate truth, the officially accepted one with greater or lesser detail that allows a more or less complete continuity according to its abundance or gaps. All that documentation answers the *what* but not the *why.* Yet the lucid or obsessive combing of this documentation on the Order fills our awareness with whys that are not reflected in the documents. Faced with this, conventional historiography proclaims that these whys do not exist. They do, however, giving evidence of their presence and challenging us to an unaccepted duel. They await our effort to unearth them, and there are no reasons to justify denying them. If we were to deny them, like Galileo we would have to shout at the disqualifying tribunal: "*Eppur, si muove!*" (But it moves!)

Only by knowing the mysterious intentions of the Templars toward the world in which they emerged can we understand the Templar mystery itself. The Order's dual position as religious institution and military organization made it the ideal body to carry out the divine war in which, as unwavering defenders of a theocracy, men of God, predestined by Providence, are given sacrosanct permission to kill. This is a prerogative the Church itself never exercised, instead handing over its convicts to the secular branches of society so they might impose law and its order. Templar ideology cannot find reflection in any document because in such testaments human decisions are proposed. Yet this Templar mentality—timidly followed subsequently by the Hospitallers and partially practiced by the Teutonic Knights—was based on presumed divine will.

The real mystery—though less admissible if we consider a strictly rationalist argument of historical reality—begins when, in order to reach its goals, the Order breaks with its usually discreet behavior, which, in theory, was to have taken the Templars to their powerful goal. Yet in such an enterprise, when the end is to universally dominate the destinies of countries, customary schemes are no longer valid. It becomes necessary to leap over what is accepted, which always implies disobedience.

Leaping over what is accepted requires taking hold of what is forbidden, taking those structures as contemporary norms. It requires embracing those schemes the majority mentality condemns and rejects as products of a malignant world that will always contrast with what we blindly accept as good and desirable—but only because those who rule over us have declared them so.

When the Church took over the reins of the Western mind-set, it organized for its parishioners a value system on which everyone patterned his behavioral guidelines. It established strict dogmas and declared satanic all attitudes and beliefs that were opposed to its schemes. But the Templar Order, founded in the Holy Land, found out that the country that had been the cradle of Christianity offered holy creeds that Christianity abominated: Islam and Judaism and those Christian variants that the Roman orthodoxy had declared heretical and condemnable.

The Templar order as a whole realized that the possession of the Axis Mundi, from which the nucleus of a universal power could emerge, obligated them to overcome the barriers of orthodoxy and to find commonalities among all the creeds living in that land, instead of pointing out, as the triumphant Church did, the ideological barriers that separated them. In this way, for example, the Templar order—a principal order with respect to its cohesive organization and its military discipline—came into contact with Islam essentially through its Shiite variant, which was more heterodox and, at that moment, more open to syncretic contacts by means of its Sufi masters. In the Templar churches of Jerusalem, as William of Tyre tells us, the brothers had managed to officiate with Islamic liturgical acts, and without changing any of its structure the Order turned the Dome of the Rock into the Temple of the Savior, knowing full well that Jacob once slept on the rock that extended from its center and that the mare Buraq poised itself on it to catapult the Prophet into the Seventh Heaven of Islam.

These fundamental circumstances were present in the Templar corporate mentality since its beginnings. But they could never be transcribed into any public document, under penalty of earning themselves the hatred and shunning of the very Church they served and that had fomented their creation as an armed force. As a monastic order, they also owned private premises in Jerusalem to which only certain individuals were permitted access. Curiously, these were located in what was left standing of the Temple of Solomon, the sacred place that, according to biblical tradition, was conceived and built from directions given by the Divinity, Yahweh, God the Father, Al'lah. If this is true—and in the Middle Ages the Bible was the primordial truth, accepted literally—this place was saturated with divine essence, and not only for these men who made up the active militia of Roman Christianity, but also for Hebrew believers and the faithful of Islam, whose faiths too were born from the Bible.

The chief office of the Templars in Jerusalem represented more than merely the main premises of the Order. The first Templar brothers solicited permission from King Baldwin II to establish themselves precisely there not on a whim, but because the Temple, or what was left of it, presented clues to an active part of a sacred tradition that had been expanded from Judaism by Christianity and that reached the Muslims at the same time that it was awakening manifestations of devotion in Eastern Christian sects, from the Coptics to the Monophysites and from the Armenians to the Nestorians. In a way, the Templars were aware that the Order, by either predestination or chance, had been born in the center of the Center of the World—and this mattered. Certainly their conservation of the Temple and their attempts to preserve it by calling themselves Templars and by reproducing a depiction of it in their seals were not mere whims, but instead the result of a visceral conviction that they were fulfilling part of a tradition. Thereby they proclaimed to the four winds, however discreetly and guardedly, their plans and ideology, giving profound clues to the Order's synarchic intentions.

This connection to the Temple is a prime aspect of the mystery surrounding the Templars that academic, conventional, rationalist historiography is incapable of recognizing. Unfortunately, the methodological norms of this historiography do not allow it to see beyond documentation, for to do so requires entering foreign territory and seizing hold of convictions for which it has no good command. As with all branches of knowledge, humanistic as well as technological, history requires certain accepted aids that many academics are bent on rejecting. History is the chronological tale of the human adventure, and that adventure, like the awareness that governs it, is so rich, varied, and complex that all facets of awareness, including dreams, beliefs, hopes, desires, and even pathologies, humors, and genetic changes, must play a part and be receptive to it.

The First Clue to the Templar Legacy: Architecture

Since the late nineteenth century, art historians and scholars of medieval architectural forms have been wrapped up in a seemingly unresolvable debate concerning Templar constructions. This questions: What model might the Templar order have used? Was this model extended to serve the construction of fortresses? And how did it figure in builders' fraternities, whose members would have had to have been brought up to speed on such sacred construction? The model for Templar architecture could have been discovered in the East, as can be seen in a study of the ruins of the Temple of Solomon, which was the established home base for the Order.

The model under debate is the polygonal structure of churches, which some attribute specifically to the Templars. Those who reject the notion that this type of structure originated and was put into standard use by the Templars look to the possibility that the Templar order, whether aware or unaware of the meaning inherent in the design of these structures, took advantage of the work of others, either by outright imitation or by employing their blueprints.

It is important to stress that the Order established its first temple, its Jerusalem see, in the Islamic sanctuary of the Dome of the Rock, which has mistakenly been called a mosque. It was surely donated to it before the Order became officially recognized. The Templars transformed into a temple the sanctuary they found on the premises and dedicated it to the Savior. According to news from the chroniclers and various Muslims

Fig. 9.1. Basing their arguments on buildings like Sant Pere el Gros, in the surroundings of Cervera, which probably was not Templar, several investigators have insisted on denying the Templar origins of all polygonal and circular religious constructions.

writings of the time, on occasion the temple may have been ceded to the Templars' Muslim friends for their religious services. The testimony of the ambassador Usama ibn Minqidh, sent by the sultan of Damascus, makes this clear: "When I visited Jerusalem, I entered the Al Aqsa Mosque that was occupied by my friends, the Templars. Next to it could be found a small mosque that the Franks have converted into a church. The Templars assigned to me this small mosque so that in it I could fulfill my prayers."[1]

The sanctuary of the Dome of the Rock was not a mere architectural model. The Temple compound, the building of which Yahweh dictated to King Solomon, first king of the world, was simultaneously a sacred place for the Templars and for their friends the Shiites of Damascus. As such, within the Order's plan, it became the sacred place par excellence, because it was sacred to those of several creeds. It is not strange that in

Fig. 9.2. In Villamurel de Cerrato, the Templars built a church around the symbol of the double door, much like the one at the Holy Sepulchre in Jerusalem.

the development of their ideals the Templars reproduced their scheme not only in other temples, especially in their European domains, but also in their seals, which were filled with symbolic elements, for the word *sigillum,* which means "seal," as in the Spanish *siglio,* "keeping a secret," "going about things stealthily," defines the very nature of the Order. It ties in with the "secret" of the temple's syncretic function under the Templars, which would never have been authorized by the Roman orthodoxy.

On the Iberian Peninsula, there are four churches that seem to mirror the architecture of the temple in Jerusalem. Of these four, three—two in Navarre and one in Castile—have suffered great doubts concerning their Templar attribution, while the fourth, in Portugal, is fortunate to have overwhelming documentation indicating its Templar origin and is part of the very complex that was once the central see of the Portuguese Templars: Tomar.

Today, La Iglesia de la Vera Cruz (Church of the True Cross) of

Segovia is the property of the Order of Malta, heir to the Hospitallers of Jerusalem, who assumed a portion of Templar holdings in Castile that together formed part of the Templar encomienda of Zamarramala. The church has twelve sides, three central arches within the polygonal structure, and a central tabernacle accessible by a staircase on its western side, from which the high altar can be seen. In the middle of the tabernacle there is an altar with *mudéjar*-styled decoration, and a bench runs around the tabernacle, possibly used at meetings with few attendants. The argument concerning its origin, which few had doubted due to the proximity of the encomienda, was raised by the study of the architect Luis María Cabello Lapiedra, who was also a member of the Order of

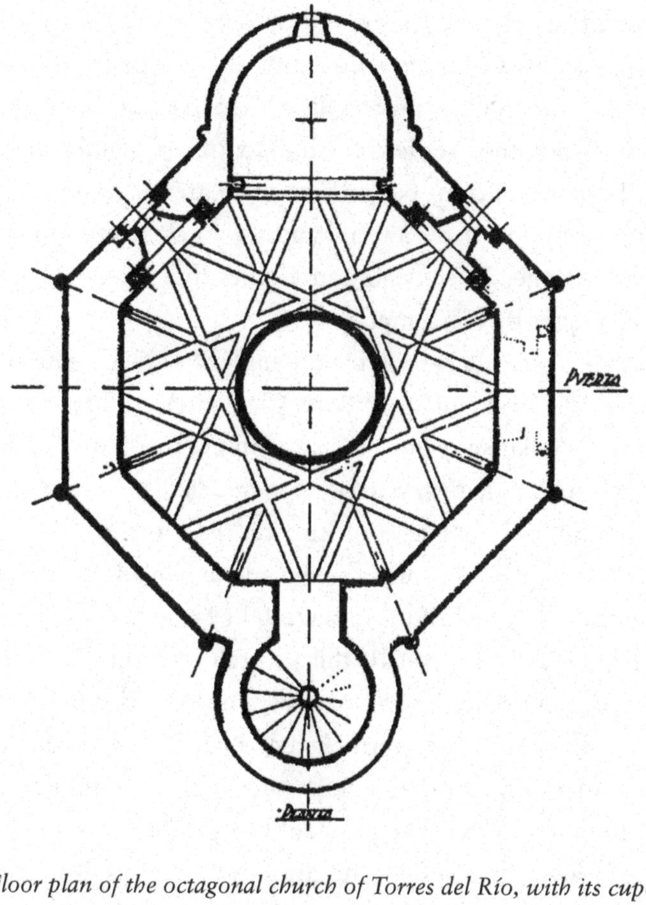

Fig. 9.3. Floor plan of the octagonal church of Torres del Río, with its cupola of Oriental design, built by the labor of mudéjar *craftsmen*

the Holy Sepulchre, which claimed this church had belonged to it.[2] His thesis, which had convinced other scholars, collapsed when there came to light in the archives of Zamarramala a brief by Honorious III, dated May 13, 1224. This brief informs us of the shipment to the Knights Templar of the relic of Vera Cruz that was worshipped in the church. The order owned the temple in question, which was situated, as the brief cites, "in the Septentrion [north] of Segovia."[3]

The Funerary Church of Eunate is found in Navarre, away from the main road that pilgrims took from Santiago and a crossbow's shot from the Templar encomienda of Puente de la Reina. In spite of this, the highest authorities of architectural investigation still insist that it is not a Templar structure, based on the absence of documents to certify such an association and a reference in obscure writings that assert its founding by a "queen" whose identity no one seems able to clarify and who could well have been one of the symbolic figures the Templars used to sanctify the sites on which they settled. In support of its Templar origins, the Chapel of Eunate conforms perfectly to the patterns of sacred construction promoted by the Order's friars and sits in close proximity to their encomienda. Further, documentation verifies that the land on which it stands was bought by the Templars.[4]

When the Hospitallers took over Templar holdings—the Vera Cruz site, for example—on orders of Pope Clement V, as often as possible they tried to eliminate any documents verifying previous Templar ownership. On some occasions, copies were falsified to specify only Hospitaller ownership. In the case of Eunate, the Hospitallers, who took over the encomienda of Puente la Reina and arranged the encomienda's documentation, stopped short of making key documents disappear.

Another aspect common to the Church of Vera Cruz and other such polygonal churches is that they were not situated precisely in the Templar encomiendas, but were placed instead near them, separated by variable distances, so that small "pilgrimages" would be required to reach them, which the friars no doubt took advantage of on specific occasions, perhaps during their initiation proceedings. Because of their locations, these churches may also have served as places of spiritual

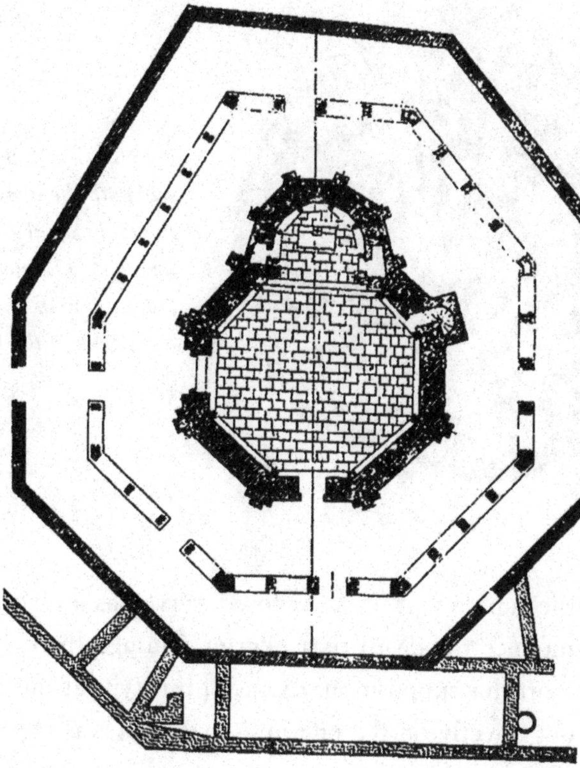

Fig. 9.4. The octagonal Church of Eunate, surrounded by a small exterior cloister similar to the one that once surrounded the Order's temple at the Dome of the Rock

retreat, somewhat apart from the encomienda. Used in these ways, it would be natural and it was no doubt intended that these structures recall the Dome of the Rock, whose spiritual significance to the Order was clear.

The Church of Torres del Río, not very far from the Church of Eunate on the same road to Santiago, is another polygonal construction that scholars have declared did not belong to the Templar order.[5] It is located a certain distance from the first house that belonged to the Templars in Navarre and later to the Hospitallers of Bargota. Its structure is perfectly octagonal, with a central arch balancing the spiral stairs that climb—as they do at Eunate—to the so-called lantern of the dead, a tiny

Fig. 9.5. The Templar seal with the image of the Holy Sepulchre, which should not be confused with that of the Dome of the Rock

room above the cupola that, it is supposed, served as a place to light a bonfire to announce the death of a pilgrim. Though there is no valid reason to support this supposition, rooms of this type at this and other, similar sites not directly on the pilgrims' route, such as the Church of Vera Cruz in Segovia, might also have served as a penitence retreat for some member of the community requesting it. Such a room also appears in the small, pre-Romanesque church of San Baudillo de Berlanga, in the province of Soria.

The Church of Torres del Río is also decorated with very specific mudéjar elements that suggest an intended parallel to the Islamic structure of the Dome of the Rock. On the church's interior cantilevers are baphometic heads, which also suggest a Templar origin.

The Chapel of San Saturnio, in the city of Soria, adjacent to the Duero River, is a seventeenth-to-eighteenth-century construction built on a rock that also contains a cave named after San Saturnio. The location of the chapel a short distance from the Templar encomienda of San Polo, the fact that to reach the chapel, we must go through the church of this encomienda, and the fact that these lands belonged to the Templars before they were transferred to the management of the Sanjuanistas lead us to think that this octagonal chapel was probably built over another octagonal structure that was taken down some time after the Templar order's demise. Other elements corroborate this supposition. First, there is a one-room sanctuary in the complex, the Heros, which has a number of similarities to the meager chapter houses of other Templar encomiendas. Second, the hall of the church is dominated by an image of San Saturnio, who is inexplicably represented as an old man with a long beard and dark skin, which matches most known ancient representations of the Sorian saint and bears a suspicious likeness to the image of the Templar baphomet repeatedly mentioned in the trials and legends that emerged from the Templar myth.

Thus, some of the most significant peninsular Templar monuments embody the architectural projection of Templar ideology, despite the fact that this relationship has been systematically rejected by conventional historical researchers. As I have said, the case of the Hispanic Templars has been and continues to be a hard bone to chew—and one on which few have wanted to set their teeth. The majority of official researchers have decided to strip from the Templar history on the Peninsula all but the Order's purpose when it first came to Iberia: to battle Islam, which turned this territory into a land of the Crusades.

Likewise, the Spanish Templars (though not the Portuguese Templars) have been systematically stripped of all the intra-historical elements they left for us so that we might one day realize the Order's authentic historical significance. For example, it is likely that all the constitutional elements of Templar occultism—and there indeed was an important Templar occultism—have been hidden from us, further obfuscating its role in our historical adventure.

Because there is not space in this book to list all Templar constructions or contributions, we must settle for a few brushstrokes to indicate the essential historical role the Templar order played in Spain and Portugal and hope that in the future we may irrefutably present all those scattered elements that cumulatively indicated a Templar history in Iberia that reaches beyond a mere recounting of events and enumeration of socioeconomic circumstances.

The Second Clue to the Templar Legacy: Patriarchal Crosses and Baphomets

Among the charges in the Templar trials were that of the presumed worship of an idol, a diabolical head with various descriptions that has been termed a baphomet, and the alleged repudiation of the cross, which novices in the Order supposedly had to spit on or kick during their vows of initiation.

Regarding the repudiation of the cross, the inquisitors chose to latch on to this Templar allegation as the most heretical, which contributed greatly to their condemnation as a whole. Some of the accused gave affirmative answers when questioned about these practices, while others said that although they did not personally engage in the practice, they heard talk of it on occasion or witnessed it in ceremonies of initiation into the Order. As for the Order's initiation rites, beyond their obvious orthodoxy, at no point do the texts of these ceremonies cite Jesus Christ or his sacrifice on the cross; they mention only God the Father and Mary. This is significant, if we consider the Order was born precisely where Jesus was born, lived, suffered the Passion, and died and that the goal of the Crusades was the recovery of the Holy Sepulchre. Though we cannot determine the motive behind it or locate documents to confirm it, in its Rule and statutes and devotional material, the Templars always tended to reject the sacredness of Christ's sacrifice. For them, the trajectory of Christ's life seems to have been deemed infinitely more worthy of devotion than its eschatological side, upon which the Church had erected a good part of its dogmatic platform.

For the Templars, therefore, the cross was not a symbol of sacrifice but of the cosmic magnitude, which it had represented since the beginnings of humanity's tradition, as in the red Greek cross, which, with slight variation, became the recognizable sign of the Order—a very different cross from the one the Church had adopted as its victorious emblem, although just as ubiquitous when it came to being schematized in the temples of Christendom. Excluding the polygonal chapels, the frequent Latin cross floor plan was avoided in the design of the Order's temples. In its place was a keylike floor plan. In these churches a rotunda—the "handle" of the key—replaces the conventional nave, and attached to the stem of the key—where its "teeth" would be—there is a small chapel (see figs. 9.6 and 9.7).

While we cannot determine here its many possible meanings, the fact remains that the Templars felt a certain aversion toward the Passion cross. Nevertheless, they loaded with meaning the Lignum Crucis, the alleged fragments of cross from Golgotha, displayed or simply protected in reliquaries that were made in the shape of a patriarchal cross or a cross with two crossbars on which were conferred virtues and miraculous capabilities that in many cases, like the so-called Cruz de Caravaca, folk tradition has extended into our times.

Fig. 9.6. Interior of the destroyed Church of the Temple in Paris. The space is designed in the shape of a key, with the central rotunda constituting the key's "handle."

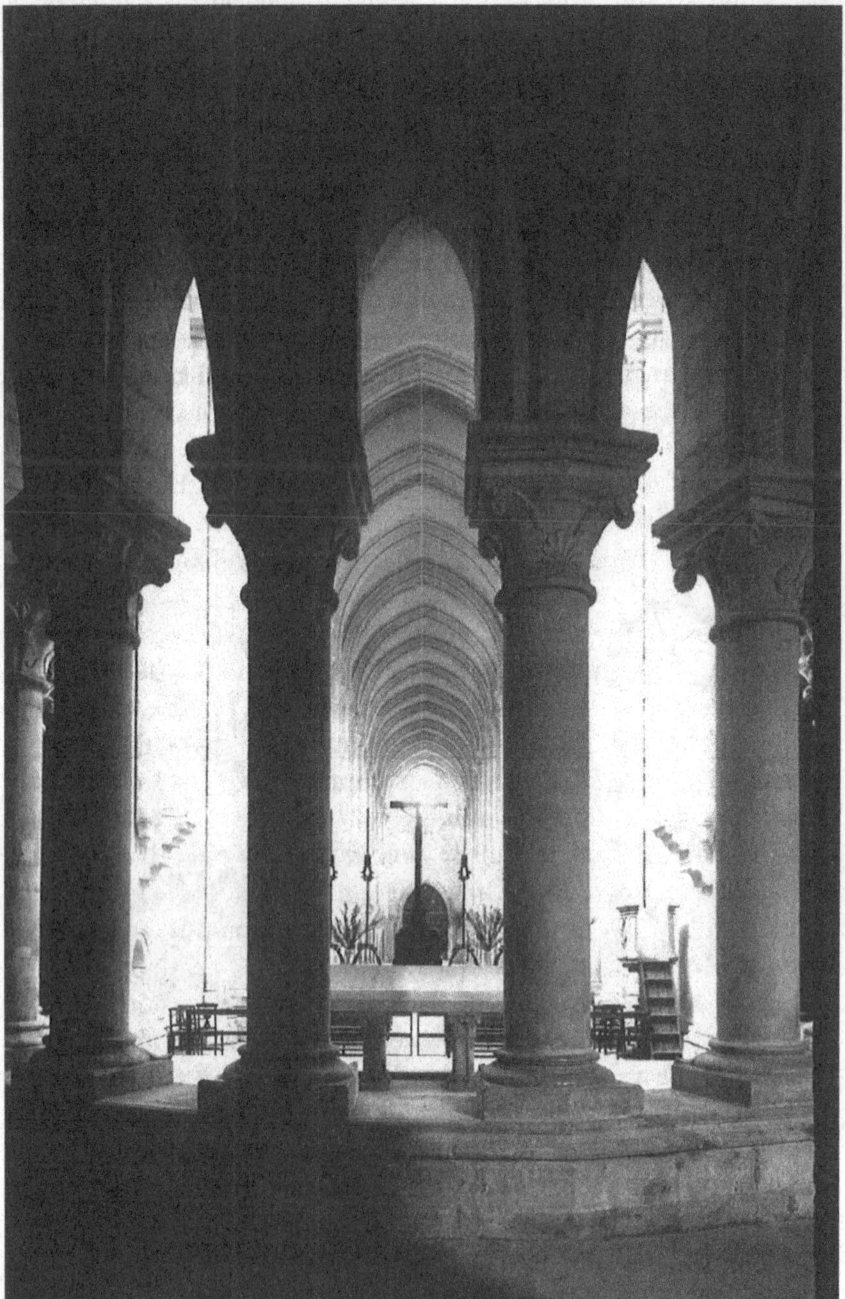

Fig. 9.7. The temple of the Portuguese monastery of Alcobaça also has a floor plan designed and built in the shape of a key. The corridor is its handle, and in the background is the lateral chapel that "opens the lock."

Without counting those relics that have disappeared but about which we have more or less reliable information, the Spanish Templar order actively encouraged the cult and the veneration of at least four of these relics, which are still preserved in their original form today:

- The Cross of Bagá was supposedly brought from the Holy Land by don Hugo de Pinós, who some later documents tried to identify as the founder of the Templars, Hugues de Payns. This relic still holds the devotion of a good part of the Catalan county of Bergadá.
- The Cross of the Cathedral of Astorga comes from the Templar castle of Ponferrada and continues to be the first object of veneration presented to new bishops when they take charge of that diocese.
- The True Cross of Segovia was given by Pope Honorius III to the Templars of the encomienda of Zamarramala. Today there seems to be a tacit agreement among the priests and the authorities of the area to prevent anyone from seeing the relic.
- The Cross of Caravaca was brought from the East by the Templars who occupied Caravaca's castle when the plaza was conquered for Castile by James I of Aragon. A curious legend was created[6] identifying it with the cross that, according to another tradition undoubtedly of Templar origin, miraculously disappeared from the patriarch's neck as he witnessed Emperor Frederick II Stafen crowning himself king in the Church of the Holy Sepulchre.

The symbol of the baphomet is described in the Catalan trials as a cat (articles 14–15) or as an idol (articles 46–57), according to Sans i Travé, who presents the text of the procedures in this way: "[T]he friars were accused of having in the different provinces some idols, in the shape of three faces or one, that represented a human skull, and which they worshipped especially during the celebration of gatherings or of chapter meetings. The Templars also believed that that head could save them and provided all the riches enjoyed by the Order; and that finally, it was its power that made the earth germinate and the trees flower."[7]

Many opinions, most of them contradictory, have been formed about the baphomet, which the Templar accusers considered an object of satanic worship. We must acknowledge that it was both a symbol and a stimulus to meditation or sanctifying memory. There is evidence that something like it remained in popular devotions. We have spoken before of the Sorian San Saturio, a head represented as dark-skinned and bearded. It is possible that it (which was black, like Romanesque Virgins) was the symbol of an ancestral devotion to the earth's fecundity, a sign of the arcane memory of the black and fertile mud of the Nile, which was turned into an object of veneration for protection of the harvest that Mother Earth gives us.

It is significant that the Cross of Caravaca is said to protect orchards and crops as, during its festival, it faces the fields from a corridor of the circular chapel that crowns the Templar castle. It is also exhibited to entice the regional protection of Extremadura's Virgin of Monsfragüe, who came from the Holy Land and became the patroness of the Aragonese military order that eventually joined the Catalan Templar Order. Even more significant is the rite of the head of St. Guillermo, which is venerated in Obanos, near the Chapel of Eunate and the Templar encomienda of Puente la Reina. During its period of veneration, this head is taken out of its sanctuary to receive the devotion of the populace. Water is made to run through the skull of the saint, and after this procedure acquires healing and fertilizing powers for both sterile women and the orchards over which it is sprinkled.

A similar rite occurs in Álava with the head of St. Felix, though in this case, wine is also passed through the saint's bones to acquire miraculous virtues. In Segovia, near Sepúlveda, next to the Hoz del Duratón, the heads of two saints who were brothers are preserved, as is the sacred head of the hermit St. Frutos. From time immemorial these heads have been viewed as irreplaceable weapons in the fight against drought. They are said to demonstrate their virtues when placed within the fountain next to their sanctuary. It is said that on a certain occasion sometime in the seventeenth century, a bishop from Segovia who did not believe in the miracle of the heads, after having given permission for the customary bathing of the relics, went near to verify the effects of the rite and was caught in such a rainfall that the poor incredulous prelate almost drowned when his carriage filled up with an enormous quantity of water from the heavens.

It is not a casual coincidence that rites of this type—and there are many more like them that can be found throughout Spain—have been preserved in proximity to the ancient Templar encomiendas. We must clarify the meaning of these rituals and, above all, the precise motive of the Templars in installing and preserving them. As for their meaning, as I have suggested, they might be linked to ancestral fecundity and fertility cults that take us back to the first religion rendered by a human being in the first stages of its awareness of Mother Earth turned creation goddess and keeper of life.[8] This worship is diametrically opposed to that of the thundering, justice-wielding God, lord of the battles of universal and imperialist religions. This feminine worship was carefully hidden from its faithful by the Church, which maintained only a marginalized devotion to the figure of the Mother of God until it was imposed more formally and overtly in the twelfth century by the Bernardine monks and the Templars.

The Third Clue to the Templar Legacy: Power through Knowledge

In the heart of the province of Soria, far from all commercial routes and the Pilgrims' Way, in a wild canyon along the Lobos River, there rises a small, transitional Romanesque church built next to the enormous mouth of a cave where, not so long ago, important prehistoric remains were discovered. This little church is all that is left of one of the most important Templar encomiendas of Castile, cited in texts such as that of San Juan de Otero. As recorded in a handful of documents, this and other locations were acquired by the Order during the last quarter of the twelfth century.[9] In the middle of the thirteenth century, however, the Templars pawned the greater part of their extensive domain to the bishopric of Osma and to various individuals and kept only the most remote of its ancient possessions—the small enclave in the canyon next to some orchards that provided their most immediate necessities.

Apparently, that encomienda was one of the poorest on the Peninsula. It lacked any strategic value and it did not even make enough money to allow its occupants to transfer obligatory contributions to the Holy Land. Yet the Order kept it until the end as a precious, hidden treasure, tended by a few friars. The documents have preserved only one of these inhabitants' names: Friar Fernán Núñez.[10] Without a doubt, this enclave was not chosen by chance.

Following a vague indication in a book by Mario Roso de Luna, I carefully measured the distance of this in relation to other places on the Peninsula. I was surprised to verify that San Juan de Otero is precisely equidistant, on a straight line, from the two extreme eastern and western points in Spain: the Cape of Creus to the east and the Cape of Finisterre to the west. It is exactly 527 kilometers and 127 meters from each. This seems to indicate that the Templar encomienda of Ucero was created and installed in the precise geographic center of the country—a location

Fig. 9.8. As seen in Tomar, symbols dominate where the Templars were established, even after they abandoned these places.

which, according to tradition, allows a person or group to exert a kind of magical domination over the place of which it is a part.

But this was not the only unusual characteristic of the enclave. It is located a stone's throw from the 42nd parallel.* If a straight line were to be traced over a map of the Peninsula, it would join Creus with Finisterre; another line parallel to this would pass through San Juan de Otero, thereby framing a strip of territory in which the entire Road to Santiago is included along with the 42nd parallel from one side of the Peninsula to the other. There is more: A series of precise and conventional lines traced with the chapel at the center of each touch the key Templar possessions on the Peninsula: Tomar, Toledo, Caravaca, and a curious enclave for which the Catalan-Aragonese Templars negotiated for more than a hundred years, until they finally made it their own twelve years before their annihilation—Culla, in the maestrazgo of Castile-León.[11]

Perhaps I am being too optimistic in exposing these presumed synchronicities, but such precise measurements could not have occurred by mere chance. They seem to indicate that the Order of the Temple, or some of its members, held geographic knowledge that in some way went beyond the scientific knowledge of the time.

Certainly, my resistance to accepting these measurements as a product of chance is not simply stubborn, for there are indications that the Templars possessed extensive knowledge of navigation and of maritime maps, which allowed them to gather an important fleet that not only reached the Mediterranean ports of the Holy Land and Egypt, but also penetrated the Atlantic from the docks that the Order controlled in France, Galicia, and Portugal. This Templar navigational tradition was faithfully continued by the Portuguese Order of Christ, which founded the nautical school of Sagres, located on the Cape of San Vicente. For this school they recruited the services of the best cartographers of the time, including the members of a Jewish family from Mallorca, the Cresques, who lived on the island in a house right next to the walls of the Templar compound. From this nautical school emerged the first

*By chance or otherwise, a good many of the more sacred places of the Occident can be found near this parallel.

navigational maps used by the first Portuguese Atlantic explorers, fueled by the enthusiasms of Henry the Navigator, who was surely grand master of the Order of Christ. There also exist indications that those maps were known by Christopher Columbus, who, while he was with the Junta of Salamanca and was laying plans for a great journey, made a mysterious trip to La Rochelle, the ancient Templar port from which Jean de Betancourt's expedition to the Canary Islands departed. Columbus returned from this trip in time for the Junta to decree viable the project the future admiral had presented to him.

These clues are coherent enough to suspect with sufficient grounds that the Templars not only planned the holy war as a goal and means to achieve their planned theocracy, but also grasped or at least tried to understand knowledge that might have contributed to the feasibility of their plan and given it a chance for success. There can be no doubt that knowledge always forms the basis of great projects that are conceived with the aim of conquering the world, for this conquest not only is, in its totality, military but also must be accompanied by a change in conscience in those who are conquered so that they may adapt to the new paradigm proposed by the conquering collective.

Unlike the knowledge imparted by academia, this conquering knowledge comes from a conscious immersion in the transcendent experience of humans and countries that has been accumulating throughout time. Through the exercising of this knowledge, those who conquer oblige us to forget who has held the power at each moment in time, for as those who would succeed in their plan know, submission is even more effective when the ignorance of the submitted is encouraged. In this way, when Christianity installed itself in power through the Church, it reversed whole centuries of human evolution, prohibiting practices and customs and knowledge that its new parishioners had preserved from times lost to memory. Islam did the same during its first days, when the conquering caliphs of North Africa ordered the library at Alexandria destroyed and its volumes burned, alleging that if those books told lies, they were contrary to the Koran, and that if they revealed truths, those truths were already included in the pages of the Koran.

On the extreme western border of a Europe that started at the Holy Land, the Iberian Peninsula had gathered the ancestral mud of all countries in their unstoppable march toward the setting sun, which was the instinctive endpoint of tradition's paths. All these peoples had left their mark on the Peninsula, including a level of knowledge jealously guarded by the collective consciousness. In a certain way, the Peninsula came to hold the transcendent essence of many cultures that, since the dawn of time, had been contributing to the region part of their vital belief systems, needs, hopes, aspirations, and even lost knowledge.

Today, it would be impossible for us to imagine the wisdom and experience of those peoples, who possessed frameworks of conscience so different from those that now govern our behavior and who lived within cultural molds so different from ours and defined so differently what we recognize as knowledge and wisdom. Yet we can rely without bias on a few keys from the past to unlock evidence that is sufficient to capture knowledge of what surrounds us today. Possibly, though it is hardly the only way, a conscious intuition that has been awakened by a meeting with its surroundings could assist us in gaining this knowledge.

Throughout human history, heterodoxy and individuals and minorities from the margins have attempted to approach the clues left by tradition in order to extract its messages. The powers that be have always rejected such attempts and indeed persecuted and condemned them. Such condemnation was also suffered by the Templars, for while we recognize that the Order was lost to the greed of the powerful, the accusations leveled in all the tribunals—at the margin of convictions and absolutions—fundamentally identified the Templars as a heretical group that, in order to prosper and achieve its goals, used the powers the Evil One confers on his faithful.

Even taking into account the previous abolitionist desire that orchestrated the fall and suppression of the Templar order, there is no doubt the Church would have defended it, despite the actions of Clement V, had it not noted among those accusations the foul smell of heterodoxy that could have become highly dangerous if it was not addressed in time. With all its economic power, the Templar order became dangerous—but if there was added to its power the evil element everyone in the Middle Ages believed a satanic pact provided—a belief that extended to the witch trials of the seventeenth century—the danger was multiplied until it became urgent to eliminate the institution that was allegedly using the services of the Evil One to attain the kind of power and influence the Templar order achieved.

For the most part, the medieval world and those who held power in it gave a profound sigh of relief when the Templar order was abolished. Its structure raised too many troubling questions and it had attained too high a concentration of power. It was surrounded by too many mysteries into which no one, no matter how influential he might be, could enter without the consent of the Templar brothers. Alas, it constituted a potential threat whose nature was unknown. Even after the Holy Land was lost, the Order was still considered an efficient weapon at the service of a Church that, with the help of the Knights of the Temple, could impose its will at any time from within different states without calling for a Crusade: Its crusaders were already inside each kingdom, governing the Church's estate, with no force daring to confront them.

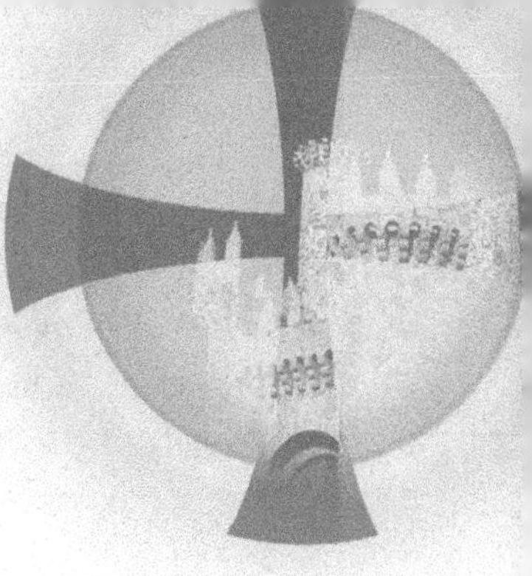

NOTES

Chapter 1: Clues to the Millennium

1. H. Foncillion, *L'An Mil* (Paris: Armond Colin, 1952).
2. Daniel le Blevic, *L'An Mil* (Paris: Presses Universitaires de France, 1976).
3. R. Folz, *L'idée d'Empire en Occident du Ve au XIVe Siècles* (Paris: Aubier, 1953).
4. Antonio Ramos Oliveira, *Los Papas y los Emperadores* (Mexico: Oasis, 1973).
5. Juan G. Atienza, *Los Monjes Españoles. Entre la Herejía y el Integrismo* (Madrid: Temas de Hoy, 1991).
6. *La Gran Conquista de Ultramar,* Biblioteca de Autores Españoles (Madrid: Ed. De Pascual Gayangos, 1951), Book 3, chapter 54.
7. Adolfa Bonilla and San Martin, *Las Leyendas de Wagner en la Literatura Española* (Madrid: Asociación Wagneriana de Madrid, 1913). See also Emeterion Mazorriaga, who extracted this section from *La Gran Conquista* and, with the intent of later conducting a study, published it under the title *La Leyenda del Caballero del Cisne* (Madrid: Librería General de Victoriano Suárez, 1914).
8. Gregorio Penco, *Storia del Monachesimo in Italia dalle Origine alla Fine del Medion Evo* (Roma: 1961).
9. G. Gabrielli, *Investarion Popografico delle Cripta Eremitiche Basiliane di Puglia* (Rome: 1934).

10. Alexandre Masoliver, *Història del Monaquisme Cristià* (Abadía de Montserrat, 1980).
11. *La Gran Conquista,* Book 3, chapter 50.5.
12. Hipòlito de Sà Bravo, *El Monacato en Galicia,* vols. 1 and 2 (La Coruña: Librigal, 1972).

Chapter 2: The Clues to God's Militia

1. Anselm Albareda, *L'Abat Oliba, Fundador de Montserrat* (Abadía de Montserrat, 1971).
2. See Ramon d'Abadal, *L'Abat Oliba* (Barcelona: Bisbe de Vic. Aedos, 1962).
3. Cited by Johannes Lehmann, *Die Kreuzfahrer* (Munich: Berthelsmann Verlag, 1976).
4. *La Gran Conquista*, Book 1, chapter 209.
5. Alexandro Ferreira, *Memória e Noticias Históricas do Célebre Orden Military dos Templários na Palestina,* vols. 1 and 2 (Lisbon: 1735), cited in Martín Fernández de Navarrette, *Españoles enlas Cruzadas* (Madrid: Polifemo, 1986).
6. J. M. Lacarra, "Documentos para el Estudion de la Reconquista y Repoblación del Valle del Ebro," *Estudios de la Edad Media de la Corona de Aragón* 2 (1946): 469–574.
7. Carlos Luis de la Vega y de Luque, "La Milicia Templaria de Monreal del Campo," *Ligarzas* 7 (1975).
8. A. Ubieto Arteta, "La Creación de la Cofradía Militar de Belchite," *Estudios De la Edad Media de la Corona de Aragón* 5 (1952), 427–34.
9. Jerónimo de Zurita y Castro, *Anales de la Corona de Aragón* (Zaragoza: Por Lorenzo Robles, 1610).
10. Alain Demurger, *Vie et Mort des Templiers* (Paris: Ed. Du Seuil, 1985).

Chapter 3: Like an Oil Stain

1. José María Bererciatúa Olarra, *La Orden de los Templarios* (Burgos: Ediciones Aldecoa, 1957).
2. Declaration of the Greek inscription on the cross of the church of San Esteban de Bagá, head of the baronetcy of Pinós, script for the army that took the Holy Land, in the year 1110, don Hugo de Bagá, first grand master of the Temple. Sign. ms. 7.377, 81–91.

3. Martín Fernández de Navarrete, *Españoles en las Cruzadas.*
4. J. Miret i Sans, *Les cases de Templers i Hospitalers à Catalunya* (Barcelona: Impr. de la Casa Provincial de la Caritat, 1910).
5. This fact contributed without specified sources by Rafael Alarcón Herrera, *La otra España del Temple* (Barcelona: Martínez Roca, 1988), 40.
6. Reproduced from Campomanes, *Dissertaciones Históricas*, 198. The *Anales* of Moret are now being reedited by the Charter Government of Navarre. *El Testamento del Batallador* can be found in Book 17, chapter 9; it appears to have been taken from the Archivo de la Catedral de Pamplona.
7. Antonio Ubieto Arteta, "Estudios sobre el Cid," *Ligarzas* 3 (1973).
8. Alarcón Herrera, *La otra España del Temple,* 46.
9. Zurita y Castro, *Anales de la Corona de Aragón,* Book 1, chapter 53.
10. Ibid., Book 1, chapter 55.
11. J. Forey, *The Templars in the Corona de Aragón* (London: Oxford University Press, 1973).
12. María Luisa Ledesma Rubio, *Templarios y Hospitalarios en el Reino de Aragón* (Zaragoza: Guara Editor, 1982).
13. Moret, *Anales,* Book 19, chapter 5.
14. *Historia de los Hechos de España,* Book 7, chapter 14.
15. *Dissertaciones Históricas*, 44.
16. Moret, *Anales,* Book 19, chapter 2.
17. Anel Alvarez de Araujo y Cuellar, *Las Ordenes Militares de Santiago, Calatrava, Alcantara y Montesa. Su Origen, Organización y Estado Actual* (Madrid: Imprenta de Fernando Cao, 1891).
18. Henri de Courzon, *La Règle du Temple* (Paris: Librairie Renouard, 1886). Facsimile edition (Paris: Libr. Honore Champion, 1977).
19. *Historia de los Hechos de España,* Book 7, chapter 10.
20. M. Asin Palacios, *El Islam Cristianizado* (Madrid: Hiperion, 1981).
21. Agnus Macnab, *España bajo la Media Luna* (Palma de Mallorca: J. Olañeta Editor, 1988). Please note that the book includes multiple historical and chronological errors.
22. Anwar G. Chejne, *Muslim Spain: Its History and Culture* (Minneapolis: University of Minnesota, 1972).
23. Rafael Alarcón has for many years promised his *Atlas Templario Peninsular.*
24. Manuel Suarez, *Historia Compostelana, o sea Hechos de don Diego Gelmirez* (Santiago de Compostela: Porto, 1950).
25. Julio González González, *Regesta de Fernando II* (Madrid: CSIC, 1943).

26. Gervasion Velo y Nieto, "*Coria y los Templarios,*" *Boletín de la Real Academia de Historia* 61.61 (1912).
27. Published by Cardinal Saenz de Aguirre, *Collection max. Concil. Omn. Hisp.* 5 (Rome: 1755).
28. *Compostelana,* Book 3, chapter 24.

Chapter 4: The Slow Ascent to the Summit

1. Rodrigo de Luz Lamarca, *El Misterio de la Catedral de Cuenca* (Madrid: Carcomo, 1982).
2. Enrique Gil y Carrasco, *El Señor de Bembibre* (Madrid: Imprenta de Mellado, 1844). Actual, prologue, and notes by Ildefonso Manuel Gil (Zaragoza: Ebro, 1982).
3. Miguel Bravo y Guarida, *Paginas Leonesas. El Castillo de Ponferrada (Memoria historico-descriptiva)* (León: Imprenta Catolica, 1923).
4. See José María Luengo y Martínez, *El Castillo de Ponferrada y los Templarios* (León: Nueva ed. Lebrija, 1980).
5. Claude Domergue, "Introduction à l'Etude des Mines d'or du Nord Quest de la Peninsule Iberique dans l'Antiguite," in *Lgio VII Gemina, Collected Works* (León: Diputación Provincial de León, 1970).
6. See Domergue, "Introduction à l'Etude des Mines d'or du Nord Quest de la Peninsule Iberique dans l'Antiguite."
7. Mercedes Durany, *San Pedro de Montes, El Dominio de un Monasterio Benedictino de El Bierzo* (León: Diputación Provincial de León, 1976).
8. Mircea Eliade *Herreros y Alquimistas* (Madrid: Alianza Editorial, 1974).
9. Juan de Villafane, *Compendio Historico de los Santuarios de la Virgen mas Celebres de Espana Salamanca, 1926.* See also Juan G. Atienza, *Nuestra Señora de Lucifer* (Barcelona: Martínez Roca, 1991).
10. Courzon, *La Règle du Temple,* 72.
11. Cited in Antonio Ribeiro in Amorim Rosa, *Historia de Tomar* (Gabinete de Estudios Tomarenses, 1965).
12. See my list of grand masters in *La Mistica Solar de los Templarios* (Barcelona: Martinez Roca, 1983).
13. The documents are preserved in the Archivo Nacional Portugues de la Torre do Tombo, cuyo legajo n. 71 reune los papeles correspondientes a la Orden del Temple.

14. Amorim Rosa, *Historia de Tomar,* 50.
15. Santos García Larragueta, *El Temple en Navarra* (Madrid-Barcelona: CSIC, 1981), citing a report of the Spanish-Portuguese Congress about military orders on the Iberian Peninsula during the Middle Ages.
16. Paulino Usón Sesé, "Aportaciones al Estudion de la Caida de los Templarios en Aragon" *Universidad* 3 (1926).
17. García Larragueta, *El Temple en Navarra.*
18. García Larragueta, *El Temple en Navarra.*
19. Moret, *Anales,* Book 31, chapters 2 and 3.
20. Fernández de Navarrete, *Españoles en las Cruzadas,* chapter 134.

Chapter 5: The Catalan-Aragonese Crown: A Templar Objective

1. Jorid Ventura, *Alfons el Cast* (Barcelona: Aedos, 1961). Also cited is Joan F. Cabestany, "Alfons el Cast" in *Biografies Catalanes,* Serie Historica no. 4 (Barcelona: Teide, 1960).
2. Ledesma Rubio, *Templarios y Hospitalarios en el Reino de Aragón,* 44.
3. Ventura, *Alfons el Cast*, chapter 13.
4. Abbé Maurice-René Mazières, "Une Curieuse Affaire du XIIe Siecle: celled u 'Puig del Lepreux' à Perpignan," in *Bulletin de la Société des Arts et des Sciences de Carcassonne* (1956).
5. Gervasion Velo y Nieto, *La Orden de Caballeros de Monsfrag* (Madrid, n.p., 1950).
6. Zurita y Castro, *Anales,* Book 2, 73 ff. (Zaragoza: 1610).
7. Antonion Ubieto Arteta, "La Reaparición de Alfonso I el Batallador," in *Argensola* 9 (1958): 29–38.
8. A. J. Forey, *The Templars in the Corona de Aragón* (London: Oxford University Press, 1973). This recounts the numerous donations of the family to the Templars and speaks of various members with the surname Torroja.
9. Zurita y Casto, *Anales,* Book 2, chapter 30 ff.
10. Antonion Ubieto Arteta, "La Reaparición de Alfonso I el Batallador."
11. According to Andrew Thomas, *Shambhalla* (Paris: Robert Laffont, 1976).
12. Ventura, *Alfons el Cast,* 197.
13. Ibid, 263.
14. Zurita y Castro, *Anales,* Book 2, chapter 47.

15. Juan G. Atienza, *La Meta Secreta de los Templarios* (Barcelona: Martínez Roca, 1981). See also *Guía de la España Templaria* (Barcelona: Ariel, 1985).
16. Cited by Ubieto in *Introducción a la Historia de España* (Madrid: Teide, 1962).
17. Abbé Maurice-René Mazières, "La Venue et Sejour de Templiers du Roussillon à la fin du XIIIe Siecle et au Debut du XIVe dans la Vallée du Bézu (Aude)," in *Bulletin de la Société des Arts et des Sciences de Carassonne:* 1957–59.
18. Pierre des Vauz de Cerney, *Hystoria Albigenses,* edited by P. Guébin and E. Lyon, vols. 1, 2, and 3 (Paris: n.p., 1951).
19. Jordi Ventura, *Pere el Católic i Simón de Montfort* (Barcelona: Aedos, 1960).

Chapter 6: The Search for the King of the World

1. *Libre dels Feyts*; *Crónica o Comentaris del rey En Jacme* (Barcelona: Ed. de Aguilo, 1873–1905); *Crónica Historica*, vols. 1 and 2 (Barcelona: Ed. Iberia, 1958).
2. Bernat Desclot, *Crónica* (Barcelona: Ed. de Coll i Alentorn, 1948); Ramon Muntaner, *Crónica* (Barcelona: Ed. de Casacuberta, 1927). The Castilian edition (Madrid: Alainza Editorial, 1970) is the one from which I extracted the texts reproduced here.
3. Ibid., chapter 5.
4. Honorio García y García, *Guillermo de Montrodón: Su Personalidad Proyectada en la Historia de España* (Vic: n.p., 1948).
5. María Teresa Oliveros de Castro, *Historia Ilustrada de la Ciudad de Monzón* (Zaragoza: Ayuntamiento de Monzón, 1974); Francisco Castillón Cortada, *El santuario de la Virgen de la Alegría de Monzón* (Zaragoza: Ayuntamiento de Monzón, 1974).
6. Cited by Ferran Soldevila, *Jaime I, el Conqueridor* (Barcelona: Aedos, 1968), 35.
7. Gabriel Almomar Esteve, *Cátaros y Occitanos en el Reino de Mallorca* (Palma de Mallorca: Luis Ripoll Editor, 1978).
8. Book 2, 92.
9. Miquel Dolc, *El Libre de Sant Jordi* (Barcelona: Biblioteca Selecta, 1952).

10. Courzon, *La Règle du Temple,* 73.
11. Jacobo de la Voragine, *La Leyenda Dorada*, vols. 1 and 2 (Madrid: Alianza Editorial, 1988).
12. Taken from ms. 889 of the Biblioteca de Cataluña and 2 F.1 of the Biblioteca de Palacio. Published for the first time in Ramon de'Alos-Moner, *Sant Jordi, Patró de Catalunya* (Barcelona: n.p., 1926).
13. Mateo Rotger y Caplonghy, *Historia de Pollensa* (Palma de Mallorca: Impr. De los Sagrados Corazones, 1967).
14. J. A. Encinas, *Pollença, Semblanza de un Pueblo* (Palma de Mallorca: n.p., 1981).
15. Atienza, *La Meta Secreta de los Templarios* (Barcelona: Martínez Roca, 1983).
16. For further discussion and other points of view concerning this polemic, see J. Amador de los Rios, *Historia Social, Política y Religiosa de los Judíos de España y Portugal* (Madrid: Aguilar, 1960), 231; and Yitzhak Baer, *Historia de los Jusios en la España Cristiana* (Madrid: Altalema Editores, 1981), 122.
17. Idries Shah, *Los Sufies,* introduction by Robert Graves (Barcelona: Luis de Caralt Editor, Barcelona, 1975).
18. Engracia Alsina Prat, "Jaime el Conquistador y sus Relaciones con los Santos Lugares," in *Jaime I y su Epoca, X Congreso de Historia de la Corona de Aragón* (Zaragoza: Institución Fernando el Catolico, 1980).
19. Of the *Libre de la Saviessa,* two manuscripts are preserved: 2.2 Codex of the Biblioteca Nacional and ms. 129 of the B. de el Escorial, where it is joined with Desclot's *Crónica.* It was published for the first time in 1908 by Gabriel Llabres i Quintana to coincide with the seventh centenary of James I, then again in late 1946 by CSIC under Professor Castro y Calvo, who conducted the preliminary study. The most recent and best Spanish edition has been J. A. Encinas, *El Libro de la Sabiduría de Jaime I, Rey* (Pollença, n.p., 1990).

Chapter 7: Twilight of the Idols

1. See the first of my books, *La Mística Solar de los Templarios.*
2. Francesco Carreras i Candi, "Entences i Templers en les montantes de Prades," in *Boletín de la Real Academia de Buenas Letras* 13 (January 1904).

3. Aurea Javierre Mur, "Aportación al Estudio del Proceso contra el Temple en Castilla" in *R.A.B.M.* 69 (1961): 47–100.
4. Demurger, *Vie et Mort des Templiers,* chapter 4.
5. Abbé Maurice-René Mazières, "La Venue it le Sejour des Templiers du Roussillon à la Fin du XIIIe Siècle et au Dèbut du XIVe dans la Vallée du Bézu (Aude)," in *Bulletin de la Société des Arts et des Sciences de Carcassonne* (1957–59).
6. Carreras i Candi, "Entences i Templers en les montantes de Prades."
7. *Quomodo Terra Sancta Recuperari Potest,* edited by Rambert-Buhor in 1954, was among Ramón Lull's Latin works published in Mallorca.
8. Ramón Garcías Palou, "Ramón Lull y la Abolición de los Templarios," in *Hispania Sacra* 5. 26, no. 51–52 (1973).
9. Carreras i Candi, "Entences i Templers en les Montantes de Prades."
10. A. De Bastard, "La Colère et la Douleur d'un Templier en Terre Sainte," in *Revue des Langues Romanes* 81 (1974).
11. Demurger, *Vie et Mort des Templiers,* 228 and ff.

Chapter 8: The Fall of the Clay Colossus

1. J. M. Sans i Travé, *El Procés dels Templers Catalans* (Lleida: Pagés Editor, 1990).
2. Carreras i Candi, "Entences i Templers en les Montantes de Prades."
3. "Crónica de Fernando IV," in *Crónicas del los Reyes de Castilla Ordenadas por don Cayetano Rosel,* vol. 66 (Madrid: Atlas, Reed, 1953).
4. Ibid., chapter 15.
5. Ibid., chapter 16.
6. Áurea Javierre Mur, "Aportación al Estudio del Proceso Contra el Temple en Castilla."
7. Sans i Travé, *El Procés dels Templers Catalans.*
8. Ibid., Diss. V.
9. The council issued its decree in the *Regnans in Coeli* bull, published August 12, 1309.
10. J. M. San i Travé, *El Procés dels Templers Catalons.*
11. Sans i Travé, *El Procés dels Templers Catalan,* 46.
12. A. Bladé Desumbila, *El Castell de Miravet* (Barcelona: R. Dalmau, 1966).
13. Sans i Travé, *El Procés dels Templers Catalan,* 282.
14. Ibid., 283.

Chapter 9: The Templars in History

1. Albert Ollivier, *Les Templiers* (Paris: Le Temps Qui Court, Seuil, 1976).
2. L. M. Cabello Lapiedra, "La Vera Cruz de Segovia Nunca fue Templaria," *Arquitectura* (June 1919), 165–69.
3. Javier Cabello Dodero, "La Iglesia de la Vera Cruz," in *Estudios Segovianos* 3 (1957).
4. Santos García Larraguets, "El Temple en Navarra" in *Actas del Congreso Hispano-Portugués Sobre Órdenes Militares en la Edad Media* (Tomar: n.p., 1971).
5. Élie Lambert, *Les Chapelles Octogonales d'Eunate et Torres del Río* (Paris: Memorial Henri Basset, 1928). See also *L'Architecture des Templiers* (Paris: Ed. Reciente por Picard, 1978); Vicente Lampérez, *Historia de la Arquitectura Cristiana Española en la Edad Media* (Madrid, 1930); José Yarnoz Larrosa, "Las Iglesias Octogonales en Navarra," in *Príncipe de Viana* 2 (1948); and M. Torres-Balbas in *Arquitectura* (November 1, 1922).
6. Juan G. Atienza, *La Mística Solar de los Templarios* (Barcelona: Martínez Roca, 1983).
7. Sans i Travé, *El Procés dels Templers Catalan,* 182.
8. *Nuestra Señora de Lucifer* (Barcelona: Martínez Roca, 1991).
9. Archivo Histórico de Soria, Protocolos Notariales de Ucero. See also Loperráez, *Historia del Obispado del Burgo de Osma.*
10. Alejandro Ayalgas Mirón, *La Ermita Templaria de Ucero* (Barcelona: Ed. del Autor, 1986).
11. I develop these matters in *La Meta Secreta de los Templarios* (Barcelona: Martínez Roca, 1981).

BIBLIOGRAPHY

Albareda y Herrera, M. *El Fuero de Alfambra.* Madrid: 1925.

Albon, Marquis d'. *Cartulaire Général de l'Ordre du Temple.* París: 1913.

Alegret, A. "Los Templarios en Tarragona." *Boletín Arqueológico* 17 (1905).

Alonso García, D. "Apuntes Históricos de la Villa de Alcanadre." *Berceo* 13 (1958) and *Berceo* 14 (1959).

Anónimo. "Los Templarios." *Ocios de Españoles Emigrados* 2 (1824).

Antolín Hernández, J. E. "Estudio Sobre Villasirga." *Boletín de la Institución Tello Téllez de Meneses* 30 (1971).

Atienza, Juan G. *La Meta Secreta de los Templarios.* Barcelona: Martínez Roca: 1981.

———. *La Mística Solar de los Templarios.* Barcelona: Martínez Roca, 1983.

———. *Guía de la España Templaria.* Barcelona: Ariel, 1985.

Ayneto, J. *Historia de los Templarios en Aragón y Cataluña.* Lérida: n.p., 1904.

———. *Hospitalarios y Templarios.* Lérida: n.p., 1914.

Barber, Malcolm. "The Origins of the Order of the Temple." *Studia Monasticae* 12 (1970).

———. *The Trial of the Templars.* Cambridge: Cambridge University Press, 1978.

Bastus y Carrera, V. J. *Historia de los Templarios, con un Apéndice Histórico de José Brissa.* Barcelona: Imprenta Verdaguer, 1834.

Benet de Capara, José María. *Estatus Temple Catalán.* s.1. ni a.

Benito Ruano, Eloy. "La Encomienda Templaria y Sanjuanista de Cantavieja." *Homenaje a José María Lacarra* 3 (1978).

Bernardo de Quirós, P. *Notas Sobre el Temple.*

Bibliographie du Temple. París: n.p. 1972.

Bladé Desumbila, A. *El Castell de Miravet.* Barcelona: R. Dalmau, 1966.

Blázquez y Jiménez, A., "Bosquejo Histórico de la Orden de Montegaudion." *Boletín de la Real Academia de la Historia* 71 (1917).

Bonavía Jacas, J., and B. Del Gaya. "El Temple en la Ribera del Ebro." *Cultura* (March/April 1959).

Bordonove, Georges. *Les Templiers: Histoire et Tragédie.* Paris: Fayard, 1977.

Bravo y Guarida, M. *El Castillo de Ponferrada: Memoria Histórica Descriptiva.* León, n.p., 1923.

Bruguera, M. *Historia General, Religiosa y Militar de los Caballeros del Temple,* 3 vols. Barcelona: n.p., 1882–89.

Cabella y Lapiedra, L. M. "La Vera Cruz de Segovia Nunca fue Templaria." *Arquitectura* (June 1929).

Cabello y Dodero, E. J. "La Iglesia de la Vera Cruz de Segovia." *Estudios Segovianos* 3 (1951).

Campomanes, Pedro R. *Dissertaciones Históricas de la Orden y Cayallería de los Templarios.* Barcelona: Reed, 1975.

Carreras i Candi, F. "La Creuada de Jaume I a Terra Santa." *Miscelánia de História Catalana* 2.

———. "Entences i Templers en les Montantes de Prades." *Boletín de la Real Academia de Buenas Letras* 2 (1904).

———. *Geografía General de Cataluñia.* Barcelona: s.f., n.d.

Castán Lanaspa, J. *Arquitectura Templaria Castellano-leonesa.* Valladolid: Secretaría de Publicaciones de la Universidad, 1983.

Cocheril, M. "Essai sur l'Origine des Ordres Militaires dans la Peninsule Ibérique." *Collectaneae Ordinis Cisterciensum Reformatorum* 20 (1958) and 21 (1959).

Colexio de Arquitectos de Galicia. *Arquitectura Románica en La Coruña.* Santiago de Compostela: COAG, 1983.

Conte Cazcarro, A. *La Orden del Temple en la Ciudad de Huesca.* Congreso Internacional Hispano-Portugués sobre Órdenes Militares en la Península Ibérica durante la Edad Media, 1972.

Delaville de Roulx, J. "Bulles pour l'Ordre de Temple Tirés des Archives de St. Gervasio de Cassolas." *Revue de l'Orient Latin* 11 (1905).

Demurger, A. *Auge y Caída de los Templarios.* Barcelona: Martínez Roca, 1987.

Dessubré, M. *Bibliographie des Templiers.* París: n.p., 1928.

"Documentos de Unión de Montegaudio al Temple." *Boletín de la Sociedad Castellana de Cultura* 9 (1928).

Doménech, A. V. *Historia General de los Santos y Varones Ilustres en Santidad del Principado de Cataluña.* Gerona, Garrich, 1630.

Durbec, J. A. "Les Templiers en Provence. Formation des Commanderies et Repartition Géographique de Leurs Biens." *Provence Historique* 9 (1959).

Dufourcq, C. E. *L'Espagne Catalane et le Maghrib aux XIIIe et XIVe Siécles.* Paris: n.p., 1966.

Eijan, S. *España en Tierra Santa.* Barcelona: Gustavo Gili, 1910.

Estepa, C. "Templarios." *Diccionarion de Historia Eclesiástica de España* 3 (1973).

———. "Las Encomiendas del Temple en Tierra de Campos." *Archivos Leoneses* 52 (1972) and *Hispania* 132 (1972).

Ferrandis, M. "Rendición del castillo de Chivert a los Templarios." *Homenaje a don Francisco Codero.* Zaragoza: n.p., 1904.

Ferrer Vives, F. de A. "Arnau de Torroja." *Sió* 149 (July 1976).

Fita, Fidel. "Coria Compostelana y Templaria." *Boletín de la Real Academia de Historia* 61 (1912).

———. "Templarios, Calatravos y Hebreos." *Boletín de la Real Academia de Historia* 14 (1889).

Forey, A. J. "The Order of Montjoy." *Speculum* 46 (1971).

———. *The Templars in the Crown of Aragón.* London: Oxford University Press, 1973.

Garcés, Marco Antonio. *San Polo.* Soria: n.p., 1979.

Garcia Escobar, V. "La Iglesia de los Templarios en Ceinos." *Semanario Pintoresco Españlo* (1853).

García Larragueta, Santos. "Fueros y Cartas Pueblas Navarro-Arragonesas Otorgadas por Templarios y Hospitalarios." *Archivo de Histoia del Derecho Español* 24 (1954).

———. "El Temple en Navarra." *Actas del Congreso Hispano-Portugués sobre Órdenes Militares en la Edad Media,* 1972.

Garcías Palou, S. "Ramón Lull y la Abolición de los Templarios." *Hispania Sacra* 26 (1973).

Guzulla, F. D. "La Orden del Santo Redentor." *Boletín de la Sociedad Castellana de Cultura* 9 (1928) and 10 (1929).

Gómez del Campillo, M. "El castillo de Monzón." *Boletín de la Real Academia de Historia* 118 (1946).

Gordillo Courcieres, J. L. *Castillos Templarios Arruinados en el sur de la Corona de Aragón.* Valencia: n.p., 1974.

Herket, K. "Das Testament Alphonso's von Aragón." *Wochenblatt Johannitterordens-Balley* 8 (1870).

Hernández Sanahuja. "Extinción de la Orden de los Templarios en la Corona de Aragón." *Revista Contemporánea* 58 (1885) and 59 (1885).

Huici, S. "Iglesia de Templarios en Torres del Río." *Revista de Obras Públicas* 1 (1923).

Íñigo y Miera, M. *Historia de las Órdenes de Caballería.* Madrid: n.p., 1963.

Javierra Mur, L., L. Áurea, and C. Gutiérrez del Arroya. "Aportación al Estudio del Proceso Contra el Temple en Castilla." *R.A.B.M.* 69 (1961).

———. *Sobre los Cartularios del Temple Existentes en el Archivo Histórico Nacional: El Archivo de San Juan de los Panetes.* Zaragoza: Publicaciones de Est. de la Edad Media de la Corona de Aragón.

King, Georgiana Goddard. *A Brief Account of the Military Orders in Spain.* New York: n.p., 1921.

Lampérez, Vicente. "La Iglesia Templaria en Villalcázar de Sirga." *Boletín de la Sociedad Española de Excursionismo* 11 (1903).

———. "La iglesia de Templarios de Eunate." *Revista de Cultura Española.* Madrid: n.p., 1907.

Lapeña Paul, and Isabel Ana. "La Encomienda de la Orden del Temple en Novillas." *Cuadernos de Estudios Borjanos* 3 (1979).

Ledesma Rubio, M. L. *Templarios y Hospitalarios en el Reino de Aragón.* Zaragoza: Guara Editorial, 1982.

Lizérand, J. *Le Dossier de l'Affaire des Templiers.* París: n.p., 1923.

López, Santiago. "Historia y Tragedia de los Templarios." *Madrid* (1813).

López Elum, P. "Aportación al Estudio de los Maestres y Comendadores de las Órdenes del Hospital y del Temple durante el Reinado de Jaime I." *Ligarzas* 2 (1970).

López Soler, Antonia. *Historia del Temple Catalán.* Nápoles: Ed. Literarias de la Ac. Int. de Pontzen, 1966.

Lozoya, Marqués de. "Monumentos de los Caballeros Templarios en España." In *Diario de Navarra* (January 6, 1945).

Luengo y Martínez, José María. *El Castillo de Ponferrada y los Templarios.* León: Reed, 1922.

De Luz Lamarca, Rodrigo. *El Misterio de la Catedral de Cuenca.* Madrid: Cárcamo, 1980.

Magallón, M. "Los Templarios de la Corona de Aragón. Índice de su Cartulario Eclesiástico del s. XII." *Boletín de la Real Academia de Historia* 32 (1897) and 33 (1898).

———. "Templarios y Hospitalarios. Primer Cutulario del AHN." *Boletín de la Real Academia de Historia* 33 (1898).

María, R. de. "Xivert y Oropesa." *Boletín de la Sociedad Castellana de Cultura* 24 (1933).

———. "La Primicia, para los Templarios." *Boletín de la Sociedad Castellana de Cultura* 25 (1934).

Marín de Espinosa, A. *Memorias para la Historia de la Ciudad de Caravaca.* Barcelona: Reed, 1975.

Meglio, G. di. *Estudios de Historia de la Iglesia.* Madrid: n.p., 1966.

Melville, Marion. *La vie des Templiers.* Paris: Gallimard, 1973.

Mercati, A. "Interrogatorio di Templari a Barcellona, 1313." *Gesammelte Aufsatze zur Kultur Spaniens* 6 (1937).

Mexia, Pedro. *Los Templarios.* Sevilla: n.p., 1542.

Miret i Sans, J. *Cartoral dels Templers de Gardeny.* Barcelona: n.p., 1899.

———. *Les Cases de Templers i Hospitalers à Catalunya.* Barcelona: Impr. de la Casa Provincial de la Caritat, 1910.

———. "Inventaris de les Cases del Temple a la Corona d'Aragó en 1289." *Boletín de la Real Academia de Buenas Letras de Barcelona* 6 (1911).

Mota Arévalo, H. "Las Órdenes Militares en Extremadura." *Revista de Estudios Extremeños* 25 (1929).

Nieto, C. "Descripción de la Iglesia que con la Advocación de Na Sa del Temple, Poseyeron los Templarios en la Villa de Ceínos de Campos." *Boletín de la Real Academia de Historia* 76 (1920).

Odriozola y Grimaud, C. *Ramón Berenger IV, conde de Barcelona, Caballero del Santo Sepulcro de Jerusalén. Memorias Históricas Referentes a la Cesión en su*

Favor de la Corona de Aragón, Hecha por la Orden Militar del Santo Sepulcro, la del Hospital y del Temple en el Año 1140. Barcelona: n.p., 1911.

Oliveira Marques, A. H. *Historia de Portugal.* Lisbon: n.p., 1978.

Oliveros de Castro, María Teresa. *Historia de Monzón.* Zaragoza: Instituto Fernando el Católico, 1964.

Ollivier, Albert. *Les Templiers.* Paris: Le Temps Qui Court, 1958.

Pascual González, B. "Los Templarios en Mallorca." *Boletín de la Asociación Española de Amigos de los Castillos* 12 (1964).

Pérez de Urbel, fray Justo. *Los Monjes Españoles en la Edad Media.* Madrid: n.p., 1930–34.

Pérez Llamazares. "La Thau de los Templarios." *Hidalguía* 4 (1956).

Quintana Prieto, Augusto. "Los Templarios en Cornatel." *Archivos Leoneses* 9 (1955).

Ramírez, T. "San Juan de Otero, Iglesia de Templarios." *Boletín de la Sociedad Castellana de Excursiones.* Valladolid, 1907.

Rodríguez, J. "Orden del Temple. Encomienda de Mayorga." *Archivos Leoneses* 1 (1947).

Rotger i Campllong, M. *Els Templers a Mallorca.* Barcelona: I Congreso de Historia de la Corona de Aragón, 1909.

Rubio, J., R. D'Alos, and F. Marturell. "Inventaris Inédits de l'Ordre del Temple a Catalunya." *Anuari de l'Institut d'Estudis Catalans* 1 (1907).

Rubion Salán, A. *Breve Noticia de Villalcázar de Sirga y de su Templo.* Publ. del Instituto Tello Téllez de Meneses, 1948.

Ruiz Pérez, J. M. *Los Templarios. Compendio Histórico de su Establecimiento y su Extinción.* Granada: n.p., 1840.

Sancristóbal Sabastián, S. *Zamarramala.* Segovia: n.p., 1978.

Sans i Travé, J. M. "Alguns Aspectes de l'Establiment dels Templars a Catalunya." *Quaderns d'História Tarraconense* 1 (1977).

———. *El Procés dels Templars Catalans.* Lérida: Pagés Editors, 1990.

Shicki, Peter. "Die Entstechung und Entwicklung des Tempelorders in Katalonien und Aragon." *Gesammte Aufsatze zur Kulturgeschichte Spaniens* 23 (1975).

Soraluce, P. M. "El Temple en Guipúzcoa." *Euskalherría* 43 (1900) and 44 (1900).

Tejada y Duque de Estrada, A. M. "La Antigua Iglesia de los Templarios en Villamuriel." *Boletín de la Sociedad Española de Excursionismo* 55 (1951).

Ubieto, Agustín. "Cofrades Aragoneses y Navarros de la Milicia del Temple." *Agagón en la Edad Media.* Zaragoza: n.p., 1950.

Uria, Riu, J. *Las Fundaciones Hospitalarias en los Caminos de Peregrinación.* Oviedo: n.p., 1940.

Usón y Sesé, M. "Aportaciones al Estudio de la Caída de los Templarios en Aragón." *Revista Universitaria* 3 (1926).

Vázquez, A. J. "El Signo de Solomón en la Iglesia del Castillo de Aracena." *Archivo Hispalenes* 26 (1957).

Vázquez Núñez, A. "Iglesias Templarias Gallegas." *Boletín de la Comisión de Monumentos de Orense* (1905).

Vega y de Luque, Carlos L. dela. "La Milicia Templaria de Monreal del Campo." *Ligarzas* 7 (1975).

Velo y Nieto, G. "Coria y los Templarios: don Fernando II de León Reconquista los Territorios de la Antigua Diócesis Cauriense." *Revista de Estudios Extremeños* 5 (1949).

———. *La Orden de Caballeros de Monsfrag.* Madrid: Ed del autor, 1950.

Vignati-Peralta. *El Enigma de los Templarios.* Barcelona: ATE, 1976.

Villar Bonet, M. *Actividades Financieras de la Orden del Temple en la Corona de Aragón.* Barcelona: VII Congreso de Historia de la Corona de Aragón, 1952.

———. *Los Bienes del Temple en la Corona de Aragón al Suprimirse la Orden.* Doctoral thesis, University of Zaragoza, 1950.

Zalba, J. "Documento Curioso: 1322. Hospitalarios y Templarios en Navarra." *Boletín de la Comunidad de Municipios de Navara* 18 (1934).

Zapater, M. R. *Cister Militante en la Campaña de la Iglesia contra la Sarracena Furia. Historia General de las Caballerías del Templo de Salomón, Calatrava, Alcántara, Avis, Montesa y Cristo.* Zaragoza: n.p., 1662.

Ziegler, Gilette. *Les Templiers.* Paris: n.p., 1975.

INDEX

BOOKS OF RELATED INTEREST